AN UNDERCURRENT OF SUSPICION

AN UNDERCURRENT OF SUSPICION

Anti-Communism in America during World War II

George Sirgiovanni

Transaction Publishers
New Brunswick (U.S.A.) and London (U.K.)

Library of Congress Catalog Number: 89-4613
ISBN: 0-88738-122-7
Printed in the United States of America

Library of Congress Cataloging-in-Publication Data

Sirgiovanni, George.
    An undercurrent of suspicion : anti-communism in America during World War II / George Sirgiovanni.
      p. cm.
    Bibliography: p.
    Includes index.
    ISBN 0-88738-122-7
    1. Anti-communist movements—United States—History—20th century. 2. World War, 1939–1945—United States. 3. United States—History—1933–1945. I. Title.
HX83.S57   1989
324.1'3'0973—dc20   89-4613
                                         CIP

To Charlie

Contents

Acknowledgments

My foremost debt is to my parents, Charles and Eleanor Sirgiovanni, who always encouraged me to pursue my intellectual interests and endeavors. I would like to thank my brother Kenneth for his enthusiasm and good humor, and I am especially grateful to my brother Robert for all the much-needed assistance he rendered on my behalf.

At Rutgers University, David Oshinsky helped me in innumerable ways throughout my years as a graduate student. Unfortunately, I doubt I ever will be able to repay him adequately for all the kindness and support he unfailingly has extended to me. Professor Oshinsky is a great role model for anyone contemplating a career in the academic profession.

Professors Norman Markowitz, John Chambers, and Donald Gibson also were good enough to read and evaluate my manuscript. All of them—Professor Markowitz in particular—disagreed with many of my views, yet I found their comments insightful and helpful. Professors John Lenaghan, Richard L. McCormick, Richard P. McCormick, Michael Seidman, and Traian Stoianovich also took an interest in me and my work as I proceeded toward my degree and the completion of this book. I am indebted as well to Dr. Barbara Bari Franzoi for her much-needed support during the last stages of this project.

I also wish to thank Dr. Irving Louis Horowitz and the fine and patient staff of Transaction Books, in particular Ms. Esther Luckett.

Several of my graduate-school colleagues made my work better than it would have been by constantly challenging me with their fresh, provocative ideas and scholarship. To the following, I can only say Thank You: Kelly Boyd, Rebecca Brittenham, Roy and Robin Domenico, Jim Hale, Peter Jakab (whose Ph.D. from Rutgers is worth twice as much as anyone else's), Chris Jespersen and Theresa Lingsch, Robert Mensel, Jonathan Nashel, Kurt Piehler, Sallie and Frank Pisani, John Rossi, Jan and Charles Sherman, John and Becky Spurlock, and Ginny Weiler. Other valued friends also have inspired and encouraged me during this phase of my career: Robert McGloughlin, Rachael Messer and her family, Peggy Ann Nerney, Michael Rubin, George Shore, and Barbara Spielman. I am especially grateful to Dr. Monika Elbert of the English Department at St. John's University.

1

Introduction

Anticommunism has been one of the most significant and enduring issues in American political history. Deep, often uncompromising hostility to domestic Communists and fellow travelers, coupled with dread and loathing for the Soviet Union, fairly describes the views of millions of Americans since the Russian Revolution of 1917. To be sure, the strength of American anticommunism as a politico-ideological force has fluctuated: less intense during the Popular Front era and the "detente" of the 1970s and late 1980s, more powerful during the Red Scare of 1919–1920 and McCarthy period. However, it was only during the U.S.–Soviet alliance of World War II that the majority of Americans put aside their anti-Soviet/anti-Communist attitudes to a really substantial degree. As a result, most historians have ignored or rapidly passed over those war-era anti-Communists who ignored the quasi-official moratorium on criticizing the Soviet allies abroad and the "ultrapatriotic" Communist party at home. Yet, some of the most resolute anti-Communists withstood the countervailing pressures of the wartime alliance from positions of leadership and influence of their own. These individuals, and the rear-guard war of ideas they fought on the American homefront of World War II, will be the subject of this study.

Those who remained hostile to foreign and domestic communism during this period can be divided into five general groupings. These include anti-Communist political figures, leaders of organized labor, prominent right-wing journalists, leading Catholics and Protestant fundamentalists, and the best-known democratic Socialists.* As the key elements of an overall study of anti-Communist, anti-Soviet sentiment during World War II, an examination of each of these groups—their attitudes, arguments, and policies as they relate to the subject at hand—is in order. The study is arranged topically. A chapter has been devoted to each group, with two chapters allotted to the politicians—one

---

*Interestingly, American businessmen were among those most supportive of the developing U.S.–Soviet friendship (lucrative trade agreements beckoned on the postwar horizon) and therefore are not a main topic of this book.

1

to explore domestic anticommunism, the other to examine foreign-policy issues relating to the U.S.–Soviet alliance. To provide necessary historical context, a background chapter will first review America's long antiradical tradition, with special focus on the conflicts engendered by the Bolshevik Revolution and the formation of the American Communist party.

Often very different in other respects, the groups we shall examine shared the belief that the fundamental nature of the Soviet Union had not changed merely because of the Nazi invasion. Having long regarded the U.S.S.R. as a repressive regime ruled by a dictator as brutal as his recent ally, Adolf Hitler, anti-Soviet Americans saw no reason to alter that assessment now that Nazi treachery had made Joseph Stalin a military partner of the United States. Anti-Soviets also were certain that Soviet–American mutual interests did not extend much beyond the battlefield. Although the United States supposedly was fighting to uphold the lofty principles espoused in the Atlantic Charter, critics of the Soviet Union predicted that Stalin would violate the charter by seizing control of Poland and Eastern Europe as spoils of war. Some Soviet-haters even questioned Stalin's good faith on military matters, because the Red Army refused to assist U.S. forces in the Pacific.

Similarly, those who harbored doubts about the American Communist party during the war believed the party members' bedrock loyalty to the Soviet dictatorship had not weakened, even though Communists were now acting like model American patriots. To anti-Communists, the reason their old foes were behaving out of character was that American and Soviet needs happened for once—probably *just* this once—to coincide. However, as soon as Hitler was defeated, the Communists could be expected to resume their hostilities to capitalist America, should Moscow so order. To believe better of either the Communist party or the Soviet government—and this was exactly what millions were doing at this time—was to engage in wishful, possibly dangerous thinking.

Although the specific groups we shall study shared a loathing for the U.S.S.R. and the American Communist party, it is significant that they often had widely divergent agendas, perspectives, and philosophies otherwise. For example, labor leaders and anti-Stalinist intellectuals considered the anti-Communist reactionaries in Congress to be at least as dangerous as the Communists themselves. William Randolph Hearst and Norman Thomas had little in common except anticommunism. Right-wing Republicans and the *Chicago Tribune* united in using communism as a partisan issue against President Roosevelt, but this line of attack would have been unthinkable to Walter Reuther of the United Automobile Workers or most officials in the Catholic church. As such, the people we shall examine did not form a "united front" of their own against communism or the Soviet Union; yet their activities as a whole kept a troubling but highly important issue before the American people.

The war years raise, and should help to answer, some of the significant questions relating to the study of American anticommunism. One starts, obviously, with why some Americans considered it so important to resist the prevailing climate of good fellowship with the Russians. Was it unthinking stubbornness or principled foresight? Both of these factors, as well as others, played roles. Motive is important in any opinion study. As such, did witch-hunting politicians and their supporters create a largely illusory domestic "menace" for purely partisan advantage? Or could it be that most Americans did not pay *enough* attention to the growing military power of the U.S.S.R.?

More broadly, does American anticommunism stem chiefly from fear of enhanced Soviet military power or from traditional American hostility to domestic radicalism? The unusual war years may offer a clue. Also, with the help of published poll data it will be possible to consider the effectiveness and popularity of anti-Communist arguments during this period. Certainly there was a considerable upsurge in pro-Soviet commentary during the U.S.–Soviet alliance, but was the turnabout in public opinion quite as far reaching as is generally believed? It also should be interesting to examine how the anti-Communist figures of World War II responded to prevailing military reality, which bound Soviet successes so closely to America's own interests. Perhaps the biggest question is this: With the considerable advantage of hindsight at our disposal, how prescient do the warnings of these individuals appear to have been? Were they implacable hate mongers who frustrated a nascent Soviet–American friendship—a partnership that, had it lasted, might have led to a long era of worldwide peace and security? Or, did the anti-Soviet holdouts raise legitimate arguments in a time of great confusion over the fundamental nature and long-term goals of the U.S.S.R.? These are controversial questions, deserving of careful reflection and research.

Anyone proposing to study those who grimly adhered to anti-Communist/anti-Soviet attitudes must continually bear in mind that these were not mainstream views during World War II. Indeed, just the opposite was the case. There was, after all, a war to be won, and the Communists and the U.S.S.R. were contributing mightily to that end. Because this unique circumstance provides the essential backdrop to our analysis, it is necessary to review briefly the pro-Soviet commentary—and corresponding diminution of antipathy toward the Communist Party USA—that emerged from the Grand Alliance and temporarily transformed anticommunism into a minority viewpoint.

Always the pragmatist, President Franklin Roosevelt realized that a climate of good feeling toward the Soviets was essential to the success of the Grand Coalition. Thus, in a Christmas Eve radio address during the war, he assured his fellow Americans that "we are going to get along with him [Stalin] and the Russian people—very well indeed."[1] For this to happen, however, a rapid shift in public perceptions of "Uncle Joe" and his regime was required, and the administration attached a high priority to effecting just such a change. The Office of War Information (OWI), Washington's official propaganda agency, consistently presented an idealized version of the U.S.S.R. to the American people. The OWI and the State Department either glossed over or ignored the substantial differences* that still plagued the "strange alliance,"[2] such as the postwar political and territorial makeup of Eastern Europe. FDR frequently praised the Soviets for their enormous contributions to the war effort, and he criticized those who remained publicly hostile to the U.S.S.R. Presidential advisor Harry Hopkins, Vice President Henry Wallace, liberal Democratic Senator Claude Pepper of Florida, Republican Wendell Wilkie, and many other high officials effusively supported the cause of U.S.–Soviet friendship. The bad relations of the past, they claimed, had been based on mutual misunderstandings and a lack of information. Former Ambassador to the U.S.S.R. Joseph Davies even suggested in his best-selling memoir *Mission to Moscow* that the Soviet purge trials of the 1930s had in fact been a far-sighted response by Stalin to potential fifth-column activity in his country.[3]

Most opinion makers outside the government also emphasized the positive aspects of the Soviet ally. Hollywood, for example, rushed to refurbish the Soviet Union's image with such films as *Mission to Moscow, Song of Russia, North Star, Counterattack,* and other motion pictures highly flattering to America's newest ally. (James McGuiness, a scriptwriter for MGM, later characterized these productions as "a form of intellectual lend lease.") In 1942, a young James Reston wrote *Prelude to Victory,* which asserted that "anti-Russian remarks" amounted to a "shabby un-American game." Eric Johnston, president of the U.S. Chamber of Commerce, claimed he could "see no cause for fear in the existence of a more or less communist system in Russia." "Marxian thinking in Soviet Russia is out," exulted the even more optimistic *New York Times,* and "the capitalist system, better described as the competitive system, is back."[4]

Other respected figures claimed that religious persecution had been curtailed in the Soviet Union. To an extent this was true: Stalin, realizing that religion would be useful in maintaining morale among his people, did permit the Russian Orthodox hierarchy to reopen some churches. Many Americans took the gesture to mean that Stalin would allow full religious freedom after

---

*The U.S. government's relations with Stalin were never as cordial as they were with British Prime Minister Winston Churchill, the third major partner in the Allied cause. Delays in lend lease shipments and in opening a second European front greatly angered Stalin, especially after Roosevelt promised Soviet Foreign Minister Vyacheslav Molotov in early 1942 that a second front would be opened later that year. Both sides (Stalin in particular) worried that the other would make a separate, self-serving peace with Germany. Perhaps most tellingly, Churchill was kept up to date on the progress of the Manhattan Project, whereas Stalin was not officially informed about the atomic bomb until his meeting with President Harry Truman at Potsdam, just after the successful testing at Los Alamos.

the war. Roosevelt even advised Soviet Ambassador Konstantine Oumansky that if Moscow could get some "publicity back to this country regarding the freedom of religion [in the USSR] ... it might have a very fine educational effect." This did not fool everyone, of course, but even some clergymen who probably knew better contributed to the prevailing mood. Reinhold Niebuhr, editor of *Christianity and Crisis* and the future president of Americans for Democratic Action, wrote that Americans would one day "thank God for the residual health of these godless Russians."[5]

Overall, the U.S.S.R. received a highly favorable wartime press. Thousands of examples could be cited, of which the most famous is the March 1943 *Life* magazine special issue on the Soviet Union. Readers learned that Lenin was "perhaps the greatest man of modern times"; that in the U.S.S.R. "divorces are harder to obtain, the family is glorified, and sexual looseness is condemned"; that "artists are the highest paid group" in the Soviet state; that the NKVD was roughly analogous to the FBI; and that the Russians, who "look like Americans, dress like Americans and think like Americans," were really "one hell of a people."[6]

Even conservative anti-Communists sometimes picked up on the new theme. While pinned down on Corregidor by the Japanese, General Douglas MacArthur conceded that "the hopes of civilization rest on the worthy banners of the courageous Red Army." After returning from a tour of the Soviet Union, World War I hero Eddie Rickenbacker offered high praise for the disciplined rigor of the Soviet work force and factory system. Capitalist businessmen, as we have noted, had little but praise for their great ideological enemy, the Soviet Union.[7]

Under these unique circumstances, many Americans came to regard the U.S.S.R. far more favorably than they had in the past. The good will produced by the alliance is well documented in Paul Willen's "Who 'Collaborated' With Russia?" and in Ralph Levering's more recent *American Opinion and the Russian Alliance, 1939–1945*. Of course, all objections to providing the Soviets with lend lease vanished immediately once the United States joined the war. Beyond this, an impressive grass-roots campaign for an early second European front emerged, which was exactly what the U.S.S.R. so desperately wanted. In some cities, orchestra halls filled with cheers when "Hymn to the Soviet Union," the Russian national anthem, was played. College students at Rutgers University held benefit dances to raise money for Russian War Relief, a cause that enjoyed wide popular support. When Red Army troops successfully defended Stalingrad and fairly assured an ultimate Nazi defeat, their gallantry inspired a tremendous outpouring of gratitude and affection among the American people. Those who criticized the Soviets during the crucial years of 1942–1943, recalled Soviet expert George Kennan, were sometimes accused of near-treasonous behavior.[8]

Although a bit of this pro-Soviet euphoria wore off as victory drew nearer, the spirit of friendship for the U.S.S.R. (which also was prevalent in England) remained viable throughout the strange alliance. In his book *The Vital Center,* Arthur Schlesinger, Jr., claims that "toward the end of the Second War, Russia had gained the admiration and confidence of all elements in the west as never before." And Stephen Ambrose, a widely read diplomatic historian, notes in his *Rise to Globalism* that "the war ended without any sharp break with the Russians. There had been innumerable strains . . . , but the United States and Russia were still allies, and . . . the possibility of continued cooperation was, if frail, alive." Significantly, during the 1944 presidential campaign, Republican challenger Tom Dewey tried to curry favor with Polish voters but decided not to criticize the U.S.S.R. directly—even though Europe's liberation was by now under way, and even though Dewey did choose to revive the old charge that Communists exercised too much influence in the Roosevelt administration.[9]

In these unusual times, even some who still viewed American Communists with contempt and *suspicion* did not necessarily consider the Communist party a serious impediment to good Soviet–American relations. The conservative journalist David Lawrence wrote in 1943 that there was no "need [for] Russia [to] be viewed through the eyes or deeds of the misguided zealots in America who have committed acts of sabotage and dissension here in the name of Communism." Yet, American Communists substantially benefited from the existing military alliance with the Soviet Union. Because no one could seriously deny that Communists were totally committed to destroying Nazi Germany, World War II was the high point of prestige for the roughly 100,000 party and Young Communist League members, and a like number of fellow travelers. Not without reason have historians described this period as "a kind of blessing to the party," "their most satisfying political experience," "exhilirating," "a recruiting harvest," and "the flood tide of their importance."[10]

In effect, the war resurrected the Popular Front, on a grander, more urgent scale. "To make America a better place to live," a one-time leader in the National Association of Manufacturers said during the war, "we must all work together, and that includes the Communists." During this period, many Communists had little difficulty in obtaining jobs in the Office of Strategic Services and other government agencies. A few Communists were elected to local offices in New York City. Julius Emspak, a Communist official in the United Electrical Workers, was appointed by FDR to the new War Labor Board, and in general Communist factions within the Congress of Industrial Organizations received a new lease on life. "Americans," wrote Communist party leader Earl Browder, "are now making a real effort to understand our Soviet ally," as they "realize that they had fallen victims to the Hitlerite campaign of misinformation and calumny against the Soviet Union." The general secretary himself benefited from the alliance in May 1942 when FDR commuted his prison sentence (he had served part of a 4-year term for passport fraud) to time served as a gesture "to promote national unity."[11]

The Communists were at least as dedicated to the war effort as other Americans, and often more so. With characteristic ardor, the party abruptly deferred the class struggle and all other divisive issues—such as civil rights for Blacks—that might have hindered the war effort. William Z. Foster and other party spokesmen urged close collaboration among all Axis enemies, regardless of class or ideology. What would be hailed as the "spirit of Teheran" provoked startling changes in the Communist movement. Louis Budenz, the managing editor of the *Daily Worker* who would later renounce communism, recalled that party members hastened "to acclaim Roosevelt [so recently a villain to them] a hero . . . according to the tone set by the chiefs of the U.S.S.R." A minister was given a regular column in the Sunday edition of the *Daily Worker*. Communists not only opposed all wartime strikes (including those called by a former ally, John L. Lewis of the United Mine Workers) but vigorously supported free enterprise and monopoly capital. Down on the farm, Archie Wright's pro-Communist monthly newsletter attacked all "fascist-minded" ploys "to disrupt the war effort," including the higher commodity prices favored by the Grange and Farm Bureau. At party gatherings, members often sang "The Star-Spangled Banner" and recited the Pledge of Allegiance.[12]

Even more surprisingly, Moscow in 1943 dissolved the Communist International, or "Comintern." A year later, the American Communist party followed suit, formally disbanding but immediately reestablishing itself as the Communist Political Association. The Young Communist League also folded up its operations. Undoubtedly the main purpose of these changes was to make the Communist movement appear less threatening at this critical time; yet, something more than mere cynicism also may have been present. George Charney, then a party member, recalled in his memoirs that "the war reunited me with my fellow Americans in a common, democratic cause." At long last, communism and "Americanism" seemed to be in harmony. As we shall see, the party flatly insisted that red baiting of any kind was a Nazi-inspired ploy to weaken Allied unity. Although for tactical reasons the Communists usually ignored their critics in the religious community, those who persisted in expressing hostile views about the U.S.S.R. or the Communist party could expect to be vilified as agents of Hitler. Having had their own patriotism called into question for so many years, the Communists were finally able to turn the tables on their long-time foes.[13]

Of course, this unique reversal was vigorously opposed by the leading American anti-Communists. Their story, largely ignored, falls broadly into three historical categories. It is a piece (admittedly a modest one) of domestic life during World War II; it examines, indirectly, the Communist movement during its most unusual and successful phase; and it contributes to our understanding of the antiradical/anti-Communist and anti-Soviet tradition in American history. In each of these three fields, the need exists for an in-depth study of anti-Soviet and anti-Communist sentiments during World War II.

Certainly the leading works on civilian life and the home front in World War II America have very little information on anti-Communist, or even pro-Communist, attitudes of this time. Most are pleasantly nostalgic and provide useful background material, but American Communists and their detractors receive passing mention at most. Geoffrey Perrett's *Days of Sadness, Years of Triumph* and Richard Polenberg's *War and Society* provide the best overviews of the political, economic, cultural, and social impact of wartime America; but again the references to the topic at hand are scattered and fairly conventional. Both briefly observe that during this period comparatively better relations with the Communist state prevailed. Perrett notes that "the core of American anti-Communism remained untouched" during these years, and that the U.S.S.R. remained "an embarrassment to the West." Yet, "the prowess of the Red Army kept the Russians high in popular esteem up to the close of the Second World War"—and their last-minute declaration of war on Japan even "triggered a boomlet of goodwill." Polenberg claims in *War and Society* that "relatively few" people thought the U.S.S.R. was "a menace to American institutions" at this time, and "[t]o some extent" a feeling of admiration for the U.S.S.R. developed out of the alliance. Concerning domestic Communists, Polenberg says that "less likely targets for repression could hardly have been found."[14]

More has been written about the American Communist party than about any political organization of comparable size and influence. In the mass of scholarly literature on this topic, the "Communism in American Life" series, begun in the late 1950s under the editorial direction of Clinton Rossiter, stands out as a particularly ambitious undertaking. This project sought to provide a comprehensive account of the Communist party, with monograph treatments of the movement's involvement and influence in specific segments—education, labor, government, the arts, religion—of American society. Useful and generally well written—Earl Latham's *The Communist Controversy in Washington: From the New Deal to McCarthy* is particularly good—these volumes are markedly hostile to the Communist movement. Together they set forth what might be called a 1950s school of academic thinking on American communism. The first volume in the series, Theodore Draper's *The Roots of American Communism,* sets the tone for the later works when it argues that the CPUSA quickly became a mere "appendage" of the Russian revolutionary state, and that "nothing else so important ever happened to it again."[15]

Two good general histories of the CPUSA are available. In 1957, Irving Howe and Lewis Coser published *The American Communist Party, A Critical History,* a lively account of the Communists' public history from 1919 to 1957.

The subtitle is accurate enough: The authors (who were once sympathetic to Trotsky) portray a dishonest, unprincipled movement that exerted a "profoundly destructive and corrupting influence upon American radicalism." A chapter on the war years discusses the "atrophy of moral sensibility" about the U.S.S.R. that created "for Stalinism ... an ideal culture in which to breed." Though still useful, the Howe–Coser study is now overshadowed by Harvey Klehr's *The Heyday of American Communism*. As a detailed account of party activities in the prewar decade of the 1930s, "those glorious years when ...[the Communists] erroneously thought the future was theirs,"[16] this volume has no equal. Throughout, Klehr is emphatic about the party's total submission to Kremlin directives and policymaking.

A broad range of specialized studies, supplementing and often surpassing the Communism in American Life volumes, have appeared. There are several interesting accounts of intellectuals and how they came to grips with Communist issues and ideas; these include William O'Neill, *A Better World;* James Weinstein, *Ambiguous Legacy: The Left in American Politics;* and Frank A. Warren, III, *Liberals and Communism, The "Red Decade" Revisited*. Many of the monographs on American Communists discuss their role in organized labor. Until recently, most of this writing was notable for an orthodox, anti-Communist approach, such as Philip Taft's well-regarded general history, *Organized Labor in American History*. This interpretation holds that Communists "created a new series of problems for the democratic unions," and they never hesitated to ignore "the interests of American workers ... when such interests did not coincide with those of the Soviet government." *The Communist Party vs. the C.I.O.*, Max Kampelman's influential anti-Communist study, asserts that nothing less than "the integrity and survival of the trade union heritage [was] at stake" in this struggle. David Saposs, in his *Communism in American Unions,* is nearly as critical of those union officials who worked with the Communists as he is of party members themselves. A supporter of the House Committee on Un-American Activities, Saposs hoped his book would intensify anti-Commmunist feeling in America; one of the chapters in this hard-line volume is entitled "Combatting Communist Domination."[17]

From a very different angle of vision, Art Preis's *Labor's Giant Step, Twenty Years of the CIO,* further contributes to the list of studies critical of the Communist party. A Trotskyist, Preis considers CIO's rise to be "the greatest event in modern American history," but his contempt for the "Stalinists" is hardly less than his scorn for those timid labor leaders who abandoned the class struggle and turned to the Democratic party to solve labor's problems. Despite this bias, Preis's work, together with Saposs's and Kampelman's studies, remained the standard critical treatments of Communists in the union movement until the publication of Bert Cochran's *Labor and Communism*. Although his criticisms are more measured than those of the previous authors,

Cochran agrees that "Communist leaders knowingly accepted every instruction from Russia as Holy Writ," and he dismisses the Communist leaders in the CIO as so many "hired hands."[18]

With the emergence of the "New Left" perspective in the late 1960s and 1970s, American Communists—particularly those involved in the labor movement—began to receive a respectful hearing from some historians. As a result, a new portrait has emerged. Communists were not slavish disciples of the Comintern or the Kremlin. They were good trade unionists. Many considered themselves to be good Americans. During the period of the Nazi–Soviet pact, the new interpretation goes, Communists were falsely accused of leading strikes intended to disrupt America's defense buildup. Subsequently, the party's expulsion from the CIO was a by-product of Cold War hysteria; their actions during the war were a negligible factor in their demise.

Roger Keeran's *The Communist Party and the Auto Workers Union* is one of the best of the newer, nontraditional interpretations of Communist party activities. Reviewed as both "a model of first-rate academic scholarship" and "an apologia of monumental naivete of the Communist party's schizophrenic career," this book is certainly the most comprehensive monograph on this topic, but the author's partiality for the Communists is obvious. James Prickett's several scholarly articles provide the most persuasive counterarguments to the charge that Communists deliberately tried to sabotage the defense industry with a series of crippling strikes in 1940 and early 1941. Harvey Levenstein's *Communism, Anticommunism, and the CIO* also treats the Communists rather charitably, although he does criticize the party for too often compromising its radical beliefs in pursuit of temporary tactical advantages. But New Left historian Nelson Lichtenstein argues in his *Labor's War at Home: The CIO in World War II* that the non-Communist leadership was responsible for taming the CIO's well-known militancy, in return for various considerations from Washington. The "filial-dependent" relationship that developed between government and organized labor foreclosed any possibility of meaningful class struggle in postwar America. Joseph Starobin, a one-time *Daily Worker* foreign news editor, concludes in his *The Crisis of American Communism, 1943–1947* that Browder's wartime attempt to reshape the movement into a left-leaning political lobby, a policy that was condemned in the famous "Duclos letter" at the end of the war, was the best strategy available to American Communists. Philip Jaffe's *The Rise and Fall of American Communism* is as close to a political biography of Earl Browder that is now available. A personal friend of Browder's and a self-described "close fellow-traveler of the American Communist Party from 1930 to 1945," Jaffe devotes only a few pages of text to the war years. Like Starobin, he is more concerned with the traumatic breakup that occurred just after the war.[19]

For the war years, a fine analysis of the party's activities is provided in Maurice Isserman's *Which Side Were You On?* Judiciously sympathetic to the Communists, Isserman attempts to humanize them, to fit them in a positive way into the broader context of American history. Anti-Communists who remained vocal during the war receive little attention from Isserman, who contends the Communists were at this time finally "moving toward a more realistic appraisal of their position in American life," until the abrupt abandonment of Browder's accommodationist policies destroyed any possibility of significant leftist participation in the American polity.[20]

However, it is highly probable that this could not have occurred under normal circumstances, given the long and virulent tradition of antiradicalism throughout U.S. history. The scholarly literature on these closely related phenomena is enormous. Studies that help put the antiradical tendency into its larger historical context will be discussed in the next chapter. Surprisingly, a balanced, first-rate general history on American anticommunism remains unwritten. But for the first flareup of anti-Bolshevik feeling, Robert Murray's excellent *Red Scare, A Study in National Hysteria 1917–1920* remains the standard account. Peter Filene's, *Americans and the Soviet Experiment, 1917–1933* also should be consulted. In the Depression decade, "anticommunism" frequently was synonymous with conservative opposition to Franklin Delano Roosevelt's New Deal. The better studies of the president and his dynamic administration provide informative material on FDR's red-baiting critics, and there are numerous specialized studies.

Publications on postwar anticommunism abound, as scores of historians have scrutinized the "Hollywood Ten," the Rosenberg and Hiss cases, HUAC and other investigative bodies, Truman's domestic response to communism, and McCarthyism. Some of these studies provide helpful background material on the long anti-Communist tradition in America, which helps set the stage for the postwar/McCarthy era.[21] But such chapters do not examine in detail the World War II years, a period in which overt American anticommunism declined to its lowest level of popularity. The gap in this field is the World War II period. The goal of this book is to bridge that discontinuity.

NOTES

1. Robert Sherwood, *Roosevelt and Hopkins: An Intimate History* (New York: Harper and Brothers, 1948), p. 804.
2. John Deane, *The Strange Alliance* (New York: Viking Press, 1947); Robert Beitzell, *The Uneasy Alliance: America, Britain, and Russia, 1941–1943* (New York: Knopf, 1972), p. 366; William O'Neill, *A Better World* (New York: Simon & Schuster, 1982), p. 58; Helen Lombard, *While They Fought* (New York: Charles Scribner's Sons, 1947), pp. 207, 278.
3. For an idea of FDR's pro-Soviet rhetoric during the war, see his congratulatory remarks in commemoration of the twenty-fifth anniversary of the U.S.S.R. in Samuel

Rosenman, ed., *The Public Papers and Addresses of Franklin D. Roosevelt*, Vol. XI (New York: Harper and Brothers, 1950), pp. 444–45, and the president's tribute to the Russians in his 7 January 1943, State of the Union address, published in Rosenman, *Papers and Addresses*, Vol. XII, p. 24; Harry Hopkins, "The Inside Story of My Meeting with Stalin," *The American Magazine*, December 1941, p. 14; Henry Wallace, "Our Friendship to Russia," *Vital Speeches of the Day*, 8 November 1942, pp. 72–3; New York *Times*, 21 May 1943; Wendell Wilkie, "We Must Work with Russia," *New York Times Magazine*, 17 January 1943, p. 5; Wilkie, "Don't Stir Distrust of Russia," *New York Times Magazine*, 2 January 1944, pp. 3–4; Joseph Davies, *Mission to Moscow* (New York: Simon & Schuster, 1941), p. 20.

4. Richard Lingeman, *Don't You Know There's a War On? The American Home Front, 1941–1945* (New York: G. P. Putnam's Sons, 1970), pp. 207–8; Robert Carr, *The House Committee on Un-American Activities* (Ithaca, NY: Cornell University Press, 1952), p. 65; James Reston, *Prelude to Victory* (New York: Knopf, 1942), p. 135; Eric Johnston, *America Unlimited* (Garden City, NY: Doubleday, Doran and Company, 1944), pp. 227–28; Robert Dallek, *The American Style of Foreign Policy: Cultural Politics and Foreign Affairs* (New York: Knopf, 1983), p. 139.

5. Ralph Roy, *Communism and the Churches* (New York: Harcourt, Brace and Company, 1960), pp. 163–74; William Langer and S. Everett Gleason, *The Undeclared War, 1940–1941* (New York: Harper, 1953), pp. 797–98; Myron Taylor, ed., *Wartime Correspondence between President Roosevelt and Pope Pius XII* (New York: MacMillan, 1947), p. 61; N. S. Timasheff, "Religion in Russia," *Current History*, February 1946, pp. 105–10; "Are You a Tory?" *Presbyterian of the South*, 31 December 1941, p. 2; "The Russians and Our Interdependence," *Christianity and Crisis*, 25 August 1941, p. 1; "Break-Through," *Time*, 27 December 1943, pp. 53–54; "Russian Orthodoxy's Offensive," *Newsweek*, 27 December 1943, p. 70.

6. Melvin Small, "How We Learned to Love the Russians: American Media and the Soviet Union during World War II," *The Historian*, May 1974, pp. 455–78; *Life*, 28 March 1943.

7. William Manchester, *American Caesar* (New York: Dell, 1978), p. 283; *New York Times*, 18 August 1943; Edward Rickenbacker, *Rickenbacker* (Englewood Cliffs, NJ: Prentice-Hall, 1967), p. 380; Harland Allen, "Looking Ahead with Russia," *Rotarian*, February 1944, pp. 25–26; Eric Johnston, "A Business View of Russia," *Nation's Business*, October 1944, pp. 21–22; Harrison Salisbury, "Russia Beckons Big Business," *Collier's*, 2 September 1944, p. 11; Junius Wood, "Russia—Customer and Competitor," *Nation's Business*, March 1944, pp. 28–30. Interestingly, though, the *Wall Street Journal* remained hostile to the U.S.S.R. (see Small, "How We Learned to Love the Russians," p. 462).

8. Paul Willen, "Who 'Collaborated' with Russia?" *The Antioch Review*, September 1954, pp. 259–83; Ralph Levering, *American Opinion and the Russian Alliance, 1939–1945* (Chapel Hill: University of North Carolina Press, 1976); *The Targum*, 11 March 1942; Edward Carter, "Russian War Relief," *The Slavonic and East European Review*, August 1944, pp. 61–74; George Kennan, *Russia and the West under Lenin and Stalin* (Boston: Little, Brown and Company, 1961), p. 359.

9. Levering offers the best account of the "ominous drift" in American opinion of the U.S.S.R. once the Axis began to crumble, see pp. 169–99; for British sentiment, see Nikolai Tolstoy, *Stalin's Secret War* (New York: Holt, Rinehart &

Winston, 1981), pp. 278–79, 287–94; "Russomania in England," *Politics*, November 1944, pp. 295–96; Arthur Schlesinger, Jr., *The Vital Center* (Cambridge, MA: Riverside Press, 1962), p. 92; Stephen Ambrose, *Rise to Globalism* (New York: Penguin Books, 1983), p. 71.

10. David Lawrence Papers (Princeton University), Dispatches, 23 February 1943; Harvey Levenstein, *Communism, Anticommunism, and the CIO* (Westport, CT: Greenwood Press, 1981), p. 158; Irving Howe and Lewis Coser, *The American Communist Party, A Critical History* (New York: DaCapo Press, 1974), p. 406; Maurice Isserman, *Which Side Were You On?* (Middletown, CT: Wesleyan University Press, 1982), p. 127; Sidney Lens, *Left, Right and Center, Conflicting Forces in American Labor* (Hinsdale, IL: Henry Regnery Company, 1949), p. 340; Bert Cochran, *Labor and Communism* (Princeton, NJ: Princeton University Press, 1977), p. 206.

11. Maurice Goldbloom, "American Communism: Party of the Right," *Common Sense*, September 1944, p. 306; Nathaniel Weyl, *The Battle Against Disloyalty* (New York: Crowell, 1951), p. 180; Earl Browder, *Victory—And After* (New York: International Publishers, 1942), p. 158; *New York Times*, 17 May 1942.

12. Wilson Record, *Race and Radicalism* (Ithaca, NY: Cornell University Press, 1964), pp. 118–21; James W. Ford, "Some Problems of the Negro People in the National Front to Destroy Hitler and Hitlerism," *The Communist*, October 1941, pp. 888–96; William Z. Foster, "Trade Unions in the War Emergency," *The Communist*, January 1942, p. 57; Louis Budenz, *This Is My Story* (New York: Whittlesey House, 1947), p. 229; Earl Browder, *Communists and National Unity* (New York: Workers Library, 1944), pp. 6, 9–10; Lowell Dyson, *Red Harvest, The Communist Party and American Farmers* (Lincoln: University of Nebraska Press, 1982), pp. 184–85.

13. John Lewis Evans, *The Communist International, 1919–1943* (New York: Pageant-Poseidon, 1973), pp. 169–77; Hans Berger (Gerhart Eisler), "Remarks on the Discussion concerning the Dissolution of the Comintern," *The Communist*, November 1943, pp. 1018–29; Freda Kirchwey, "The End of the Comintern," *Nation*, 29 May 1943, p. 762; Jane Degras, ed., *The Communist International, 1919–1943, Documents*, vol. III (London: Oxford University Press, 1965), pp. 476–81; George Charney, *A Long Journey* (Chicago: Quadrangle Books, 1968), p. 133.

14. Geoffrey Perrett, *Days of Sadness, Years of Triumph* (New York: Coward, McCann, and Geoghegan, 1973), pp. 421–25; Richard Polenberg, *War and Society, The United States 1941–1945* (Philadelphia: J.B. Lippincott Company, 1972), pp. 39–40.

15. Theodore Draper, *The Roots of American Communism* (New York: Viking Press, 1957), p. 395. Other titles in this series include Daniel Aaron, *Writers on the Left* (New York, 1961); Theodore Draper, *American Communism and Soviet Russia* (New York, 1960); Nathan Glazer, *The Social Basis of American Communism* (New York, 1961); Robert Iverson, *The Communists and the Schools* (New York, 1959); Frank Meyer, *The Moulding of Communists, The Training of the Communist Cadre* (New York, 1961); Clinton Rossiter, *Marxism: The View from America* (New York, 1960); David Shannon, *A History of the Communist Party since 1945* (New York, 1959); Roy, *Communism and the Churches*.

16. Howe and Coser, pp. 436, 499; Harvey Klehr, *The Heyday of American Communism, The Depression Decade* (New York: Basic Books, 1984), p. 416.

17. Philip Taft, *Organized Labor in American History* (New York: Harper and Row, 1964), pp. 618–19.

18. Art Preis, *Labor's Giant Step, Twenty Years of the CIO* (New York: Pioneer Publishers, 1964), p. 3; Cochran, pp. 9, 100.
19. The review quotes are by Norman Markowitz, in *Political Science Quarterly*, Spring 1981, pp. 161–62; and Bert Cochran, in *American Historical Review*, April 1981, pp. 475–76; James Prickett, "Communists and the Communist Issue in the American Labor Movement, 1920–1950," (unpublished Ph.D. dissertation, UCLA, 1975), pp. 247–61; Prickett, "Communism and Factionalism in the United Automobile Workers, 1939–1947," *Science and Society*, Summer 1968, pp. 257–77; Prickett, "Some Aspects of the Communist Controversy in the CIO," *Science and Society*, Summer–Fall 1969, pp. 299–321; Philip Jaffe, *The Rise and Fall of American Communism* (New York: Horizon, 1975), p. 12.
20. Isserman, *Which Side Were You On?*, p. 17.
21. Examples of such overview chapters include Athan Theoharis, *Seeds of Repression* (Chicago: Quadrangle, 1971), pp. 3–12; Alan Harper, *The Politics of Loyalty* (Westport, CT: Greenwood Press, 1969), pp. 5–19; and David Oshinsky, *A Conspiracy So Immense* (New York: Free Press, 1983), pp. 85–102.

2

America's Antiradical Tradition

Barely a week after the Japanese attack on Pearl Harbor, a columnist for the *Daily Worker* predicted that "the Hitlerite nexus" in the United States would "try again and again" to split the "fighting alliance" with the U.S.S.R., thus permitting Adolf Hitler to "conquer America." As the war progressed, Earl Browder, head of the American Communist party, confessed to having underestimated the strength and scope of the Nazi-inspired "strike wave conspiracy" then under way in the United States.[1]

Quite unintentionally, these men were contributing to a dark tradition deeply rooted in America's political and social culture. Simply stated, this tradition involves an insistent, often exaggerated belief that vast internal conspiracies are afoot to undermine the American way of life, to deprive the people of their liberties, and to supplant freedom with dictatorship in the United States.[2] Economic upheavals and attendant social dislocations have been routinely attributed—most often by politically conservative Americans—to the designs of evil, scheming men. American political history is replete with these accusations and countercharges of complicity in treasonous conspiracies. Frequently, the accusers claim that an unfriendly foreign country is encouraging or directing these "un-American" activities. Those most commonly identified as responsible for these plots include immigrants, Catholics, labor unions, and radical groups of every stripe, especially the American Communist party.

For most of the present century, communism has been the bête noire of those Americans who have believed their country to be imperiled by enemies from within—and beyond. Members of the Communist party have been subjected to unsparing criticism and official persecution, on the grounds that they are under secret orders from the U.S.S.R. to help overthrow the U.S. government. Although the Soviet–American alliance of 1941–1945 substantially weakened the "red bogey" phenomenon, many Americans—no doubt including the Communists themselves—were puzzled and frustrated by the survival of anti-Soviet, anti-Communist opinion, amid even this unique crisis. Perhaps they failed to appreciate the extended tradition of conspiracy theory, anti-radicalism, and hatred of bolshevism that lay behind these convictions. As such, a review of this tradition provides a necessary prologue to an extended discussion of the hardy anti-Communist credo that survived the U.S.–Soviet alliance of World War II.

The United States proclaimed their independence from England in a crescendo of egalitarian rhetoric—and conspiracy theory. Deeply influenced by the conspiracy-laden ideas and rhetoric of eighteenth-century British opposition political theorists, America's revolutionary leaders justified their cause by maintaining that London was engaged in a plot to deprive them of their rights as Englishmen. In Bernard Bailyn's reconstruction of the colonists' impression of these events, the Stamp Act, Townshend Duties, Boston Massacre, and Coercive Acts all "added up to something greater, [and] more malevolent than their simple sum." Aroused, the colonists struck back and defeated what Thomas Jefferson called this "deliberate, systematical plan of reducing us to slavery." However, the American people might have squandered their triumph had they listened to those who branded the proposed Constitution of 1787 the handiwork of an "infernal junto of demagogues" seeking to repeal the rights of individual citizens and the several states.[3]

Even as President George Washington nobly presided over the new nation, America's first party system began taking shape amid impassioned accusations of unholy conspiracies and secret sellouts to foreign powers. Similar charges would resurface in future party conflicts, but probably never with as much sound and fury as when the Federalists and Democratic-Republicans competed for power in the last years of the eighteenth century. Ironically, the upheaval of 1789 in faraway France served as a primary focus of this interparty strife. Federalists, horrified by the violent excesses of this revolution, looked upon the Jeffersonians' apparent approval of these activities with fear and dismay. These concerns rapidly coalesced into full-blown, partisan charges that the Jeffersonians were conspiring with the French revolutionaries to bring the plague of Jacobinism to American shores. The Federalist propaganda mill also linked their rivals to the allegedly subversive activities of the "Bavarian Illuminati," a small, secret society attached to the European freemason movement.* Contemporary concerns about the power of the Illuminati melded effectively into the Federalists' broader attacks on the patriotism and good intentions of their Jeffersonian rivals.[4]

---

*Ultraconservative, pro-Federalist preachers like Timothy Dwight and Jedediah Morse were largely responsible for spreading fear about this shadowy organization. Before long the furor quieted down, dormant but not dead: Many decades later, Nelson Rockefeller was accused of financing the organization. (See *The Herald of Freedom and Metropolitan Review,* IV, No. 3, 13 September, 1963. Found in Radical Literature Special Collection, Rutgers University, Box 25, No. 6100.)

Republicans countered with the charge that the Federalists (sometimes even Washington was included) supported their leader Alexander Hamilton in his mad dream of reimposing the monarchy in America. When Jeffersonians examined the terms of "Jay's Treaty" with Britain, they denounced this agreement as the final proof of a Federalist-sponsored betrayal of America's hard-fought independence from the Crown. This treaty, barely approved by the Senate in 1794, became a major issue in the presidential contest of 1796. In an astonishingly bitter campaign, the two principals—Jefferson, and the victorious John Adams—were each accused of high treason by his rival's party press.[5]

When an undeclared naval war with France broke out in 1798, Federalist congressional leaders rammed through the infamous Alien and Sedition Acts, perhaps the most repressive legislation in American history. These laws gave the president authority to deport "dangerous" aliens and to imprison them without trial in wartime; in addition, penalties were established for saying or writing anything "with the purpose of . . . aiding and abetting a foreign nation in hostile design against the United States." Although the Federalists badly underestimated the internal strength of the country they governed, their suspicions were not entirely groundless. French agents operating in the United States did try to help the Republicans politically. When the "Revolution of 1800" swept the Jeffersonians into national power, relations with France improved, and the much-maligned acts were allowed to expire. They endure, however, as a symbol of the antiradical, antiforeign attitudes that have played a conspicuous role in American life and politics from the earliest years of the country's history.[6]

The more egalitarian spirit of Jeffersonian democracy, cresting in the age of Andrew Jackson, hatched its own great conspiracy panic, the remarkable Anti-Mason movement. In 1829, the unexplained disappearance of a disaffected Mason who had threatened to reveal his fraternal order's secrets touched off an explosion of antimasonic activity in the northeastern states. Almost overnight, the Masons' loyalty to their country came under widespread suspicion. With their secret loyalties, mysterious rituals, and hidden wealth, the "grand kings" of the "Masonic empire" somehow seemed to threaten America's democratic folkways and institutions. Shrewd politicians like Thurlow Weed of New York soon realized that what has been called the "unbridled fanaticism" of antimasonry could be exploited for partisan political advantage.[7]

In general, the antimasonic cause was embraced by politicians not aligned with the Democratic party. Using the rhetoric of antimasonry, Whigs postured as the opponents of conspiring, power-hungry elites—the very trick the Jacksonians used so effectively in their "common man" tirades against the "Monster Bank" and other symbols of unfair privilege. Antimasonry played a brief but significant role in the political wars of its time; and historians continue to debate the merits, if any, of this curious movement. From a modern perspective, antimasonry serves as another early example of the American people's persistent inclination to believe that their country is under secret siege, threatened by conspirators determined to destroy the American way of life.[8]

For most citizens living in the early nineteenth century, the "American way of life" had a distinctly Protestant cast; but by the 1830s this, too, was coming under attack. The new threat originated from across the seas: the first great wave of immigration in American history, mainly from Ireland and Germany, resulting in a vast increase in the country's Roman Catholic population. This rapid demographic shift in America's ethnoreligious makeup inspired a vicious upsurge in nativism and related religious bigotry, especially as the "Romanists" were seen as an impediment to the revivalistic fervor and evangelical-inspired reform movements of this time. The resulting "Protestant Crusade" to defeat the alleged Papist menace took a variety of forms. In 1843, a group of anti-Catholic ministers formed the American Protestant Association "To awaken the community to the dangers which threaten... these United States from the assaults of Romanism." A so-called "no-Popery" press grew in circulation. Prominent evangelical ministers delivered fiery anti-Catholic sermons, sometimes provoking riots and other violence against American Catholics.[9]

Religious identification and related ethnocultural attitudes and issues often were decisive factors in determining mass voting behavior during the Young Republic—indeed for most of the nineteenth century.[10] The Democratic party usually won the allegiance of these new voters, whereas nativist issues tended to be raised by the Whigs, some of whom acquired reputations as antiforeign bigots. When the sectional crisis fatally fragmented the Whig party, nativist and anti-Catholic passions found a political outlet in the American, or "Know-Nothing" party.* This group demanded a sharp reduction in immigration, a lengthened naturalization period, and limitations on the political rights of those immigrants already in the United States. With nativist fears running especially high, the American party temporarily enjoyed remarkable success: they captured several state legislatures, elected a half-dozen governors, sent some 75 Congressmen to Washington, and collected more than 20 percent of the popular vote in the presidential election of 1856.[11]

Slavery and other sectional issues raised havoc in the Know-Nothing movement, just as they did within the other major parties. Nativism, however, found a new vehicle of political expression in the Republican party, whose leaders made a deliberate effort to appeal to these still-extant xenophobic and

---

*Members routinely responded "I know nothing" when asked about their secret organization; hence the nickname.

nativist fears, especially after the Civil War.* During the great wave of immigration that followed the war, the arrival of so many Catholic Italians and Poles triggered a virtual replay of what had occurred in the antebellum period. Once more Catholic-hating Protestants charged that the "foreign prince" in the Vatican was masterminding a conspiracy to bring the United States under his autocratic authority. Once again nativists depicted the immigration process as a Trojan Horse through which treasonous-minded foreigners gained access to America.** And again a host of anti-Catholic and nativistic organizations sprang up in the 1870s and 1880s, all determined to expose and destroy this supposedly great threat to America's survival.[12]

These decades also witnessed America's entry into the Industrial Age, a process that enormously increased the nation's overall material wealth—but at a terrible human cost. Seemingly all-powerful business moguls ruthlessly exploited immigrant and native-born laborers alike in their drive for ever-greater profits. In turn, what has been described as a "loose community of revolt"—made up of Greenbackers, Grangers, single taxers, antimonopolists, Populists,*** Socialists, "Coxey's Army" marchers, anarchists, trade unionists, and others—emerged to redress the imbalances wrought by industrialism. Most of these groups favored specific, fairly limited reforms and were not anticapitalist as such; almost none acquired much political power. Yet, among the general public all were widely regarded as the advance agents of "foreign ideas," mob rule, class conflict, and the destruction of the free-enterprise system.[13]

Trade unionism, the most enduring of these reform movements, had been vilified for decades as dangerously un-American, but these forebodings grew much stronger as the labor movement gained limited momentum after the Civil

---

*The penchant for conspiracy theories contributed to the uncompromising sectional rhetoric of this era. The "Slave Power" symbol so effectively invoked by Republican orators borrowed heavily from this tradition. Of course, the evils of slavery could hardly have been overstated; yet, historian Eric Foner has argued that many Republicans believed that "the ultimate intention of the South was to spread slavery into the North, and to destroy civil liberties in the free states." This was nonsense, but the fact that so many Republicans thought this way made an already volatile situation worse. See Eric Foner, *Free Soil, Free Labor, Free Men* (New York: Oxford University Press, 1978), pp. 97–102; and David Brion Davis, *The Slave Power Conspiracy and the Paranoid Style* (Baton Rouge: Lousiana State University Press, 1969).

**Of course, the Chinese, Jews, and other immigrants encountered at least as much bigotry and discrimination in America as did the "Papists." But Catholics were viewed as the greatest *menace* at this time, because of their greater numbers and because of their confessed allegiance to a foreign head of state, the Pope.

***The Populists peddled their own conspiracy theory, insisting that the farmers' economic woes in the 1890s were the result of secret manipulations by unscrupulous Jewish Wall Street bankers. See Richard Hofstadter, *The Age of Reform* (New York: Vintage Book, 1955), pp. 60–93; but also Norman Pollack, 'The Myth of Populist Anti-Semitism,' *American Historical Review*, October 1962, pp. 76–80.

War. Such events as the lawless activities of the "Molly Maguires," the Great Railroad Strike of 1877, the Haymarket Square bombing of May 4, 1886, in Chicago; the steelworkers' strike against Andrew Carnegie's Homestead plant in 1892, and the Pullman walkout of 1894 seemed to confirm the charge that labor unions nurtured foreign-inspired agitators, domestic instability, and proletarian revolt. For the most part, the public supported the government's harsh, unyielding crackdowns against those involved in these events.[14]

Similar fears were aroused by the appearance and early successes of the Socialist party, which was organized in 1901 under the leadership of Eugene Debs, Victor Berger, Morris Hillquit, and others. Initially benefitting from the idealistic impulse of the Progressive Era, the party grew impressively in most regions of the country: by 1912, party membership stood at 118,000, more than 1,000 Socialists held public office (mainly on the local level), and Debs, the party's perennial presidential candidate, received nearly 6 percent of the popular vote. Mainstream opinion makers and political figures, sensing serious competition from the left, denounced this "rising tide of socialism" as a dire threat to democracy and basic American values. Theodore Roosevelt considered the Socialist party "far more ominous than any populist or similar movement in time past," and he bruited his Bull Moose campaign of 1912 as "a corrective to socialism and an antidote to anarchy."[15]

However, in actual practice the American Socialist party proved to be more of a reformist organization, radical only by virtue of its formal ideological opposition to capitalism. Without excessive complaint, most Socialists pragmatically accommodated themselves to the established political and trade union institutions in the United States. This was why more militant Socialists like William "Big Bill" Haywood left the party in 1905 to organize the anarchosyndicalist Industrial Workers of the World.[16] After the Bolshevik Revolution, of course, the disaffected had an even more radical alternative, the American Communist party. At least in the short term, however, such defections did little to improve the Socialist party's reputation with a broad segment of apprehensive and suspicious Americans.

Socialists encountered the full brunt of antiradical antagonism after they refused to support U.S. involvement in World War I. The government prosecuted a number of Socialists, including Debs, under the newly enacted Espionage Act, which made it illegal "to promote the success" of America's enemies. In addition, local police forces around the country broke up Socialist meetings, and party members frequently suffered public abuse, physical attack, and loss of employment during the war. The "Wobblies," who also refused to support the war effort, suffered even more repression, for they were in a position to hinder the war effort directly in the plants and war-production industries in which they were organized. The IWW's refusal to suspend strike activity infuriated the predominantly conservative press; for example, the *Chicago Tribune* demanded the jailing of all IWW men. In September 1917, the Justice Department launched a nationwide raid on IWW offices and arrested at least 200 union officials. Authorities did little to protect those Wobblies victimized by beatings, tar-and-featherings, and even lynchings during the war.[17]

For encouraging the darkest antiradical, antiforeign impulses in the American character, the Wilson administration must bear heavy responsibility for these excesses. Wilson appointed the journalist George Creel to head the newly created Committee on Public Information, the country's first federal propaganda agency. The CPI urged citizens to sign up with local superpatriot groups and to keep a watchful eye on their neighbors, acquaintances, and friends. "Not a pin dropped in the home of any one with a foreign name," Creel boasted, "but that it rang like thunder on the inner ear of some listening sleuth." After all, the enemies spies were everywhere.[18]

Unfortunately, this climate of official intolerance and suspicion long outlasted the war-ending armistice of November 11, 1918. In fact, thanks to the Russian Revolution of 1917 and the assumption to power by Vladimir Lenin and his followers, antiradicalism grew even stronger in 1919–1920. What emerged has been labeled the *Great Red Scare,* which, in the words of its foremost historian, "unleashed a wave of hatreds and hysteria unmatched in modern American history."[19]

It was certainly hatred that governed initial U.S. relations with the new Union of Soviet Socialist Republics. Woodrow Wilson, having sent American troops into eastern and northern Russia to assist the remaining counterrevolutionary forces, refused to grant diplomatic recognition to the victorious Bolsheviks. There were many justifications given for this policy: the immense destruction and violence of the Russian Revolution, the Soviets' decision to take Russia out of World War I, the confiscation of U.S. property and disavowal of Tsarist debts, the religious repression in the new regime, and of course, a concern that the Bolsheviks would follow through on their threat to conspire with radicals abroad to extend communism to other parts of the world, including America.

A spate of incidents occurring soon after the war appeared to confirm this suspicion. May Day disturbances erupted in various cities in 1919. Pro-Soviet rallies were held in Washington, D.C., and elsewhere. Radical newspapers seemed to be more readily obtainable than in the past. Letter bombs were mailed to prominent business and civic officials; in one month alone bombs supposedly built by people "connected with Russian bolshevism" exploded in nine American cities. "There *is* an American Bolshevism," insisted a contributor to the monthly journal *Forum.* "It is today infecting democracy with the virus of a vicious propaganda that has come across the seas and seeks to organize revolution against law, order, and politics."[20]

A serious crisis in organized labor exacerbated these tensions. Among the thousands of strikes called during this period were several of the most memorable in U.S. labor history. In February 1919, the Central Labor Council of Seattle, Washington, called a general strike to support local shipyard workers involved in a labor dispute. The ensuing shutdown, which one of the president's key aides called "the first appearance of the Soviet in this country," lasted 5 days, until Mayor Ole Hanson called upon the militia to help him crush the strike. But 7 months later a policemen's strike in Boston opened the door to several days of looting, violence, and terror in that city. Observing the turmoil, the *Wall Street Journal* predicted: "Lenin and Trotsky are on the way."[21]

As events unfolded in the Bay State, 350,000 steelworkers walked off their jobs, an act that Senator Miles Poindexter of Washington termed "a revolutionary movement." The coal industry was next, when almost 400,000 miners ignored a court's restraining order and refused to enter the pits, just as the winter of 1919 was approaching. When the miners demanded the nationalization of all coal-mining operations, many viewed it as yet another indication that Communistic ideas had taken root in America. In the frenzied Red Scare atmosphere of the time, it was easy to believe that all these strikes were part of an overall plan to "soften up" the country for a Bolshevik takeover. An alarmed public backed the tough stance that business and government took toward these strikes; this was a prime reason why the police and steel strikes were defeated, and the miners settled for much less than they had demanded.[22]

Intolerance was the order of the day. "We must smash every un-American and anti-American organization in the land. We must put to death the leaders of this gigantic conspiracy of murder, pillage and revolution," read one newspaper advertisement highly revealing of Red Scare sentiment. In February 1919, a jury in Indiana deliberated for all of 2 minutes before acquitting a man who had killed an alien heard shouting, "To Hell with the United States." In early 1920, a man in Waterbury, Connecticut, received a 6 months' jail sentence for having referred to Lenin as "the brainiest," or at least "one of the brainiest," political figures in the world. In Centralia, Washington, four American Legionnaires died in a clash—the "Centralia Massacre"—with local IWW members. Hundreds of Wobblies were arrested, and a handful were convicted of second-degree murder for their role in the Legionnaire slayings.[23]

The government's response to the crisis only made matters worse. In early 1919, a subcommittee of the Senate Judiciary Committee conducted an investigation of pro-Bolshevik propaganda activities in America. Headed by Lee Overman, of North Carolina, the subcommittee heard testimony from individuals who claimed that the Soviets had brought mass murder, "free love" bureaus, the "nationalization of women," and other evils to Russia. In New York State, the legislature expelled several elected Socialist representatives and established a committee, chaired by State Senator Clayton Lusk, to investigate groups and activists accused of sedition. In a frantic rush to obtain evidence of conspiracies, the Lusk committee authorized spectacular raids on the IWW offices, the Russian Soviet Bureau, Socialist meeting rooms, the Rand School, and other suspected centers of radical activity.[24]

New York did not embark on its anti-Bolshevik crusade alone. Almost every state adopted various types of criminal anarchy, syndicalist, sedition, loyalty-oath, and "Red flag" statutes. The so-called Red flag laws prohibited any public display of this traditional symbol of international radicalism. Reportedly, some accused radicals were made to kiss the red-white-and-blue banner of the United States as a way of enforcing public respect for the land of the free.[25]

One individual stands out as the central figure in America's first great Red Scare: Attorney General A. Mitchell Palmer, a man with presidential ambitions and himself an intended victim of a bomb left at his home. Palmer believed that if the people saw him doing what was necessary to quell this "blaze of revolution" that "was sweeping over every American institution," they might elect him president in November 1920. To this end, Palmer initiated a ruthless, sweeping campaign of repression against suspected radicals. At his directive, federal men raided the offices of the Union of Russian Workers in a dozen cities, detaining hundreds of immigrants suspected of subversive activity. Next, some 249 aliens, most of them anarchists who had committed no specific crime, were put aboard the cargo ship *Buford*—nicknamed the "Soviet Ark"—and deported to Finland, from where they were sent by train to the U.S.S.R. Palmer authorized additional raids in early January 1920, including a 1-night, 37-state roundup of 5,000 suspects. Most of these arrestees had to be released when no formal charges could be pressed against them.[26]

Gradually, it dawned on people that in actual fact the "Bolsheviks" had not committed so many crimes, after all. The country began to recover its senses. Palmer was slow to realize this and inadvertently hastened this salutary process by repeatedly warning of a massive Bolshevik uprising scheduled for May Day 1920. When the promised rebellion failed to materialize, the public relaxed into laughter, the worst of the Red Scare was over, and the attorney general looked like a fool. Briefly a national hero, his prominent role in this ugly affair will always be his legacy. Yet, he was by no means the only one in his time—to say nothing of other periods in U.S. history—to stoke the public's antiradical fears in a bid for political advancement. Moreover, Palmer's actions—destructive and self-serving though they were—merely reflected the mood of a nation that was, to quote one contemporary English observer, positively "hagridden by the specter of Bolshevism."[27]

Warren Harding's promise in 1920 to return America to "normalcy" provided an additional salve to the wounds opened by the Red Scare. But not entirely. Attesting to the continuing strength of the Red "specter" in the 1920s were such events as the Sacco–Vanzetti trial and executions, the continued efforts to restrict immigration, the enduring popularity of superpatriot groups, Protestant fundamentalist attempts to equate communism with Darwinism, the reemergence of the Ku Klux Klan (black Americans, it was feared, were "sufficiently discontented and sufficiently unbalanced to make good Communists"), and the involvement of the U.S. Army and the recently established FBI in counterespionage work, often with a reckless disregard for suspects' civil liberties. Sinclair Lewis's archetypical George Babbitt gloried in his country's united stand against "foreign ideas and communism" but warned that "the worst menace to sound government is not the avowed socialists but a lot of cowards who work under cover." One resident of Robert and Helen Lynd's *Middletown,* reflecting on his neighbors' deep prejudices and strong sense of conformism, perceptively remarked, "These people are all afraid of something."[28]

To a limited extent, these apprehensions had a basis in fact, because the successful Bolshevik Revolution did galvanize the energies of radical elements in the United States and elsewhere. In America, the Socialist party's left wing, believing that the Soviets had discovered a short cut to victory in the international class struggle, broke away from the more cautious group that remained. This split in the Socialist ranks produced two new political groups, the Communist and Communist Labor parties, both of which joined the Soviet-led Third International, or "Comintern." In 1921 these parties obeyed a Moscow directive to merge into a single Communist party; from then on, the Communist movement in America faithfully subscribed to the often-fluctuating policy directives laid down in Moscow.[29]

Not surprisingly, the Kremlin's domination of a domestic American political movement, no matter how small, only worsened the Soviet regime's already-bad reputation. Long after the Red Scare had subsided, the American press continued to portray the U.S.S.R. as a land governed by ruthless criminals determined to instigate world revolution. One writer compared American news coverage to "a poison gas attack against the Soviet Union." Of course, editorial-page attacks on domestic radicalism, both real and imagined, also continued apace. Red baiting made exciting copy and sold newspapers. Ironically, the individual who perfected this formula, William Randolph Hearst, initially admired the U.S.S.R., but in time he set his mighty press empire on a relentless crusade against both the Soviets and their supporters—"incurable malcontents" and "unbalanced college professors" who "want the bloody despotism of Communism in our free America." One of the few publishers to match the near-hysterical tone of Hearst's editorials was Colonel Robert McCormick, owner of the most influential newspaper in the Midwest, the *Chicago Tribune.* The colonel subjected more than 1 million daily readers to his insistent attacks against the despotic Soviet leaders and their disciples in the United States.[30]

Staunchly Republican in its editorial policy, the *Tribune* applauded the anti-radical views of the trio of men who presided over the "Republican Ascendancy" of the 1920s. Harding, although not personally obsessed by the Red bogey, had the typical small-town businessman's abhorrence of domestic radicalism. After his death in 1923, the Republican National Committee tried to brand congressional investigators of the Teapot Dome scandals as so many "senatorial Bolshevists"; the GOP also red-baited Robert LaFollette's third-term presidential candidacy in 1924. Calvin Coolidge's published writings on "enemies of the republic" confirm this president's unyielding Yankee repugnance for everything tainted with radicalism.* He refused to consider granting diplomatic recognition to the U.S.S.R. unless its leaders complied with a series of unrealistic demands, including a formal declaration of "words meet for repentance." Both Harding and Coolidge relied heavily on the advice of Secretary of State Charles Evans Hughes, who opposed recognition in part because of the "persistent propaganda spread throughout this country by the Soviet regime" and its American sympathizers. President Herbert Hoover blamed some of his many problems—including the Bonus Army crisis of 1932—on Communist revolutionaries. As for the Soviet Union, Hoover's view remained unchanged from the day he had advised President Wilson against recognition because "The Bolsheviki has [sic] resorted to terror, bloodshed and murder to a degree long since abandoned even amongst reactionary tyrannies." Accordingly, Hoover resisted the prorecognition arguments of Senator Charles Borah, of Idaho, and those businessmen eager to sell goods to the potentially huge Soviet market.[31]

The irony of big business' support for granting diplomatic recognition to the U.S.S.R. is all the greater when compared to the stridently anti-Soviet, anti-Communist views of the American Federation of Labor, the leading force in U.S. organized labor. From its inception in 1881, the AFL's conservative, business-unionist leadership had stressed "pure and simple" labor issues, while refusing to endorse broad social reform and large-scale government intervention in the national economy. The AFL's founder, Samuel Gompers, had been attracted in his youth to left-wing causes, but as the long-time president of the federation he attacked the Socialists, Wobblies, and Communists as heatedly as any corporate magnate might have done.[32]

Gompers' antiradical views set the pattern for future AFL policy. William Green, elected president after Gompers died in 1924, was perhaps even more rigidly anti-Bolshevik than his predecessor. During his 24-year tenure as AFL president, Green crusaded relentlessly against American communism, "the pet child of the Moscow master strategist, Stalin." Otherwise an ineffective,

---

*Coolidge owed his presidency to the Red Scare. As governor of Massachusetts during the police strike, he won national praise by declaring that there was "no right to strike against the public safety by anybody, anywhere, anytime." This led to his fortuitous nomination as vice president at the GOP convention in 1920.

colorless personality, Green served as a figurehead–spokesman for a claque of craft-union chieftains who sat on the federation's powerful executive council. To these very conservative men—William Hutcheson, of the Brotherhood of Carpenters, John Frey, of the Metal Trades Department, Dan Tobin, of the Teamsters, Matthew Woll, of the Photo Engravers Union, and others—the Communists posed a dangerous threat to the stability and future survival of America's capitalist order.[33]

Given the public's historical tendency to associate trade unionism with radical activity, anticommunism was a shrewd policy for the AFL to embrace—though even this did not completely shield the federation from ultraconservative red-baiting attacks. The fact was, however, that as early as the Red Scare the federation tried to position itself as America's most important bulwark against bolshevism. The Communist party's Trade Union Educational League, led by the former steelworkers' organizer William Z. Foster, encountered stiff resistance when it abandoned the party's initial underground phase and tried "boring from within" the established AFL unions. Known or suspected followers of what Gompers had called "the Russian will-o-the-wisp" were ruthlessly expelled from most AFL affiliates. The most intense battles occurred in the New York needle trades' unions, where few Socialist leaders in the AFL struggled to maintain control of their organizations. David Dubinsky, a Socialist who fought through the Communists to assume command of the International Ladies' Garment Workers' Association, forever after hated communism; indeed, in one prominent historian's judgment he became "probably its most resourceful enemy within the ranks of organized labor."[34]

After repeatedly failing to infiltrate the AFL, the Communists replaced the TUEL with the equally unsuccessful dual-unionist Trade Union Unity League. This organization was an important component of another, more independent phase—the so-called "Third Period"—in Communist party strategy. However, the federation's attitude remained constant: AFL conventions in the 1920s, 1930s, and beyond routinely denounced the U.S.S.R. and communism. In 1921, the AFL approved an executive council report that condemned the Soviet system "of labor compulsion or enslavement." In 1935 the federation amended its constitution with a provision that "no organization officered or controlled by Communists, or any person espousing Communism . . . shall be allowed representation or recognition in any Central Labor Body or State Federation of Labor."[35]

The Roman Catholic religious convictions of several leading executive council members also was a factor in the AFL's adoption of a rigidly anti-Communist policy. Green, Woll, and Secretary-Treasurer George Meany were devout Catholics, undoubtedly influenced by the uncompromisingly anti-Communist views of their church. The Vatican's position on the subject was very clear. *Rerum novarum,* the 1891 encyclical issued by Pope Leo XIII on the world's social and labor problems, had rebuked Socialists because they "act against natural justice." Leo, who also criticized laissez-faire capitalism, wrote: "The main tenet of Socialism, the community of goods, must be utterly rejected." Pope Pius XI, in his *Quadragisimo Anno,* updated and elaborated upon his predecessor's instruction. In a sharp attack on the Communists, Pope Pius said that "when they have attained power it is unbelievable, indeed it seems portentous, how cruel and inhuman they show themselves to be .... . Their antagonism and open hostility to Holy Church and to God Himself are, alas! but too well known and proved by their deeds." In March 1937, Pius XI issued his encyclical *Divini Redemptoris,* in which he declared that, "Communism is intrinsically wrong and no one who would save Christian Civilization may give it assistance in any undertaking whatsoever."[36]

Most of the Protestant denominations in America also criticized the "godless" Communists but none did so as vehemently as the evangelical fundamentalists, who insisted that communism's collectivist value system undermined the concept of personal salvation. "If I had my way," the famed evangelist Billy Sunday said, "I'd fill the jails so full of them [Communists] that their feet would stick out the windows ....Let them rule? We'll swim our horses in blood up to the bridles first." Sunday had few equals, though he would have many imitators in the years ahead.[37]

It is highly significant that conservative Catholic opinion makers like Patrick Scanlan of the Brooklyn *Tablet* and Father James Gillis of *Catholic World* would have wholeheartedly applauded Sunday's anti-Communist thunder—even if they would have found little else comforting about his sermons. Although Catholics and fundamentalists hated communism equally, the issue was especially beneficial to Catholics in a way that many of them perhaps only subconsciously understood. By condemning the "Red Menace" as virulently as even the most fiery, soul-saving Protestant, a Catholic could flaunt his "Americanism" without compromising his fealty to the Church. Better still, the public at large now considered the Soviet Union and the Communist party, not the Church and its believers, to be the main threat to the American way of life. Regrettably, some Church leaders took to branding as Communistic any ideas or policies that they believed were hostile to Catholicism.[38]

In the political arena of the 1930s, Franklin Roosevelt's New Deal was eviscerated by its conservative critics as a blueprint for the bolshevization of America. From the start, FDR's embittered enemies insisted that he had turned the federal government into a haven for left-wing intellectuals, Socialists, and Communists. In fact, most of the New Dealers detested communism, and the Communist party itself pushed an anti-Roosevelt line during the first years of his presidency.[39] Nevertheless, the notion that FDR sympathized with communism became an abiding article of faith—a rallying cry—for some of his most implacable foes.

Among the right-wing radicals who made this charge, two of the most important were men of God: Father Charles Coughlin and the Reverend Gerald L. K. Smith. Coughlin used his national radio program to berate Roosevelt's "Jew Deal" and its supposed partnership with international bankers and Communists. Smith, an anti-Semitic fundamentalist minister who had been one of Huey Long's lieutenants until the Kingfish's assassination in 1935, elbowed his way into the national spotlight by calling upon all "true" Americans to "drive the Communists out of the country" and their friend President Roosevelt out of office. In 1936, Smith joined forces with Coughlin and another colorful maverick, Francis Townsend,* to form the short-lived Union party, whose presidential candidate, William Lemke, polled some 880,000 votes, about 2 percent of the overall vote.[40]

Republicans offered a more serious challenge to Roosevelt's reelection, but of course voters still held them responsible for the Great Depression. Even in 1932, the GOP had tried to stave off disaster with a comical effort to portray John Nance Garner, FDR's Texas-conservative running mate, as a Communist; now, as the president's popularity continued to soar, the "Communists in government" issue was still about all Republicans had to take before the voters. Former President Hoover, grousing that his successor was creating a society "a lot worse than Communism," served as the titular head of Republican conservatism and as a hero–spokesman for the Liberty League, a "Tory" pressure group with the self-appointed goal of uprooting the "Communist element" now running the country. During the ill-fated presidential run of Alf Landon in 1936, the desperate GOP tried to link the administration to communism. Landon's running mate, Frank Knox (a former executive in the Hearst organization), charged that FDR had "been leading us toward Moscow." Although the Republican party suffered another crushing defeat in this election, its leading Republicans refused to abandon the issue: Senator Robert Taft, of Ohio, predicted that FDR was "bound" to become a communist if he were not one already; and Rep. Hamilton Fish, of New York, claimed the Roosevelt "regime" was filled with "fashionable apologists for Communism and its bloody master, Stalin."[41]

Significantly, the "Reds" issue also caused disruption within the New Deal coalition itself. Despite FDR's wide appeal among blue-collar workers, the AFL loudly disapproved of the president's decision in 1933 to grant diplomatic recognition to the U.S.S.R. The Catholic community, for the most part pro-Roosevelt, also objected to this policy shift. The president even had to contend with Red-baiting attacks from disaffected politicians within his own party. Al Smith, the standard-bearer in 1928, thought the New Deal was Communistic;

---

*Townsend's solution to the Depression was ingenious: everyone sixty or older would receive a government pension of two hundred dollars a month—provided he or she spent the money within a month. The economy, stimulated by so much forced spending, would be pulled out of the Depression.

more seriously, so did segments of the entrenched Southern-conservative congressional bloc. Notwithstanding the unparalleled success that Roosevelt had brought to their party, Dixiecrats like John Rankin, Carter Glass, Harry Byrd, Martin Dies, and others firmly believed that the party of their fathers had been captured by radical bureaucrats and Communists. "Let's don't allow a bunch of Reds to have four more years in office," pleaded Georgia's Governor Eugene Talmadge in 1936, as he tried to organize a grass-roots Southern Democrat revolt against FDR's renomination.[42]

FDR overcame this challenge easily enough, but he was never able to win over a host of hostile newspaper publishers, in particular the Hearst chain and the *Chicago Tribune*. Hearst, initially a Roosevelt supporter, soon concluded that "much of the Administration is more Communistic than the Communists themselves." The *Tribune*, probably the single-greatest bastion of the antiadministration press, waged a relentless campaign to persuade Americans that they could save their country from communism only by voting out the entire New Deal crowd, and restoring Republican rule in Washington. Joe Patterson, Col. McCormick's cousin and the publisher of the *New York Daily News*, did not turn against FDR until early 1941, over the isolationist issue; Eleanor "Cissy" Patterson, owner of the *Washington Times-Herald*, followed her brother's lead. Thus, by the time America entered World War II, the entire McCormick–Patterson news chain was subjecting Roosevelt to furious red-baiting editorial attacks.[43]

The durability of the Red bogey as a political issue is especially remarkable if one considers that, by any objective standard, the Soviet Union hardly posed much of a threat to the distant United States. As for the American Communist party, it had only 7,000 dues-paying members in 1929, the year the stock market crashed. The ensuing Depression brought in some new blood, but the party's go-it-alone approach during the third period eliminated any possibility of cooperation with Socialists or most other progressive, leftist elements. Joseph Stalin, having acquired full power by 1929, brought the policies of the American Communist party even more rigidly in accord with the needs of the Soviet Union. Trotskyists, "Lovestoneites," and other dissenters were branded as traitors and expelled, further narrowing the movement's appeal.[44] In 1932 some 52 leading intellectuals and artists signed a public letter of support for William Z. Foster's presidential candidacy, but this window-dressing could not obscure the fact that the Communist party of the early 1930s was an isolated, widely despised, near-negligible force in the United States.

In 1935 the Comintern ordered an abrupt change of direction: henceforth, all Communist parties were to deemphasize the class struggle and seek "collective security" with all antifascist forces against the growing Hitler menace. Thus began the "Popular Front" phase of international communism.[45] The movement enjoyed a fair degree of success, for several reasons:

the lingering Depression; the party's less strident, broadly inclusive rhetoric and approach; the Comintern's support of Republican Spain during its 1937–1938 civil war with Francisco Franco's fascist army; party members' special enthusiasm for a strategy that allowed them to feel like fully assimilated citizens; and of course the looming might of German–Italian fascism, which posed a far more immediate danger than the Soviet Union. During the Popular Front, the Communist party improved its image with liberals (many of whom joined such Communist-led groups as the American League for Peace and Democracy and the United Front Against Fascism), some urban blacks, and a few of the more liberal state Democratic party organizations.

However, the party's greatest coup was its successful penetration of the Congress of Industrial Organizations, whose establishment roughly coincided with the Popular Front directive. Under the determined leadership of United Mine Workers chieftain John L. Lewis, the renegade CIO abandoned the AFL's outmoded craft-union structure for the more practicable policy of industrial unionism. This brought hundreds of thousands of unskilled, minority, and immigrant workers employed in the mass-production industries into the union movement. Lewis invited Communists into the CIO only because he knew they were highly dedicated and disciplined organizers, whom he desperately needed if his master plan was to succeed. The party initially opposed the CIO rebellion, presumably in the hope that it might yet find a place in the AFL, but before long the Communist party was describing the federation's suspension of the CIO unions as "a reactionary crime against the working class."[46]

The turnabout proved to be fortuitous. Lewis's invitation not only rescued the communists from near oblivion in the American labor movement, it also gave the Communist party its first taste of genuine power in the United States. Communists assumed control of about a dozen CIO internationals,* they led important factions in the United Automobile Workers and the shoe-workers' union: they occupied several key posts in the national organization, and they controlled a few state and local CIO federations.

These achievements did not go unnoticed or unchallenged by the party's numerous critics. David Dubinsky, who briefly brought the garment workers' union into the CIO but soon returned to the AFL fold, attacked the Communist

---

*The United Electrical, Radio and Machinists; State County and Municipal Workers; the Maritime Federation of the Pacific and the International Longshoremen and Warehouse Workers; Mine and Smelter Workers; Fur Workers; American Communications Association; United Cannery, Agricultural, Packing and Allied Workers; and International Woodworkers of America were under Communist control at some point in their history. In addition, the Communist party, with cooperation from fellow travelers dominated the Transport Workers Union, American Newspaper Guild, Furnitiure Workers Union and the Teachers Union.

presence in the organization he had helped to create. John Frey spoke for most of the AFL leadership when he testified before Congress that the CIO was riddled with Communists. Many Catholic church officials interested in organized labor agreed with this assessment. Other conservative groups and individuals routinely portrayed CIO strikes—especially sit-down strikes—as Red-tinged rehearsals for revolution.[47]

In retrospect these apprehensions seem very exaggerated. The CIO was not, as its critics contended, the leading front group for the Communist party. The Communist party never assumed control of the national CIO, partly because the majority of CIO leaders, from conservatives like James Carey to Sidney Hillman and other liberal advocates of what Ronald Radosh has called "social unionism," basically shared the AFL's fundamental allegiance to America's corporate, capitalist structure. Significantly, so did Lewis, a notorious red-baiter who allowed the Communists a role in his CIO venture solely to advance his own purposes. Always, Lewis assumed that he could destroy his Communist colleagues whenever he chose to do so—"John L. Lewis knows how to do that sort of thing," he once assured Secretary of Labor Frances Perkins. His successor Philip Murray, a devout Catholic who took over the CIO presidency in late 1940, also despised the Communists, but like Lewis he cooperated with them when it was expedient to do so.[48]

Walter Reuther, who succeeded Murray in the CIO presidency, was a special case. An immensely ambitious leader in the United Automobile Workers (the CIO's flagship union), Reuther had a leftist background of his own. He was raised by a Socialist father, he had worked and traveled in the Soviet Union as a young man, and he was a member of the Socialist party when he put aside his tool-and-die-making trade to plunge into the ferocious political and organizing wars of the fledgling UAW in the mid-1930s. Reuther—who may even have briefly joined the Communist party[49]—and his followers, many of whom were Socialists, joined a "unity caucus" with the Communists in order to remove the incompetent Homer Martin from the UAW presidency. After this, however, Reuther's desire for the top post in his union proved to be far stronger than any admiration he had for left-wing ideologies. He quit the Socialist party, observed that his erstwhile allies the Communists now stood in his way, and proceeded to engage them in a protracted struggle for control of the UAW. In the process, Reuther hardened into one of the Communists' most resourceful and dangerous enemies in all of organized labor.

Just as many misread the extent of the Communist influence in the CIO, so too have some exaggerated the success of the Popular Front. If American communism enjoyed its "heyday" in the 1930s, this was only in comparison to its earlier—and subsequent—experiences. Significantly, the Communists failed to make an alliance with the Socialist party, now led by Norman Thomas. Having listened to the Communists so recently condemning him and his associates as "social fascists," Thomas rejected what he called this "new

Communist opportunism." He also feared that the U.S.S.R. would destroy the "dreams of Socialism," as did other anti-Stalinists on the left. As a political force, American Socialism never recovered from the repression of World War I, the broader appeal of the New Deal's reforms, and the defection of those conservative, Old Guard Socialists who organized as the Social Democratic Federation in 1936. Nevertheless, anti-Stalinist leftists like Bertram Wolfe, Sidney Hook, and others would provide some of the clearest, most principled opposition to Soviet-style communism and its followers in the United States.[50]

A rather different anti-Communist perspective was provided by the Special U.S. House Committee for the Investigation of Un-American Activities (HUAC), empaneled by Congress in 1938. Patterned after two similar investigative efforts of this decade, HUAC was responsible for investigating both fascist and Communist groups and individuals. Although the committee did accumulate some useful information on pro-Nazi elements in the United States, Chairman Martin Dies, a right-wing demagogue from Texas, turned HUAC into a forum for attacking the New Deal and the network of Communist spies and sympathizers who supposedly had infiltrated the government under FDR's friendly aegis. Dies was an especially rabid critic of "New Deal Socialist philosophy," which he thought was "pushing us" in the direction of communism. But his ranking Republican colleague, J. Parnell Thomas of New Jersey, was just as extreme: He condemned the New Deal's Federal Theatre and Writers Project for producing plays that were "sheer propaganda for Communism."[51]

Very rapidly, the Dies committee acquired a deserved reputation for anti-Communist witch-hunting. By one count, in the course of only several days, committee witnesses linked some 640 organizations, 483 newspapers, and 280 labor unions to communism. At one point the efforts of the Boy Scouts and Camp Fire Girls to "increase international understanding" were unfavorably noted; and Shirley Temple's name came up when one witness, J. B. Matthews (who would later serve as the committee's chief of staff) criticized her press manager for some kind words he had written to a Communist newspaper in France. Civil libertarians, labor officials, anti-Communist liberals, and Roosevelt himself, who tried to hurt Dies politically by cutting off federal projects in his district, hoped that Congress would kill off the committee. But the House consistently voted to permit Dies to continue his war against the "Trojan Horse in America." Dies also had his supporters in the media: The Hearst press and *Chicago Tribune* hailed the committee as a guardian of American freedom; the *Tribune* called HUAC "the only government agency endeavoring to discern and to disclose the communistic penchants of the New Deal."[52]

As all anti-Communists enjoy pointing out, the Communist party has performed several of the most dazzling policy pirouettes in modern political history. But its most astonishing reversal followed the shocking announcement of a nonaggression pact signed by representatives of the Soviet Union and its arch-nemesis, Nazi Germany. Earl Browder, head of the American Communist party, had recently assured followers that there was less chance of this occurring than of his being elected president of the U.S. Chamber of Commerce. Now, overnight, anyone wishing to stay in the party had to support the Soviets' deal with the Nazis—who, having removed the possibility of a two-front campaign, promptly launched World War II by invading Poland. After taking eastern Poland for itself, the Soviet Union's position on the war was officially neutral. Accordingly, the Communist party took the view that a rival imperialists' struggle now raged between the French–British forces and Germany. The lofty rhetoric of the Popular Front was abandoned; in its place, one Soviet official remarked that fascism now was to be considered "a matter of taste."[53]

This was too much for many party members, whose only option was to quit in disgust. Jewish Communists, obviously, had an especially difficult choice. Although an outright revolt within party ranks failed to occur, the pact was disastrous to party fortunes: it destroyed the Popular Front; it cost Communists the sympathy and forebearance of many liberals and fellow travelers, and it had to hurt morale among the hardy party liners who had to endure the self-satisfied jibes of their enemies. "The mask of friendly comradeship with democratic peoples," declared *American Legion Magazine,* "has been torn from Communism's face by the alliance of Stalin and Hitler." Westbrook Pegler crowed that the Reds finally had stepped into their "true light," arm in arm with their Nazi brothers-under-the-skin of ideology.[54]

When the Red Army launched an invasion of neighboring Finland in November 1939 (to be followed by their annexation of the Baltic states and part of Rumania), the public's reaction was almost unanimously negative. Even the extremely liberal *New York Post* labeled the venture as one motivated "solely" by "lust for empire." A Finnish relief fund, with Herbert Hoover serving as national chairman, received thousands of contributions from citizens outraged by this unprovoked assault on a small, pro-American country. President Roosevelt, addressing the Communist-led American Youth Congress soon after the invasion, bluntly told his audience that the Soviet Union was "a dictatorship as absolute as any other dictatorship in the world."[55]

At least one historian has argued that a brief Red Scare broke out during the pact period, lasting until Germany invaded the U.S.S.R. in June 1941. The point is well taken. Rep. Dies, now at the height of his popularity, stepped up HUAC's anti-Communist investigations, while virtually ignoring Nazi subversives. Several states joined the hunt by establishing so-called "Little Dies" committees to unearth conspiracies close to home. In 1940 Congress passed the Smith Act, which made it illegal to advocate the desirability or need for overthrowing the U.S. government, and the Alien Registration Act, which required all organizations "subject to foreign control" to register with the Justice Department. Earl Browder was convicted on an old charge of passport violations and given a 4-year sentence. Lesser party officials received jail terms for technical violations of voter-registration regulations and other laws, and party candidates for elective office were removed from the ballots of 15 states shortly before the 1940 elections.[56]

During this campaign, party spokesmen accused both President Roosevelt, now seeking a third term, and Republican standard-bearer Wendell Wilkie of being the servants of Wall Street warmongers. Ironically, the party's new "The-Yanks-are-not-coming" stance on the war left them working for the same goal as both Socialist Norman Thomas and their numerous conservative enemies in America First,* the leading isolationist pressure group of this period. Thomas agreed to share a platform with this group in an antiwar rally, but no one in America First solicited the Communist party's assistance, advice, or support.[57]

Far more worrisome to the party was its loss of support and influence within the CIO. At their 1940 national convention, CIO delegates approved a resolution that denounced "the dictatorships and totalitarianism of Nazism, Communism and Fascism as inimical to the welfare of labor, and destructive of our form of government." The UAW approved a Reuther-sponsored resolution condemning "the brutal dictatorships and wars of aggression" of the U.S.S.R. and Axis powers. Similar measures were approved by other CIO affiliates. The Communists even lost the grudging support that Lewis had given them when he left the CIO after the rank and file overwhelmingly rejected his claim that a third term for FDR "will result in the nation's involvement in war."[58]

The Communists further eroded their standing by supporting several defense-industry strikes, which brought a rush of charges that the party was deliberately sabotaging America's defense preparations. When Roosevelt heard that "Communistic influences" were responsible for a walkout against the North American Aviation plant in Inglewood, California, he ordered Army troops to break the strike. Although several historians have argued that the Communists were not involved in any conspiracy to weaken the United States, this was not what most contemporary observers believed. Indeed, had it not been for yet another abrupt change in the Communists' policy, they might well

---

*A very conservative group, America First employed many of the arguments that left-liberal groups and individuals raised against America's participation in the Vietnam War. America First Chairman Robert Wood wrote that "we are faced with a Presidential war in violation of the Constitution, and this threat must be answered in no uncertain terms by every patriotic American." (See America First papers, Northwestern University, Box 1, Folder 3.)

have been summarily purged from the CIO before the United States entered World War II.[59]

Nazi Germany provided the next surprise in this terrible war by invading its erstwhile ally on June 22, 1941. Naturally, the Communists immediately reversed course once again. Dismissing the pact as "fully vindicated," the party abandoned its isolationist propaganda, denounced all strikes in defense factories, and demanded that the United States immediately provide all assistance possible to the beleaguered Soviet army. Historian Maurice Isserman has raised the interesting argument that the Communists, for all their genuine concern, reacted to the invasion with "a sense of relief, even of exhilaration," because at last they were freed from defending the Nazi–Soviet Pact. If so, this exhilaration came only after the initial shock had worn off: "The first hour," *Daily Worker* columnist Mike Gold wrote, "was awful. I shall never forget it. Now it had come—the thing we so feared for five, ten, twenty years."[60]

Meanwhile, other Americans reacted to the news with unqualified exhiliration. "If we see that Germany is winning we ought to help Russia," Senator Harry Truman gloated, "and if Russia is winning we ought to help Germany and that way let them kill as many as possible." The *Chicago Tribune,* for once agreeing with a Democrat friendly to the administration, declared that "no outcome in this war in the east can be viewed without dismay except one in which the two hateful systems destroyed each other." In more colorful prose, Henry Luce's *Time* also declined to distinguish between the belligerents: "Like two vast prehistoric monsters lifting themselves out of the swamp, half-blind and savage, the two great totalitarian powers of the world now tore at each other's throats."[61]

This same *Time* article warned Americans that the new development in the war ought not to lull them into forsaking vital defense-preparedness efforts. Roosevelt, faced with this ultimate responsibility, determined that Germany posed a more tangible threat to U.S. security; therefore, the U.S.S.R. should receive American assistance. Predictably, his decision provoked considerable controversy.[62]

The opposition came from diverse quarters: Abraham Ziegler wrote in *Modern Socialism* that the invasion had neither democratized nor pacified the "Stalinist beast"; Herbert Hoover claimed that assisting the Soviets—FDR's "gargantuan jest"—would make "the world safe for Stalin." Isolationists adopted this line of reasoning in their continuing crusade to keep the United States clear of the European conflict. Germany's invasion of the U.S.S.R., they contended, had exploded the interventionists' claim that the war pitted democracy against dictatorship. In a statement released the day after the German attack, America First's executive committee declared that the "intervention issue" had been settled for good: "The war party can hardly ask the people of America to take up arms behind the red flag of Stalin."[63]

Other well-known anti-Communists gave additional reasons for denying assistance to Hitler's latest victim. Hearst and his hero Martin Dies predicted that any Lend Lease shipments to the "doomed" U.S.S.R. would be taken by the soon-to-be-victorious Nazi invaders. The *Chicago Tribune* warned that "The Red ally of today might be the Red Terror of tomorrow." The fundamentalist *Christian Beacon,* noting that "the double-crosser has been double-crossed," said that a victorious U.S.S.R. would attempt to "determine the set-up in Europe." Senator Taft, saying that Stalin remained "the most ruthless dictator in the world," insisted that "the victory of communism . . . would be far more dangerous to the United States than the victory of fascism." Charles Lindbergh, the most illustrious figure in the isolationist movement, even said he would prefer a German-American alliance to a military partnership with the U.S.S.R. Such remarks eroded public confidence in the famed aviator, and even many America Firsters disavowed Lindbergh after he delivered a speech that was sharply critical of American Jews.[64]

Father Charles Coughlin frequently resorted to anti-Semitic slurs in his stridently isolationist attacks against FDR. Although more responsible figures in the Catholic community were embarrassed by Coughlin, they also tended to oppose the president's aid-to-Russia policy. Isolationism was very popular with many Church opinion makers—and any gesture of friendship made to the atheistic fellow-conqueror of Poland was certain to trouble Catholics. Father James Gillis, editor of *Catholic World,* called the policy a "Covenant with Hell." The Denver *Catholic Register* lamented that "we now find ourselves in some sort of a stupid alliance with Stalin, a man whose norm of life is mass murder." Concerned that such criticisms might weaken his popularity with an important constituency, FDR sought political help from such influential Catholics as Philip Murray, Justice Frank Murphy, and Postmaster General Frank Walker. However, even after the policy had become a *fait accompli,* skeptics remained vocal. Just 4 days before the attack on Pearl Harbor, Washington, D. C.'s Archbishop Michael Curley denounced Roosevelt's determination to extend aid to Stalin, "the greatest murderer of men the world has ever known."[65]

As of 7 December, 1941, the president no longer needed to justify lend lease aid to the Red Army. Thanks to the Japanese, the U.S.S.R. and the United States were now full partners in the "Grand Coalition" to defeat the Axis powers. "The Communist party pledges its loyalty, its devoted labor and last drop of its blood in support of our country in this greatest of all the crises that ever threatened its existence," read a statement released by the party's national committee just after the Pearl Harbor attack. "There were," historian Harvey Klehr has stated, "no Americans more patriotic than the Communists" during World War II.[66] As they would soon discover, however, the antagonism toward them and the U.S.S.R. did not pass from the scene. Such sentiments were too closely woven into a tradition strong enough to withstand even the countervailing pressures of total war.

NOTES

1. *Daily Worker*, 16 December 1941; Earl Browder, "The Strike Wave Conspiracy," *The Communist*, June 1943, pp. 483-94.
2. Among the leading works on this phenomenon are Seymour Martin Lipset and Earl Raab, *The Politics of Unreason* (Chicago: University of Chicago Press, 1978); Richard Hofstadter, *The Paranoid Style in American Politics and Other Essays* (Chicago: University of Chicago Press, 1965); Murray Levin, *Political Hysteria in America* (New York: Basic Books, 1971); J. Wendell Knox, *Conspiracy in American Politics, 1787–1815* (New York: Arno Press, 1972); Daniel Bell, ed., *The New American Right* (New York: Criterion Books, 1955); David Brion Davis, "Some Themes of Counter-Subversion: An Analysis of Anti-Masonic, Anti-Catholic, and Anti-Mormon Literature," *Mississippi Valley Historical Review*, September 1960, pp. 205–24; David Brion Davis, ed., *The Fear of Conspiracy, Images of Un-American Subversion from the Revolution to the Present* (Ithaca, NY: Cornell University Press, 1971).
3. Bernard Bailyn, *The Origins of American Politics* (New York: Random House, 1970), p. 12; Bailyn, *The Ideological Origins of the American Revolution* (Cambridge, MA: Harvard University Press, 1967), p. 120; Cecilia Kenyon, ed., *The Antifederalists* (Indianapolis, IN: Bobbs Merrill, 1966), p. 71.
4. John C. Miller, *The Federalist Era* (New York: Harper and Row, 1963); Marshall Smelser, "The Federalist Period as an Age of Passion," *American Quarterly*, Winter 1958, pp. 391–419; William Nisbet Chambers, *Political Parties in a New Nation* (New York: Oxford University Press, 1963), pp. 42–43; Clinton Rossiter, *Conservatism in America* (New York: Random House, 1962), pp. 109–110; Esmond Wright, *Fabric of Freedom, 1763–1800* (New York: Hill and Wang, 1964), pp. 207–8; Winfred Bernard, *Fisher Ames, Federalist and Statesman, 1758–1808* (Chapel Hill: University of North Carolina Press, 1965), p. 236; Vernon Stauffer, *New England and the Bavarian Illuminati* (New York: Columbia University Press, 1918); Kenneth Silverman, *Timothy Dwight* (New York: Twayne, 1969), pp. 99–100; Joseph Philips, *Jedidiah Morse and New England Congregationalism* (New Brunswick, NJ: Rutgers University Press, 1983), p. 82.
5. Merrill Peterson, *The Portable Thomas Jefferson* (New York: Penguin, 1980), pp. 470–71; Lance Banning, *The Jeffersonian Persuasion* (Ithaca, NY: Cornell University Press, 1978), pp. 285–87; Chambers, p. 116; Saul Padover, *Jefferson* (New York: New American Library, 1955), p. 113.
6. James Smith, *Freedom's Fetters: The Alien and Sedition Laws and American Civil Liberties* (Ithaca, NY: Cornell University Press, 1956); Samuel Eliot Morison, *Harrison Gray Otis* (Boston: Houghton Mifflin, 1969), pp. 102–7, 121; Miller, p. 195.
7. For a good sample of antimasonic rhetoric, see the appendix to Michael Holt, "The Antimasonic and Know Nothing Parties," in Arthur Schlesinger, Jr., ed., *History of U.S. Political Parties*, I (New York: Chelsea House, 1973), pp. 575–679; Charles McCarthy, "The Antimasonic Party," in *Annual Report of The American Historical Association*, I (Washington, DC: U.S. Government Printing Office, 1903), p. 545; Robert Remini, *Martin Van Buren and the Making of the Democratic Party* (New York: Columbia University Press, 1959), p. 186;

Glyndon Van Deusen, *Thurlow Weed: Wizard of the Lobby* (Boston: Little, Brown and Company, 1947), pp. 38–52.

8. Daniel Howe, *The Political Culture of the American Whigs* (Chicago: University of Chicago Press, 1979), pp. 54–57; Marvin Meyers, *The Jacksonian Persuasion* (Stanford, CA: Stanford University Press, 1957), pp. 6–23; Ronald Formisano and Kathleen Kutolowski, "Antimasonry and Masonry: The Genesis of Protest, 1826–1827," *American Quarterly*, Summer 1977, pp. 130–65; William Gribbin, "Antimasonry, Religious Radicalism, and the Paranoid Style of the 1820's," *The History Teacher*, February 1974, pp. 239–54.

9. Martin Marty, *Righteous Empire: The Protestant Experience in America* (New York: Dial Press, 1970), pp. 127–30; John Higham, *Strangers in the Land* (New York: Atheneum, 1966), p. 6; Clifford Griffin, *Their Brothers' Keepers, Moral Stewardship in the United States, 1800–1865* (New Brunswick, NJ: Rutgers University Press, 1960), pp. xiii, 140–42, 208–13; William McLaughlin, *Revivals, Awakenings and Reform* (Chicago: University of Chicago Press, 1978), pp. 3–4; Carroll Noonan, *Nativism in Connecticut, 1829–1860* (Washington, DC: Catholic University of America Press, 1938), p. 100; Ray Billington, *The Protestant Crusade, 1800–1860* (Chicago: Quadrangle Books, 1964), p. 439; Samuel F. B. Morse, *Imminent Dangers to the Free Institutions of the United States through Foreign Immigration* (New York: Arno Press, 1969), p. 25 (originally published in 1835); Lyman Beecher, *Plea for the West* (Cincinnati, OH: Truman and Smith, 1835), p. 139.

10. The major studies in the "ethnocultural" school of political history include Lee Benson, *The Concept of Jacksonian Democracy, New York as a Test Case* (Princeton, NJ: Princeton University Press, 1961); Ronald Formisano, *The Birth of Mass Political Parties: Michigan, 1827–1861* (Princeton, NJ: Princeton University Press, 1971); Michael Holt, *Forging a Majority: The Formation of the Republican Party in Pittsburgh, 1848–1860* (New Haven, CT: Yale University Press, 1969); Paul Kleppner, *Cross of Culture: A Social Analysis of Midwestern Politics, 1850–1900* (New York: Free Press, 1970); Richard Jensen, *The Winning of the Midwest, Social and Political Conflict, 1888–1896* (Chicago: University of Chicago Press, 1971); Samuel McSeveney, *The Politics of Depression: Political Behavior in the Northeast, 1893–1896* (New York: Oxford University Press, 1972); Frederick Luebke, *Immigrants and Politics, The Germans of Nebraska, 1880–1900* (Lincoln: University of Nebraska Press, 1969); Richard L. McCormick, "Ethno-Cultural Interpretations of Nineteenth-Century American Voting Behavior," *Political Science Quarterly*, June 1974, pp. 351–72.

11. Louis Scisco, *Political Nativism in New York State* (New York: AMS Press, 1968), pp. 190–91; Griffin, pp. 215–16; Formisano, p. 203; Howe, pp. 248–49, 276; Carleton Beals, *Brass Knuckles Crusade, The Great Know-Nothing Conspiracy: 1820–1860* (New York: Hastings House, 1960).

12. Michael Holt, *The Political Crisis of the 1850s* (New York: John Wiley and Sons, 1978), pp. 162–80; Josiah Strong, *Our Country* (Cambridge, MA: Harvard University Press, 1963), p. 86 (originally published in 1886); Charles Chiniquy, *Fifty Years in the Church of Rome* (Chicago: Craig Press, 1892); Donald Kinzer, *An Episode in Anti-Catholicism: The American Protective Association* (Seattle: University of Washington Press, 1964); Lipset and Raab, pp. 79–92; John Higham, "The American Party, 1886–1891," *Pacific Historical Review*, February 1950, pp. 37–46.

13. Irving Howe and Lewis Coser, *The American Communist Party* (New York: DaCapo Press, 1974), p. 1; John Sproat, *The Best Men: Liberal Reformers in the*

Gilded Age (New York: Oxford University Press, 1968); Samuel Hays, *The Response to Industrialism, 1885–1914* (Chicago: University of Chicago Press, 1957); Lawrence Goodwyn, *The Populist Moment* (New York: Oxford University Press, 1978); John Hicks, *The Populist Revolt* (Minneapolis: University of Minnesota Press, 1931); Norman Pollack, *The Populist Response to Industrial America* (Cambridge, MA: Harvard University Press, 1962); Henry George, *Progress and Poverty* (New York: D. Appleton and Company, 1884); Henry Demarest Lloyd, *Wealth against Commonwealth* (New York: Harper and Brothers, 1894); Edward Bellamy, *Looking Backward* (Cambridge, MA: Belknap Press, 1967), originally published 1888; Dennis Nordin, *Rich Harvest, A History of the Grange, 1867–1900* (Jackson: University Press of Mississippi, 1974); Irwin Unger, *The Greenback Era* (Princeton, NJ: Princeton University Press, 1964); Donald McMurry, *Coxey's Army* (Boston: Little, Brown and Company, 1929).

14. Anthony Bimba, *The Molly Maguires* (New York: International Publishers, 1970); Philip Foner, *The Great Labor Uprising of 1877* (New York: Monad Press, 1977); Gerald Grob, "The Railroad Strikes of 1877," *The Midwest Journal*, Winter 1954–1955, pp. 16–34; Robert Bruce, *1877: Year of Violence* (Indianapolis, IN: Bobbs-Merrill, 1959); Paul Avrich, *The Haymarket Tragedy* (Princeton, NJ: Princeton University Press, 1984); Harold Livesay, *Andrew Carnegie and the Rise of Big Business* (Boston: Little, Brown and Company, 1975), pp. 140–44; Leon Wolff, *Lockout, The Story of the Homestead Strike of 1892* (New York: Harper & Row, 1965); Stanley Buder, *Pullman* (New York: Oxford University Press, 1967).

15. Ira Kipnis, *The American Socialist Movement, 1897–1912* (New York: Columbia University Press, 1952); John H. M. Laslett and Seymour Martin Lipset, *Failure of a Dream? Essays in the History of American Socialism* (Berkeley: University of California Press, 1984); James Weinstein, "The Socialist Party: Its Roots and Strength, 1912–1919," *Studies on the Left*, Winter 1960, pp. 5–27; Ray Ginger, *The Bending Cross* (New Brunswick, NJ: Rutgers University Press, 1949); Nick Salvatore, *Eugene V. Debs: Citizen and Socialist* (Urbana: University of Illinois Press, 1982); Robert Hoxie, "The Rising Tide of Socialism," *The Journal of Political Economy*, October 1911, pp. 609–31; H. Wayne Morgan, *Eugene V. Debs, Socialist for President* (Syracuse, NY: Syracuse University Press, 1962), p. 85; John Gable, *The Bull Moose Years* (Port Washington, NY: Kennikat Press, 1978), p. 86.

16. Daniel Bell, "The Background and Development of Marxian Socialism in the United States," in Donald Egbert and Stow Persons, eds., *Socialism and American Life*, I (Princeton, NJ: Princeton University Press, 1952), p. 285; Albert Fried, *Socialism in America* (Garden City, NY: Doubleday, 1970), p. 12; Norma Pratt, *Morris Hillquit: A Political History of an American Jewish Socialist* (Westport, CT: Greenwood Press, 1979), p. 198; Peter Carlson, *Roughneck, the Life and Times of Big Bill Haywood* (New York: W.W. Norton, 1982).

17. David Shannon, *The Socialist Party of America* (Chicago: Quadrangle Books, 1955), pp. 100–01; James Weinstein, *The Decline of Socialism in America, 1912–1925* (New York: Monthly Reviw Press, 1967), pp. 170–173; Melvyn Dubofsky, *We Shall be All, A History of the Industrial Workers of the World* (Chicago: Quadrangle Books, 1969); Patrick Renshaw, *The Wobblies* (Garden City, NY: Doubleday, 1967); Paul Brissenden, *The I.W.W., A Study of American Syndicalism* (New York: Russell and Russell, 1957), pp. 346–48; John Gambs, *The Decline of the I.W.W.* (New York: Columbia University Press, 1932), pp. 48–49.

18. William Preston, *Aliens and Dissenters, Federal Suppression of Radicals, 1903–1933* (Cambridge, MA: Harvard University Press, 1963), pp. 11–34; George Creel, *How We Advertised America* (New York: Harper and Brothers, 1920), p. 168.

19. Robert Murray, *The Harding Era* (Minneapolis: University of Minnesota Press, 1969), p. 87. The foremost work on this subject is Murray's *Red Scare, A Study of National Hysteria, 1919–1920* (New York: McGraw-Hill, 1955); Burl Noggle, *Into the Twenties* (Urbana: University of Illinois Press 1974), pp. 84–121; Frederick Lewis Allen, *Only Yesterday* (New York: Bantam, 1931), pp. 45–69.

20. *Washington Post*, 3 July 1919. Quoted in Stanley Coben, "A Study in Nativism: The American Red Scare of 1919–20," *Political Science Quarterly*, March 1964, p. 60; Lewis Allen Browne, "Bolshevism in America," *The Forum*, June 1918, p. 717.

21. Robert Friedman, *The Seattle General Strike* (Seattle: University of Washington Press, 1964); John Blum, *Joe Tumulty and the Wilson Era* (Hamden, CT: Archon Books, 1969), p. 206; Francis Russell, *A City in Terror: 1919—The Boston Police Strike* (New York: Viking Press, 1975); Levin, *Political Hysteria in America*, p. 130.

22. David Brody, *Labor in Crisis: The Steel Strike of 1919* (Philadelphia: Lippincott, 1965); Murray, *Red Scare*, pp. 153–65; Philip Taft, *Organized Labor in American History* (New York: Harper & Row, 1964), pp. 341–60.

23. Shannon, pp. 122–23; Coben, p. 52.

24. August Ogden, *The Dies Committee* (Washington, DC: Catholic University of America Press, 1945), pp. 16–18; Murray, *Red Scare*, pp. 97–102.

25. Coben, p. 70.

26. Stanley Coben, *A. Mitchell Palmer: Politician* (New York: Columbia University Press, 1963); A. Mitchell Palmer, "The Case Against the 'Reds,'" *The Forum*, February 1920, p. 174.

27. For examples of Palmer's rivals in political red-baiting, see: Lawrence Sherman, "The Aims of the Republican Congress," *The Forum*, December 1918, p. 740; Will Hays, "The Living Issues of the Republican Party: What it Stands for and Against," *Current Opinion*, February 1920, p. 168; William de Wagstaffe, "What Poindexter Stands For," *The Forum*, February 1920, pp. 197, 200–201; Howard Allen, *Poindexter of Washington* (Carbondale: Southern Illinois University Press, 1981), pp. 200–225; Murray, *Red Scare*, p. 17.

28. Francis Russell, *Sacco and Vanzetti: The Case Resolved* (New York: Harper & Row, 1986); Higham, *Strangers in the Land*, pp. 264–330; Paul Murphy, *The Meaning of Freedom of Speech, First Amendment Freedoms from Wilson to FDR* (Westport, CT: Greenwood Press, 1972), pp. 184–219; Ray Ginger, *Six Days or Forever?* (Chicago: Quadrangle Books, 1958), p. 11; William Leuchtenburg, *The Perils of Prosperity, 1914–32* (Chicago: University of Chicago Press, 1958), pp. 204–24; David Chalmers, *Hooded Americanism: The First Century of the Ku Klux Klan* (Garden City, NY: Doubleday, 1965); R. M. Whitney, *Reds in America* (New York: Beckwith Press, 1924), p. 189; David Oshinsky, *A Conspiracy So Immense* (New York: Free Press, 1983), p. 89; Sinclair Lewis, *Babbitt* (New York: Harcourt, Brace and World, 1922), p. 187; Robert and Helen Lynd, *Middletown, A Study in American Culture* (New York: Harcourt, Brace and Company, 1927), p. 493.

29. Shannon, *Socialist Party of America*, pp. 165–68; David Shannon, *The Decline of American Communism* (Chatham, NJ: Chatham Bookseller, 1959), p. 371; Theodore Draper, *The Roots of American Communism* (New York: Viking Press,

1957), p. 395; Harvey Klehr, *The Heyday of American Communism* (New York: Basic Books, 1984), pp. x, 8–10.

30. Albert Rhys Williams, *The Bolsheviks and the Soviets* (New York: Rand School of Social Science, 1919), p. 26; Ferdinand Lundberg, *Imperial Hearst* (New York: Equinox Cooperative Press, 1936), pp. 243–44; John Winkler, *William Randolph Hearst* (New York: Hastings House, 1955), pp. 274–75; Joseph Gies, *The Colonel of Chicago* (New York: E.P. Dutton, 1979), p. 109.

31. Randolph Downes, *The Rise of Warren Gamaliel Harding, 1865–1920* (Columbus: Ohio State University Press, 1970), p. 361; Robert James Maddox, "Keeping Cool With Coolidge," *Journal of American History*, March 1967, p. 778, n. 22; John Hicks, *Republican Ascendancy, 1921–1933* (New York: Harper and Brothers, 1960), p. 100; Calvin Coolidge, "Enemies of the Republic," *Delineator*, June, July, and August 1921; Coolidge, "Whose Country is This?" *Good Housekeeping*, February 1921, p. 72; Coolidge, "Everyman's Property," *Collier's*, 23 July 1932, p. 90; Donald McCoy, *Calvin Coolidge, The Quiet President* (New York: Macmillan, 1967), pp. 181–84; Robert Paul Browder, *The Origins of Soviet-American Diplomacy* (Princeton, NJ: Princeton University Press, 1953), p. 19; Ethan Ellis, *Republican Foreign Policy, 1921–1933* (New Brunswick, NJ: Rutgers University Press, 1968), p. 76; Herbert Hoover, *The Memoirs of Herbert Hoover*, Vol. 2 (New York: Macmillan, 1952), p. 182; Hoover, *Memoirs*, Vol. 3, pp. 224–25; Richard Norton Smith, *An Uncommon Man, The Triumph of Herbert Hoover* (New York: Simon & Schuster, 1984), p. 92; Peter Filene, *Americans and the Soviet Experiment, 1917–1933* (Cambridge, MA: Harvard University Press, 1967), pp. 101–29, 211–39, 243, 269, 271; J. H. Wilson, "American Business and the Recognition of the Soviet Union," *Social Science Quarterly*, September 1971, pp. 349–68.

32. John Laslett, "Reflections on the Failure of Socialism in the American Federation of Labor," *Mississippi Valley Historical Review*, March 1964, pp. 634–51; Samuel Gompers, *Seventy Years of Life and Labor: An Autobiography*, Vol. I (New York: E. P. Dutton, 1925), pp. 391–427; Fred Greenbaum, "The Social Ideas of Samuel Gompers," *Labor History*, Winter 1966, pp. 54–55.

33. William Green, *Report on Communist Propaganda in America* (Washington, DC: American Federation of Labor, 1935), p. 8; Matthew Woll, *Labor, Industry and Government* (New York: D. Appleton-Century Company, 1935), pp. 326–29; Woll, "Labor Had Better Watch Out—Or It Will Lose Everything," *Liberty*, February 1936, pp. 6–7; Maxwell Raddock, *Portrait of an American Labor Leader, William Hutcheson* (New York: American Institute of Social Science, 1955), pp. 159–66; Archie Robinson, *George Meany and His Times* (New York: Simon & Schuster, 1981), p. 123.

34. Murray, *Red Scare*, pp. 58, 106, 114; James Prickett, "Communists and the Communist Issue in the American Labor Movement, 1920–1950," (unpublished Ph.D. dissertation, UCLA, 1975), p. 51; Walter Galenson, *The CIO Challenge to the AFL* (Cambridge, MA: Harvard University Press, 1960), p. 320; David Schneider, *The Workers (Communist) Party and the American Trade Unions* (Baltimore: The Johns Hopkins Press, 1928), pp. 87–104; David Dubinsky and A. H. Raskin, *David Dubinsky: A Life with Labor* (New York: Simon & Schuster, 1977), p. 56; William Z. Foster, *History of the Communist Party of the United States* (New York: Greenwood Press, 1968), pp. 252–54; Irving Bernstein, *Turbulent Years* (Boston: Houghton Mifflin, 1960), p. 82; Gompers, *Autobiography*, Vol. II, p. 401.

35. Philip Taft, *The A.F. of L. in the Time of Gompers* (New York: Harper and Brothers, 1957), p. 450; Taft, *The A.F. of L. From the Death of Gompers to the Merger* (New York: Harper and Brothers, 1959), p. 431.
36. Marc Karson, *American Labor Unions and Politics* (Carbondale: Southern Illinois University Press, 1958), pp. 212–84; David Saposs, "The Catholic Church and the Labor Movement," *Modern Monthly*, June 1933, p. 298; Claudia Carlen, ed., *The Papal Encyclicals, 1878–1903* (Raleigh, NC: McGrath, 1981), p. 244; Carlen, ed., *Encyclicals, 1903–1939*, p. 432; George Flynn, *Roosevelt and Romanism* (Westport, CT: Greenwood Press, 1976), p. 138. For one indication of Stalin's views on religion, see Robert Conquest, ed., *Religion in the U.S.S.R.* (New York: Frederick A. Praeger, 1968), p. 19.
37. Robert Wenger, "Social Thought in American Fundamentalism, 1918–33," (unpublished Ph.D. dissertation, University of Nebraska, 1973), pp. 275–79; William Gatewood, Jr., *Controversy in the Twenties* (Nashville, TN: Vanderbilt University Press, 1969), p. 24, 114; Ralph Roy, *Apostles of Discord* (Boston: Beacon Press, 1953), pp. 228–50; Murray, *Red Scare*, p. 83; Leo Ribuffo, *The Old Christian Right* (Philadelphia: Temple University Press, 1983).
38. David O'Brien, *American Catholics and Social Reform* (New York: Oxford University Press, 1968), pp. 81–82, 95–86.
39. Arthur Schlesinger, Jr., *The Politics of Upheaval* (Boston: Houghton Mifflin Company, 1960), pp. 190–91, 195.
40. James Shenton, "The Coughlin Movement and the New Deal," *Political Science Quarterly*, September 1958, pp. 352–73; Sheldon Marcus, *Father Coughlin* (Boston: Little, Brown, 1973); Charles Tull, *Father Coughlin and the New Deal* (Syracuse, NY: Syracuse University Press, 1965); David Bennett, *Demagogues in the Depression, American Radicals and the Union Party, 1932–1936* (New Brunswick, NJ: Rutgers University Press, 1969).
41. James Farley, *Behind the Ballots* (New York: Harcourt, Brace and Company, 1938), p. 162; Joan Hoff Wilson, *Herbert Hoover, Forgotten Progressive* (Boston: Little, Brown and Company, 1975), p. 212; Frederick Rudolph, "The American Liberty League, 1934–1940," *American Historical Review*, October 1950, p. 19; Donald McCoy, *Landon of Kansas* (Lincoln: University of Nebraska Press, 1966), pp. 279, 296, 307, 326; Schlesinger, *The Politics of Upheaval*, pp. 619–25; Richard Fried, *Men against McCarthy* (New York: Columbia University Press, 1976), p. 7; Robert Ingalls, *Point of Order* (New York: G.P. Putnam's Sons, 1981), p. 30; James Patterson, *Mr. Republican* (Boston: Houghton Mifflin, 1972), pp. 152, 156; Hamilton Fish, *FDR, The Other Side of the Coin* (New York: Vantage Press, 1976), pp. 7–8, 38, 41–42. See also *The Roosevelt Record in Red!* (Washington, DC: Republican National Committee, 1940), pp. 67–69.
42. See William Green's opposing arguments in "Should the United States Government Recognize Soviet Russia?" *Congressional Digest*, October 1933; John Frey interview, Columbia Oral History Project, Vol. 4, no. 225, 7 February 1955, p. 579; Leo Kanawada, *Franklin D. Roosevelt's Diplomacy and American Catholics, Italians, and Jews* (Ann Arbor: University of Michigan Press, 1982), pp. 3–19; George Flynn, *American Catholics and the Roosevelt Presidency, 1932–1936* (Lexington: University of Kentucky Press, 1968), pp. 122–49; Richard O'Connor, *The First Hurrah, A Biography of Alfred E. Smith* (New York: G. P. Putnam's Sons, 1970), pp. 281–84; Oscar Handlin, *Al Smith and His America* (Boston: Little, Brown and Company, 1958), pp. 179–80; James Patterson, *Congressional Conservatism and the New Deal* (Lexington: University of

Kentucky Press, 1967); Schlesinger, *The Politics of Upheaval*, pp. 515–23; Hamilton Basso, "Our Gene," *New Republic*, 19 February 1936, p. 36.

43. Raymond Swing, *Forerunners of American Fascism* (New York: Julian Messner, Inc., 1935), p. 144; John Tebbel, *The Life and Good Times of William Randolph Hearst* (New York: E. P. Dutton and Company, Inc., 1952), pp. 258–60; Rodney Carlisle, *Hearst and the New Deal, The Progressive as Reactionary* (New York: Garland Publishers, 1979), pp. 242–76; Schlesinger, *The Politics of Upheaval*, p. 85; Gies, pp. 127–38; James MacGregor Burns, *Roosevelt: The Lion and the Fox* (New York: Harcourt, Brace and World, 1956), p. 241; Leo McGivena, *The News* (New York: News Syndicate, 1969), pp. 308–13; Alice Albright Hoge, *Cissy Patterson* (New York: Random House, 1966), pp. 181–85.

44. Constance Myers, *The Prophet's Army, Trotskyists in America, 1928–1941* (Westport, CT: Greenwood Press, 1977); Theodore Draper, *American Communism and Soviet Russia* (New York: Viking Press, 1968), pp. 357–76, 405–30.

45. Klehr, *The Heyday of American Communism*, pp. 167–385; Howe and Coser, *The American Communist Party*, pp. 319–86; Kermit McKenzie, "The Soviet Union, the Comintern and World Revolution: 1935," *Political Science Quarterly*, June 1950, pp. 214–37; James Martin, *American Liberalism and World Politics, 1931–1941*, Vol. I (New York: Devin-Adair, 1964), p. 596; Maurice Isserman, *Which Side Were You On?* (Middletown, CT: Wesleyan University Press, 1982), pp. 3–14.

46. Harvey Levenstein, *Communism, Anticommunism, and the CIO* (Westport, CT: Greenwood Press, 1981), pp. 36–37; Rita Simon, ed., *As We Saw the Thirties: Essays on the Social and Political Movements of a Decade* (Urbana: University of Illinois Press, 1967), p. 232; Saul Alinsky, *John L. Lewis* (New York: G. P. Putnam's Sons, 1949), pp. 153–55. The Communists had acquired a formidable reputation for being good organizers: see McAlister Coleman, *Men and Coal* (New York: Farran and Rinehart, 1943), p. 171; Frances Perkins interview, Columbia Oral History Project, Vol. 8, Part 3, 3 May 1955, p. 478. Earl Browder, *The People's Front* (New York: International Publishers, 1938), p. 41.

47. Levenstein, pp. 106, 133–35; David O'Brien, "American Catholics and Organized Labor in the 1930's," *Catholic Historical Review*, October 1966, pp. 336–37; Sidney Fine, *Sit-Down, The General Motors Strike of 1936–1937* (Ann Arbor: University of Michigan Press, 1969), pp. 190–91; Benjamin Stolberg, *The Story of the CIO* (New York: Viking Press, 1938), pp. 92–122; Gies, pp. 139–140; Joseph Kamp, *Join the C.I.O. and Help Build a Soviet America* (New Haven, CT: Constitutional Educational League, 1937).

48. Ronald Radosh, "The Corporate Ideology of American Labor Leaders from Gompers to Hillman," *Studies on the Left*, November–December, 1966, pp. 66–88; Sidney Lens, *The Labor Wars* (Garden City, NY: Doubleday, 1973), p. 234; Levenstein, p. 47; Bert Cochran, *Labor and Communism* (Princeton, NJ: Princeton University Press, 1977), pp. 97, 265–66.

49. Roger Keeran, *The Communist Party and the Auto Workers Union* (Bloomington: Indiana University Press, 1980), pp. 186–204, 313, n.17; Foster, *History of the Communist Party of the United States*, p. 353. One of the best of several biographies of Walter Reuther is by his brother, Victor Reuther, *The Brothers Reuther* (Boston: Houghton Mifflin Company, 1976).

50. M. H. Child, "The American Social Fascists," *The Communist*, August 1932, pp. 708–15; Vaughn Bornet, "The Communist Party in the Presidential Election of 1928," *Western Political Quarterly*, September 1958, p. 515; Earl Browder, *The Meaning of Social-Fascism, Its Historical and Theoretical Background* (New

York: Workers Library, 1933); Browder, *What is Communism?* (New York: Workers Library, 1936), p. 77; "Which Road for American Workers, Socialist or Communist?" (New York: *Socialist Call*, 1936), p. 18 (This pamphlet is a transcript of a debate between Thomas and Browder held on 11 November, 1935); W. A. Swanberg, *Norman Thomas, The Last Idealist* (New York: Charles Scribner's Sons, 1976), p. 175; Norman Thomas, *After the New Deal, What?* (New York: Macmillan, 1936), p. 218; Harry Fleischman, *Norman Thomas* (New York: W.W. Norton and Company, 1969), p. 184; Bertram Wolfe, *A Life in Two Centuries* (New York: Stein and Day, 1981), pp. 548–67; William O'Neill, *A Better World*, (New York: Simon & Schuster, 1982), p. 14.

51. For the Dies Committee's predecessors, see Earl Latham, *The Communist Controversy in Washington, From the New Deal to McCarthy* (New York: Atheneum, 1969), pp. 28–38; Walter Goodman, *The Committee* (New York: Farrar, Straus and Giroux, 1968), pp. 3–13; Robert Carr, *The House Committee on Un-American Activities, 1945–1950* (Ithaca, NY: Cornell University Press, 1952), pp. 1–18; Ogden, pp. 14–37; Martin Dies, *Martin Dies' Story* (New York: Bookmailer, 1963), pp. 173, 205; Eric Bentley, ed., *Thirty Years of Treason* (New York: Viking Press, 1971), pp. 3–47; Goodman, p. 43.

52. William Leuchtenburg, *Franklin D. Roosevelt and the New Deal, 1932–1940* (New York: Harper & Row, 1963), pp. 280–81; Ted Morgan, *FDR, A Biography* (New York: Simon & Schuster, 1985), pp. 564–68; Martin Dies, *The Trojan Horse in America* (New York: Dodd, Mead and Company, 1940); Oshinsky, p. 92; Goodman, p. 139; *Chicago Tribune*, 16 December 1938 (Quoted in Ogden, p. 103).

53. Soviet Foreign Minister Molotov made this remark (Isserman, p. 16), but for his official explanation of events, see "The Meaning of the Soviet-German Non-Aggression Pact," *Communist International*, 19 September 1939, pp. 951–57. Molotov claimed (as have many others, subsequently) that the U.S.S.R. was forced into this agreement because earlier attempts to negotiate collective-security deals with Britain and France were rejected. But see Anna Louise Strong, *The Soviets Expected It* (New York: *Soviet Russia Today*, 1942), which argues that the pact also was a cagey ploy by Stalin to gain additional time for the Red Army to prepare for war.

54. Frank Warren, III, *Liberals and Communism, The "Red Decade" Revisited* (Bloomington: Indiana University Press, 1966), pp. 193–215; "They Did not Die in Vain," *American Legion Magazine*, November 1939, p. 25; Westbrook Pegler, "What Strange Bedfellows!" *American Legion Magazine*, November 1939, p. 10.

55. O'Neill, p. 43; *New York Post*, 1 December 1939, quoted in Ralph Levering, *American Opinion and the Russian Alliance, 1939–1945* (Chapel Hill: University of North Carolina Press, 1976), p. 32; Records of the Finnish Relief Fund (Special Collections Archives of Rutgers University); Isserman, p. 60; for a defense of the invasion, see I. Salonen, *Finland in Hitler's War* (New York: Eteenpain, 1942).

56. Isserman, *Which Side Were You On?*, pp. 67–73.

57. *Campaign Book, Presidential Elections 1940* (New York: Workers Library, 1940), p. 17; Howe and Coser, *American Communist Party*, pp. 387–405; Wayne Cole, *America First, The Battle Against Intervention, 1940–1941* (New York: Octagon Books, 1971).

58. *Proceedings of the Third Constitutional Convention of the Congress of Industrial Organizations*, November 18–22, 1940, p. 226; Keeran, p. 210; Art Preis, *Labor's Giant Step, Twenty Years of the CIO* (New York: Pioneer, 1964), p. 124;

David Oshinsky, "Labor's Cold War: The CIO and the Communists," in Robert Griffith and Athan Theoharis, eds., *The Specter* (New York: Franklin Watts, 1974), p. 123; Alinsky, pp. 161–91; John L. Lewis Papers, Wisconsin State Historical Society, Reel 1, "Radio Talk by John L. Lewis," 5 November, 1940.

59. Victor Riesel, "The Communist Grip on Our Defense," *American Mercury*, February 1941, pp. 202–10; "Our Immediate Obligation," *American Federationist*, July 1941, p. 20; Max Kampelman, *The Communist Party vs. the CIO* (New York: Frederick Praeger, 1957), pp. 25–27; Keeran, pp. 212–20; Levenstein, p. 145; James Prickett, "Communists and the Communist Issue in the American Labor Movement, 1920–1950," (unpublished Ph.D. dissertation, UCLA, 1975), pp. 247–61; Oshinsky, "Labor's Cold War," p. 123; Norman Markowitz, "From the Popular Front to Cold War Liberalism," in Griffith and Theoharis, p. 98; Thomas Brooks, *Toil and Trouble* (New York: Delacorte Press, 1971), p. 227.

60. "Why This Is Our War," *New Masses*, 8 July 1941. This article is representative of the Communists' rationale for what turned out to be their final change of mind regarding World War II. See also Max Weiss, *Destroy Hitlerism* (New York: New Age Publishers, 1941); Isserman, p. 104; *Daily Worker*, 25 June 1941.

61. *New York Times*, 24 June 1941; *Chicago Tribune*, 30 July 1941; *Time*, 30 June 1941, p. 11.

62. Raymond Dawson, *The Decision to Aid Russia, 1941* (Chapel Hill: University of North Carolina Press, 1959); George Herring, Jr., "Lend-Lease to Russia and the Origins of the Cold War, 1944–1945," *Journal of American History*, June 1969, p. 94.

63. Abraham Ziegler, "Russia," *Modern Socialism*, Fall 1941, p. 6; James MacGregor Burns, *Roosevelt: The Soldier of Freedom* (New York: Harcourt Brace Jovanovich, 1970), p. 111; Herbert Hoover, *Addresses Upon the American Road, 1940–41* (New York: C. Scribner's Sons, 1941), p. 93; Joan Hoff Wilson, *Herbert Hoover, Forgotten Progressive* (Boston: Little, Brown and Company, 1975), p. 247; New York *Times*, 6 August 1941; Cole, *America First*, p. 85.

64. Goodman, *The Committee*, p. 124; *New York Journal-American*, 27 June 1941; *Chicago Tribune*, 30 July 1941; "Liberty in Russia," *Christian Beacon*, 9 October 1941; Patterson, *Mr. Republican*, pp. 245–46; Cole, *America First*, p. 85; Wayne Cole, *Charles A. Lindbergh and the Battle Against American Intervention in World War II* (New York: Harcourt, Brace Jovanovich, 1974).

65. Cole, *America First*, pp. 134–38; James O'Gara, "The Catholic Isolationist," in *Catholicism in America: A Series of Articles from 'The Commonweal'* (New York: Harcourt, Brace, 1954), p. 116; James Gillis, "Covenant with Hell," *Catholic World*, August 1941, pp. 513–17; Denver *Catholic Register*, 26 June 1941. Similar attitudes were expressed in "Dining With Stalin," *America*, 22 November 1941; Brooklyn *Tablet*, 28 June 1941; *Catholic Universe Bulletin*, 27 June 1941; Leonid Strakhovsky, "America, the Savior of Red Tyranny?" *Catholic World*, November 1941, pp. 140–44; Flynn, *Roosevelt and Romanism*, pp. 152–53, 168; *New York Times*, 3 December 1941. Not all Catholic officials opposed aiding the U.S.S.R. during this period: see St. Augustine, Florida's Bishop Joseph Hurley's remarks in Fight for Freedom Archives (Princeton University, Box 19, "Communists" Folder).

66. *Daily Worker*, 8 December 1941; Klehr, *The Heyday of American Communism*, p. 410.

3

The Politics of Anticommunism in
Wartime America

Even as America confronted the greatest external crisis in its history, some in wartime Washington continued to believe that internal communist conspiracies most threatened the nation's security. Although the United States was locked into a military alliance with the world's only communist state, the familiar "Red bogey" still preyed in the minds of some congressmen. In particular, Martin Dies, the New Deal-hating Democratic chairman of the House Committee on Un-American Activities, remained busy hunting "Red" subversives in the government, organized labor, and elsewhere in American society. Anticommunism also was an important theme in the 1944 presidential campaign between Republican challenger Tom Dewey and President Franklin Roosevelt, then seeking an unprecedented fourth term. Dewey accused his opponent of truckling to the totalitarian-minded communists who allegedly dominated the powerful political action committee set up on Roosevelt's behalf by the Congress of Industrial Organizations. The GOP's attempt to red-bait its way into the White House was assisted by the Democratic-controlled Dies Committee, which also assailed PAC and its president, Sidney Hillman, as agents of international communism. FDR won again, of course; but the "anti-Red" bloc had succeeded in maintaining at least a foothold in the American political arena of World War II America.

As they had in the past, demagogic speechmakers took the floor of Congress to offer drastic solutions for solving the communist problem, once and for all. Democratic Representative John Lesinski, of Michigan, believed that the appropriate authorities should "just load them all on a boat and send them back ... Stalin, no doubt, can use them to good advantage. Certainly, the people of America, with true American ideals, have no use for them." Such proposals were fairly rare during the war, but congressional white supremacists like John Rankin, of Mississippi, and Joe Starnes, of Alabama—both Democrats—still blamed the communists for trying to "stir up race trouble" in the South and in northern cities, such as Detroit. Rankin even charged that communists were behind the effort to remove labels indicating a donor's race from the military's blood-bank supplies. When Stalin dissolved the Comintern in June 1943 as a gesture of reassurance to his new allies, Representative Fred Busbey, Republican of Illinois, sarcastically commented that now "everyone should be free to speak about communism in the United States without someone yelling saboteur, Nazi collaborator, or [sic] accused of undermining the war effort of the so-called United Nations."[1]

In addition, the old argument that the communists and their left-liberal sympathizers were secretly but steadily expanding their destructive influence in the federal government remained an article of faith among hard-line anticommunists during the war. A conservative Democratic Senator, Guy Gillette, of Iowa, echoed the concerns of many when he spoke out about alleged advocates of state socialism and international utopianism within his own party. An ultraconservative Republican from Michigan, Representative Clare Hoffman—who charged, in June 1942, that the communist party was "now openly and boldly aiding the cause of the Japs and of Hitler" by trying to destroy freedom in America—insisted that the New Deal radicals who controlled the Washington bureaucracy "have done their darnedest ... to establish a dictatorship and to bring about communism, fascism, or some other form of foreignism." In a meeting with FDR, Democratic Senator Burton Wheeler, of Montana, sternly warned: "I think I know the Communists. They want to channel your mind and unless they can do it one hundred per cent, they'll cut your heart out!"[2]

Unfortunately, the most intense anti-New Dealers thought that FDR's mind already had been "channeled" by the communists, and some believed that he had given his heart to them, as well. The president's decision to free Earl Browder from federal prison in May 1942 served to confirm this suspicion. Denounced by the American Legion, an important conservative pressure group, Browder's release was too much for some hard-liners to bear. When John Vorys, a Republican congressman from Ohio, heard the news, he stammered, "I am too shocked to say anything—I can hardly believe it." Raymond Willis, Republican U.S. senator from Indiana, fumed that granting freedom to Browder amounted to "the greatest contribution to disunity in America that has taken place since the war began." Senator Taft said that he saw "no good reason to pardon Browder just because he is a communist." Democratic Senator Richard Russell, of Georgia, stated that he would not have commuted Browder's sentence had he the power to do so. Representative J. Parnell Thomas, of New Jersey, the ranking Republican on HUAC, said that Browder's release was "conclusive proof that the New Deal is garroted by communism." In a telegram to FDR, Thomas darkly added that he would attempt to make "the New Deal-communist marriage" the committee's "first order of business" at its next session.[3]

Behind this arrogant threat lay an obvious truth: The freedom to denounce communism as a "menace" to America often counted for little without a corresponding power to investigate allegations of Communist-inspired subversion of American institutions. Investigatory efforts of this nature continued in wartime America, despite the awkwardness created by the military partnership with the U.S.S.R.. In New York, the state legislature's Rapp–Coudert committee, established in 1941 to investigate subversive activites in the state's public schools and universities, continued to function, despite the efforts made by Communists and others to close down its operations. In April 1942, the committee issued a report that included this admonition:[4]

> If ... the Communists succeed in extending their influence under cover of their present pseudo-patriotic garb, while we naively take them at face value and permit ourselves to be hoodwinked into a false sense of security, we will find to our sorrow that the problem will be more acute in days to come than it has been in the past.

On the west coast, a Fact-Finding Committee on Un-American Activities was established in the 1941 session of the California state legislature. Headed by State Senator Jack Tenney, it gave about equal investigative attention during the war years to pro-Axis organizations and the Communist party, the "tool and agent" of the Soviet Union. In a report to the California legislature, the "Tenney" committee noted that the Communist party was for once supportive of U.S. interests only because the war effort corresponded "in every detail with the foreign policy, ambition and need of the Comintern." But because the "Communist Fifth Column" remained loyal to Marxism, "even in the chameleon cloak with which they have now enshrouded themselves," Tenney's committee predicted that party followers could be expected to use these fortuitous circumstances "for their own future, sinister purposes." Notwithstanding their temporary change of tactics, the Communists remained as determined as ever to destroy "the American way of life."[5]

Important in their own right, these state-level activities were overshadowed by Congress' own Committee on Un-American Activities and its chairman, Martin Dies. Wielding his authority to the fullest, Dies used the committee as his personal vehicle for waging a demagogic crusade against a supposed Communist-directed plot to subvert the liberties of the American people. War or no war, this was a mission that Dies firmly believed was far too important to be sidetracked merely because it might injure the feelings of a military ally. "Those who feel that it has become indelicate even to speak of the Communist fifth column," Dies intoned, "seem to think that the Russians' heroic fight ... is good ground for closing our eyes to the nature and ultimate aims of the Communist party." This was a view that Dies found "wholly devoid of logic," because Hitler's defeat "would not make Communism one iota more compatible with the American way of life." Dies took it upon himself to assist an apparently reluctant American public to "look that fact squarely in the face." A sympathetic colleague, E. E. Cox, an antilabor Democrat from Georgia, said that so long as the Communists were "boring away," intent on "making over" the United States, "there is work for the Committee to do." Representative Harry Coffee, Democrat of Nebraska, agreed: No one wanted "to stir up any fight or any friction" with the Russians, he said, but "we still have the job of preserving Americanism in this country."[6]

Dies resumed this preservation effort on December 19, 1941—less than 2 weeks after Pearl Harbor—when he successfully offered an amendment to a House bill requiring the registration of foreign agents; this amendment specified that Communist party members, as well as those belonging to the German-American Bund and the Kyffhauserbund, were subject to this law. Hamilton Fish, a Republican colleague who was as ardently anti-Communist as Dies, warned his colleagues that this was no time to "pussyfoot and shadow-box to avoid the issue, which is very simple . . . [and] which almost ninety-nine percent of the people back home want done." Approved by the House, the amendment was rejected in the Senate and did not become law. According to the *San Francisco Examiner,* admittedly a biased, antiadministration source, the Roosevelt administration heavily pressured the conference committee to remove the Dies amendments from the bill.[7]

White House hostility to the Texas congressman was to be expected; the chairman was, in the words of Interior Secretary Harold Ickes, nothing but "a hair shirt for the Administration." Dies's hatred for the generally progressive-looking philosophy of the New Deal was so intense that he assumed, instinctively, that anyone who supported the administration had to be acting out of the most sinister motives. Having already accused the administration in the recent past of harboring Communists in various agencies of the government, Dies took the House floor on January 15, 1942, to announce "that the flow of Communists and Communist sympathizers into Government positions has not entirely ceased." Some of them, according to "reliable evidence, which I am not at liberty to disclose at the present time," had penetrated America's defense agencies, where, Dies said, they "consider themselves strategically placed for purposes of revolutionary change in our form of government and economics if and when some great crisis engulfs us." As proof, Dies cited by name the left-wing literary critic Malcolm Cowley ("one of the most ardent Communist intellectuals in this country"), then serving as chief information analyst for the Office of Facts and Figures. For good measure, Dies charged that the Office of Civilian Defense was also infested with Communists.[8]

Cowley was forced to resign his post, but Dies was intent on proving that the Communist conspiracy reached even higher. Undaunted by the prospects of wounding his own political party, Dies trained his sights on vice president Henry Wallace. The vice president, Dies charged, had knowingly permitted some 35 officials with Communist-front backgrounds to remain on the Board of Economic Warfare, an agency that Wallace then headed. Characteristically, Dies transmitted his complaints in an "open letter" that was published in many major newspapers. Wallace, a skilled political infighter in his own right, responded with a well-publicized, stinging rejoinder to Chairman Dies. Saying that the congressman's letter "might as well have come from Goebbels himself" and was the product of a "witchcraft mind," Wallace charged that the effect of the chairman's broadside "on our morale would be less damaging if Mr. Dies were on the Hitler payroll." HUAC's liberal enemies applauded Wallace's vigorous counterattack, and the vice president received numerous complimentary letters, including one that said that Dies's unscrupulous tactics, a "major nuisance" even before Pearl Harbor, had "now become an actual national menace."[9]

Having sparred with Roosevelt's vice president and drawn little blood, Dies next directed his wrath at Attorney General Francis Biddle. The attorney general, who was pushing hard for the deportation of Harry Bridges, would have seemed invulnerable to charges of being soft on communism, but Dies was a demanding inquisitor. In 1941, the chairman had given Biddle a list of some 1,123 government employees who allegedly had belonged, or continued to belong, to one or more Communist-front organizations. The committee's investigatory methods were notoriously unsound, however, and after a lengthy Justice Department review, only two persons on this HUAC list were fired. Biddle followed this up with some disdainful remarks about "amateur investigations of espionage" that wasted taxpayers' money and hindered the "trained, coordinated, responsible action" of the FBI and military intelligence units. The chairman tried to even the score against Biddle by criticizing him in one of his many personal-privilege speeches on the House floor, and in the committee's summary 1941–1942 report to Congress.[10]

Even before this self-congratulatory report appeared, HUAC issued, in late June 1942, its *Special Report on Subversive Activities Aimed at Destroying Our Representative Form of Government*. This report lashed out at the Union for Democratic Action (UDA), a recently established proadministration lobbying organization. Without benefit of any hearings, the committee declared that unnamed leaders of the UDA had become, through extensive collaboration with Communist-party front groups, "a significant part of the interlocking directorate of the Communist movement in the United States." Acting in concert with such publications as *Time, PM, New Republic, Daily Worker,* and *New Masses,* the UDA was attempting to undermine the public's trust in Congress, which according to Dies was the first tactic employed by "the Bolshevists, the Nazis, the Fascists, all of these groups who believe in totalitarianism in one form or the other." Once this smear campaign had destroyed Congress as a co-equal, independent branch of government, all power would belong to the administration and its Communist allies. Jerry

Voorhis of California, the lone liberal on the committee, filed a dissenting minority report that argued that those who criticized the Congress were engaging in "a sort of national pastime," not conducting a conspiracy to destroy the U.S. government. Representative Thomas promptly labeled Voorhis's observations "nothing more than a whitewash of the New Deal," and Voorhis, outvoted and under pressure from liberal admirers to resign his seat on HUAC in protest over the committee's anti-New Deal bias, quit the committee in February 1943.[11]

Voorhis's disgust was shared by a number of his Congressional colleagues. Democratic Representative Thomas Eliot of Massachusetts wanted the Committee's appropriations terminated because HUAC "divides the Nation and plays into the hands of our enemies" through its persistent criticism of communism and the Soviet Union. Representative Adolph Sabath, an Illinois Democrat, favored the committee's dissolution because it had not investigated the "Fascists and Nazis . . . that are really the greatest danger to our country." The most ardent of the committee's congressional enemies was Vito Marcantonio, the pro-Communist Independent Representative from New York City. In a 1942 speech opposing the continued funding of HUAC, Marcantonio accused it of "interfering with the successful prosecution of our war against the fifth column." A man whose own patriotism was (and would be) continually called into question, Marcantonio freely associated his colleague–antagonist from Texas with the Fuehrer: "While Americans are gloriously fighting at Guadalcanal and North Africa and the Red Army is smashing the enemy at Stalingrad and Rostov," Marcantonio said in exasperation, "Hitler and Mr. Dies are still crusading against communism."[12]

Leftists in particular liked to use this line of argument in their efforts to discredit Dies' anti-New Deal, anti-Communist crusade. *The Nation,* one of the two major left-leaning journals of opinion, contended that because the unscrupulous Chairman Dies was "pro-fascist in the deepest and most dangerous sense of the word," it was natural that he would pretend periodically to be antifascist "if that seemed the only way of continuing his career." (Of course, anti-Communists always accused their enemies of similar deceptions, for exactly the same reason.) The *New Republic,* the other main left-liberal journal of this period, cuttingly predicted that "there will presently be many American fathers and mothers of sons dead on the battlefield who may begin to ask themselves why Mr. Dies doesn't ever, not ever, do anything to help our war effort instead of hurting it." The National Lawyers Guild, a legal group highly sympathetic to leftist causes, accused the committee and its congressional collaborators of "seeking to pave the way for fascism in the United States" and of being "the secret weapon with which Adolf Hitler hopes to soften up our Nation for military conquest." Another fellow-traveling organization, the National Federation for Constitutional Liberties, accused HUAC of treasonously shielding the "agents of the Axis."[13]

As for the Communists, they joined the attack against their great nemesis with relish, calling HUAC a fifth-column organization whose anti-Communist attacks were designed to foment disunity in the country and among the allies. William Z. Foster, writing in *The Communist,* accused the committee of engaging in the "Hitlerian tactics of Red-baiting and sniping the Roosevelt Administration," with the purpose of "sowing dissension among the United States and its allies." All the Communist diatribes directed at HUAC had a simple logic: Because America and the U.S.S.R. were allies against the Nazis and because Martin Dies continued to oppose communism, it followed that he must be doing so out of sympathy for nazism. "With what glee must Hitler, Goering, and Goebbels read the reports of Martin Dies at their desks in Berlin!," Browder exclaimed in righteous and wrathful indignation.[14]

Indeed, Radio Berlin did broadcast some of Dies's statements, undoubtedly to promote the sort of divisiveness among the Allies that so many Americans, perhaps the Communists in particular, greatly feared. Nevertheless, there is no basis to the charge, so routinely asserted by Dies's critics, that the chairman was sympathetic to fascism or that he hoped Nazi Germany would win the war. Over the years, he and the committee repeatedly denounced profascist groups and individuals operating in the United States, and these criticisms were publicized by HUAC with great fanfare, especially when the House was considering its appropriations for the upcoming year. Nazis, Dies asserted, were nothing more than the "ideological bedfellows" of Communists, with one meaningful difference: Nazism posed an "immediate threat" to American interests, whereas communism represented a "greater long-term" danger to American security. Accordingly, Dies felt justified in directing the bulk of his committee's energies toward unearthing the Communist conspiracy that he believed was afoot in America, especially because the Communist party and its sympathizers could be expected to "utilize the present situation" to pose as ardent, pro-American patriots.[15]

Dies, together with other anti-Communists at this time, was certain that this pro-American posture was an expedient hoax, to be dropped as soon as the Soviet Union was out of danger and no longer needed the assistance of the United States. As for the alliance itself, Dies contended that the American people would be well-advised to reflect upon Soviet–American relations "with the frankest realism." Recalling that Stalin entered the war not "because he has been converted from communism to democracy" but "because Hitler invaded Russia," Dies concluded that the destruction of Hitlerism was the only point at which the interests of the two nations converged. He took it for granted that once this mutual goal was achieved, America would find itself once again in fundamental conflict with Stalin's regime.[16]

As such, Earl Browder was partly right when he branded Dies's "whole work" as a plan "to establish, nourish, and spread the idea that our Ally, the

Soviet Union, is really the most serious and deadly and almost the single enemy of the United States." It was the last part of this accusation—the part designed to do the most damage to Dies's credibility and political standing—that was, much in the tradition of the committee itself, inaccurate and unfair. The Dies committee deserved a lot of the criticism it received, but it was unjust to label the chairman the "clearest and most consistent exponent of Hitler's policies and slogans within the United States," as Browder and other Communists charged. To believe that communism posed a greater danger than nazism is not the same as being pro-Nazi, yet this falsehood lay at the core of much of the criticism leveled at the committee during the war and the U.S.–Soviet alliance.[17]

Similarly, Dies's irrational crusade to demonstrate that Communists ran the administration may have been an especially unwelcome complication for a government fighting a war, but his fixation on the "Communistic" New Deal predated World War II by several years, at least. Thus, he and his committee clearly did not embark on their anti-Roosevelt campaign to injure the war effort, though of course they also made no effort to soften these attacks out of any consideration for domestic unity or the U.S.–Soviet alliance. This may have been a vindictive misjudgment of the national interest. However, at the time HUAC was only a special committee of the House, so Congress could have terminated Dies's operations had it believed this step was warranted or necessary. By healthy margins (291-64; 302-94; 331-46), the direct representatives of the people consistently voted to keep the Un-American Activities Committee in operation, apparently believing that a list of subversive elements still active in the United States would not be complete unless it included the American Communist party.

In 1943, a comparatively quiet year for the committee, there were inquiries and reports about the Japanese relocation centers and American pacifist groups, but Communist activities remained uppermost in Chairman Dies's conspiratorial mind. On 1 February 1943, he delivered a wide-ranging, blistering address to the House, demanding that some 39 federal employees with "radical and crackpot" backgrounds be relieved of their positions. Because the administration had been slow to move against such people in the past, Dies suggested that Congress simply refuse to appropriate money for their salaries. Despite bipartisan misgivings about this procedure, the House voted to terminate (but subsequently restored) the salary of William Pickens, a black economist in a minor Treasury Department post.[18]

In an unsuccessful effort to forestall any further harassment of executive-branch employees by the Dies Committee, FDR appointed a panel to review charges of subversive penetration of the various executive-branch departments. At the same time, the proadministration House leadership empaneled a special subcommittee of the Appropriations Committee and charged it with much the same responsibility. One of HUAC's staunchest defenders, Clare

Hoffman, labeled the new subcommittee an attempt to "get rid of the Dies committee by kicking it out the back door." But Hoffman's fear proved to be premature. Communist influence in the government and the American political process would continue to be the committee's major matter of concern, as indicated in HUAC's brief summary report, published in early 1943. Roughly half the total report was related to alleged Communist activities, compared to three final paragraphs tacked on that mentioned Axis-front operations in the United States. With the overwhelming support of House Republicans and conservative Democrats, HUAC received a fresh appropriation of $75,000 (for a total of $625,000, the most ever granted to a special committee) for 1944, a year that would prove to be the committee's most momentous to date.[19]

In February of this election year, Dies announced that his committee's next investigative target would be the CIO's recently established Political Action Committee. Directed by Sidney Hillman of the CIO's Amalgamated Clothing Workers union, the PAC was established to mobilize the working-class vote for Roosevelt's expected bid for a fourth term, and for liberal congressional candidates across the country. This in itself was enough to arouse Dies's suspicions, though the chairman's antipathy for the "Communist-infested" CIO had been well-established before the PAC even came into existence. Now the CIO was trying to influence American elections by financing this new organization, whose parentage, Dies said, could be traced directly to the Communist party. Flatly predicting that "Sidney Hillman will soon succeed Earl Browder as head of the Communists in the United States," Dies declared that PAC's leaders were illegally financing their operation by "levying tribute upon every worker in their organization," all with the long-range purpose of "destroying parliamentary government" by electing "men who will serve as their stooges in the Congress of the United States."[20]

These remarks were but preliminary to the appearance, on 26 March, of the committee's *Report on the C.I.O. Political Action Committee*. This report accused PAC of violating the Smith–Connally Act, which forbade labor organizations from making direct contributions to political campaigns. It also outlined the substantial number of Communist-front associations of many of the officers and other personnel in CIO–PAC. "In its main outline," the report read, CIO–PAC was "a subversive Communist campaign" designed to subject Congress "to its totalitarian program." Though the report noted that Hillman had cooperated with Communists at other points during his long career in organized labor, this latest venture stood alone as "by far the most sinister of all his Communist coalitions." Eighteen of PAC's 49 executive board members were Communists, and although this did not constitute a majority, the report contended that "as long as the C.I.O. shelters so large a number of leaders who are subversive, the entire organization wears a dark blot upon its escutcheon."[21]

This report read like a call to arms, but on 12 May 1944, Dies stunned admirers and detractors alike by announcing that he would not seek reelection for an eighth term in Congress. He cited a throat ailment and a fear of becoming a "professional politician" as the reasons for his surprise announcement, but many observers suspected that a well-financed, PAC-endorsed challenger for his seat also hastened the chairman's retirement. Dies may well have lost this election had he run because some new defense installations had been built in his district, leaving him more vulnerable than in the past to the labor vote. By retiring, the chairman likely saved himself the fate suffered by two other committee Democrats targeted for elimination by the PAC, Frank Costello and Joe Starnes, both of whom lost their primary-election contests.[22]

This early demonstration of political muscle inspired HUAC's conservative members to intensify their attacks against the PAC. In the time remaining to them in Congress, they were grimly determined to influence events in the only way they knew: by "stepping boldly and deeply," as the *New York Times* put it, into the upcoming presidential contest.[23] As we shall see, their anti-PAC activities amounted to an auxiliary effort on behalf of the Republicans' presidential campaign against President Franklin Roosevelt.

Although he professed to want nothing more than to return home to Hyde Park, FDR firmly believed that he was by far the best-qualified (if not indispensable) leader to help construct a stable postwar settlement, and he eagerly sought reelection to a fourth term. Although in retrospect his victory seems to have been almost foreordained, this was by no means apparent at the time.

Indeed, Republicans began the 1944 campaign with high expectations of victory. They had done exceedingly well in the 1942 congressional elections, capitalizing on the public's disenchantment with all the inconveniences of war to gain 44 seats in the House and 9 in the Senate, sharply narrowing the Democratic majorities and strengthening the Southern Democrat-conservative Republican coalition that had been frustrating FDR's domestic agenda since 1938. The *Daily Worker* attributed this reversal to national dissatisfaction "with the inexcusable delay in unfolding our military offensive" in Europe; in fact, public resentment over rationing, shortages, and wage controls had more to do with the Republican windfall. In addition, a campaign by liberal activists to elect a "victory Congress"—in other words an attempted "purge" of the right-wing congressmen running for reelection—failed badly, as most of the conservatives in both parties were returned to Washington. Nebraska's Harry Coffee claimed that the purge's real purpose was "to eliminate those members of Congress who have been actively combating the subversive influence of communism"; John Rankin jibed that "nothing ever did me more good politically" than for the people of Mississippi to know that leftists wanted him out of Congress. The ultraconservative Clare Hoffman, another congressman who had frustrated the liberal-progressive attempt to unseat him, jubilantly called the elections "a clear-cut mandate to get rid of the bureaucrats, the crackpots, the Communists, and the New Dealers." And when a string of off-year elections in 1943 were won by the GOP, syndicated columnist Raymond Clapper observed that, "the Democratic Administration is living now on borrowed time," and *Life* magazine proclaimed: "The U.S. is now a Republican country." GOP hopes for capturing the White House soared.[24]

The principal contenders for the Republican presidential nomination included New York's Governor Tom Dewey, Ohio's conservative Governor John Bricker, Minnesota's former Governor Harold Stassen, General Douglas MacArthur, and 1940 candidate Wendell Wilkie. As the most recent standard-bearer of his party, Wilkie was the best known candidate; he had received more votes for president in 1940 than had any previous candidate except for Roosevelt's own total that year. Yet, Wilkie was something of an outsider in his own party: He had endorsed many "New Dealish" policies, he had established a good personal relationship with the president, and he had articulated a strong "internationalist" position on foreign affairs, which some took as a sign of softness toward Stalin.* His book *One World* (hailed by the Communist press as "a great patriotic service"), his well-publicized tour of the U.S.S.R., and his belief that there was "a chance to influence Mr. Stalin's judgment," won plaudits from liberals but further alienated Old Guard Republican opinion against him. For example, as far as Senator Kenneth Wherry, of Nebraska, was concerned, Wilkie still needed to "earn his spurs" with the party, whereas Clare Boothe Luce bluntly advised him "to stop drinking, lose forty pounds and adopt a more realistic understanding of the Communists' announced plan to conquer the world." He did none of these things, and after Dewey's convincing victory in the Wisconsin primary of 4 April, a thoroughly repudiated Wilkie abandoned his presidential dreams. His unexpected death only a few months later was lamented by the *New Republic* as "a heavy blow to American liberalism," but within his own party, Wilkie died unmourned. He did not even receive an invitation to what would be the last Republican convention of his life.[25]

Dewey's strong showing in Wisconsin made him the clear front-runner for the nomination. An intelligent moderate, he was a party regular who had enough sense not to oppose the most popular New Deal reforms. In addition, Dewey was acceptable to those conservative elements in the GOP practical enough to realize that the governor of New York was by far their most electable candidate against President Roosevelt. Still, some hard-right Republicans considered him too sympathetic to "internationalism" or "world state"

---

*Stalin, of course, displayed no such softness toward Wilkie after the American included some very mild criticism of the Soviet regime in an otherwise friendly *New York Times Magazine* article. For this he was immediately rebuked in *Pravda,* much to the amusement of conservative Republicans. (See *Times,* 2, 9 January 1944.)

schemes. Actually, Dewey simply realized that isolationism no longer served the interests of the nation. He was never a "one worlder" or at all liberal in his views on communism and the U.S.S.R. By the time the convention met in Chicago in late June, the New Yorker had secured more than enough delegates committed to his candidacy. The final tally was unanimous, except for the one delegate who declared: "I am a man, not a jelly fish. I vote for MacArthur." To appease the more conservative wing of the party, Dewey selected Governor Bricker as his running mate.[26]

Nor was the conservatives' traditional anti-Communist theme ignored at this gathering, despite the ongoing alliance. "No problem exists which cannot be solved by American methods," the party platform read. "We have no need of either the communistic or the fascist technique." Another plank optimistically appealed for support from a traditional Democratic constituency by stating that "the American labor movement and the Republican party, while continuously striving for the betterment of labor's status, reject the communistic and New Deal concept that a single group can benefit while the general economy suffers."[27]

Even though most Republicans realized that a concerted attack on the Soviet Union would be politically unwise at this time, former President Hoover was unable to resist a few hostile remarks about the country that both he and many of his listeners on the convention floor so thoroughly despised. "We have seen a series of independent actions by Russia which seem to be the negative of restored sovereignty to certain peoples," Hoover said, adding that "the Atlantic Charter has been sent to the hospital for major amputations of freedom among nations." The former president's speech called for the independence of Poland and "every other country which desires to be free from alien domination." On the upcoming election, Hoover commented, "The Communists and the fellow travelers are spending vast sums to reelect this regime. Would they spend their money to support the freedom of men?"[28]

Political attention next focused on the Democratic convention, also held in Chicago, where the only real suspense concerned the vice-presidential nomination. There was clear opposition to retaining Henry Wallace in this post; for example, a state Democratic convention in Virginia instructed its delegation to vote against Wallace because he was a convert to "foreign doctrines and ideologies." Wallace, one of the few mainstream politicians whom American Communists admired, had indeed become an effusive cheerleader for U.S.–Soviet friendship during the war. To a gathering of the Congress of American-Soviet Friendship in Madison Square Garden, Wallace had proclaimed that America, suffering from "an excess of political democracy," could learn some things from Stalin's regime. (The U.S.S.R., he claimed, permitted too much "economic democracy.") Even with the unusual conditions created by the alliance, remarks like this exposed Wallace to political criticism, such as when Alf Landon called upon "real Democrats" to join with Republicans in preventing Wallace and "his fellow travelers" from taking "us down the same disastrous primrose path which Hitler has led his people."[29]

This sort of appeal was not entirely ineffective: journalist Allen Drury reported that the ultraconservative Mississippi delegation sent to the convention nearly voted to support Wallace's renomination "on the deliberate assumption that he would be the best choice to *weaken* the ticket." The *Daily Worker* called this "anti-Wallace movement" an "anti-Roosevelt movement that has become diverted because the President is too popular." This was not entirely true, but conservative Democrats knew that although Roosevelt's renomination in Chicago was assured, Wallace was quite vulnerable to their machinations, especially after FDR refused to fight to keep him on the ticket. When a coalition of big-city bosses and conservative Southern Democrats, fearing that Roosevelt would not live out the full 4 years of another term, refused to renominate Wallace, the vice president was rather disingenuously dropped from the ticket in favor of Senator Harry Truman, of Missouri.[30]

The deposed vice president remained loyal to the Roosevelt cause, but his noncandidate status did much to eliminate him as an issue in the ensuing campaign. Thanks in large part to the Dies committee, however, Republicans found themselves with an even better figure to help them link the Democratic party with the Communist cause. This new focus of controversy was Sidney Hillman, one of Roosevelt's closest supporters in organized labor. In mid-1943 the politically savvy Hillman proposed to his CIO colleagues that their organization mobilize its considerable financial and manpower resources to help reelect FDR, get other candidates friendly to labor elected to Congress, and thereby halt what Hillman termed the "powerful reactionary trend" that had surfaced in the 1942 elections. Julius Emspak, a prominent CIO official with close ties to the Communist party, has described the PAC's formation as "one of those things that just happened. It was not a carefully thought out business at all." Perhaps not, but the PAC, founded on 7 July 1943, readily showed itself to be well financed, energetic, and politically formidable.[31]

With a national headquarters in New York City, branch offices across the country, and local operations organized to the ward and precinct level, PAC had a formidable staff of dedicated professionals and volunteers. NC–PAC, the National Citizens' Political Action Committee, was a sister organization set up to solicit nonunion contributions and to circumvent a provision in the Smith–Connally act that prohibited direct union contributions to federal elections. (Over the considerable protests of the GOP, Attorney General Biddle denied that either CIO–PAC or NC–PAC had violated the law on political contributions.) With this organizational muscle supporting his cause, Roosevelt hoped that he could avoid the sort of divisive and ideological campaign that might hurt the war effort. But the CIO–PAC carried with it a potential liability, as well, for among those whose services Hillman accepted were members of the Communist party.

Ironically, over the years, Hillman—who never was a Communist himself—had frequently been at odds with the Communists in his clothing-workers' union. Now, however, he adopted what his biographer, Matthew Josephson, called a policy of "moral neutrality." Hillman knew the Communists could be of great help to him, at least in the short term, and his actions were based on political opportunism, not ideology. Because Stalin clearly hoped that FDR would be reelected (the Soviet press criticized the GOP while calling the incumbent "the most plausible candidate"), the Communists dutifully reversed their 1940 disavowal of the president. They praised his enlightened outlook, as compared to the GOP's desire to "scuttle Teheran." Already deeply involved in CIO affairs, Communists moved easily into positions of authority within PAC, with Hillman's tacit blessing. As usual, the Communists were nothing if not thoroughly dedicated to the task at hand. Historian Maurice Isserman has described the Communists' pro-Roosevelt work in 1944 as "the greatest electoral effort of their history," and Richard Rovere, writing in *Harper's,* noted that the Communists made up "the backbone" of the PAC's operations in several key urban areas, including New York City.[32]

Recognizing that New York was especially vital to victory, Hillman strengthened his political organization there by collaborating with the Communists in a takeover of the American Labor party, a small, left-wing party that could hold the balance of power in a close election. David Dubinsky and the other anti-Communist Socialists who lost out in this power struggle to the Hillman–Communist forces angrily abandoned the Labor party and organized the new Liberal party, which also gave FDR its endorsement. Governor Dewey, watching these skirmishes from the sidelines, could now cite a prominent labor leader, Dubinsky, as an authority on the way Sidney Hillman had allowed himself to become a "front for Communists."[33]

Richard Norton Smith, in his biography of Dewey, says that a "dearth of winning issues" forced the candidate to use the Communist bogey against Roosevelt in 1944. His point is well taken. With military victory nearing and the employment issue temporarily neutralized by the wartime economy, the Republicans needed a compelling issue to arouse voters enough for them to retire their commander-in-chief. The "Russian problem" loomed as the most likely potential weak point in FDR's stewardship over foreign policy, and political figures in both parties had raised the issue. Within the GOP, even confirmed internationalists like Wallace White, a sponsor of the "Mackinac Pledge" to support a "postwar cooperative organization among sovereign nations," still insisted that "our first duty is to America," not any ally. Of course, more reactionary Republicans would have welcomed explicit criticism of the Soviets. In April 1944, Hamilton Fish said that he was "convinced the

Administration has no foreign policy but to appease Soviet Russia," an assessment echoed much later in the campaign by Mrs. Luce. Senator Taft was advised by a friend and correspondent to "play up the idea of commitments unfavorable to us but favorable to Russia and England," whereas Republican Senator H. Alexander Smith, of New Jersey, was reminded by one correspondent that there were some 5 million Polish–American voters who were waiting to hear something more specific than the party platform's ritualistic call for a "just" peace in this part of the world. Indeed, the Polish–American Congress, a potentially formidable political pressure group created in the spring of 1944, formally requested that the president work toward "the ultimate vindication of our ideals as expressed in the Atlantic Charter and the Four Freedoms."*[34]

As we shall see in the following chapter, FDR largely abandoned these "ideals"—and Poland—at the 1943 "Big Three" conference with Winston Churchill and Stalin in Teheran. But in the campaign of 1944, FDR was concerned enough about these Polish-related anxieties to keep secret the concessions he had made to Stalin regarding Poland's postwar borders. Instead, Roosevelt neutralized the potentially explosive issue with characteristically duplicitous reassurances, including his posing for a photograph that included a large background map of Poland, with its prewar eastern boundaries heavily marked. This picture, taken while Roosevelt was meeting a delegation of the Polish–American Congress, was widely distributed in areas with large Polish–American constituencies. A fuming Dewey, saddled with the GOP's isolationist image, and lacking any solid evidence to support a claim that Poland would be "sold out" to the U.S.S.R. after the war, was not in a good position to counteract this kind of ploy. Herbert Hoover had predicted that if the war were over by September or early October, "Uncle Joe's activities are going to be plain to the American people and they will be pretty distasteful." But the war did not end before the election, which allowed liberals like Senator Claude Pepper, of Florida, to say that "Russia would not trust a Republican administration," and moderate Democrats like Senator Connally to claim that FDR, rather than some "inexperienced stranger" to Stalin, could "best influence Russia." There was little that Dewey could say in response. At one point, the candidate did note that the president "has not yet even secured Russian recognition of those whom we consider to be the true Government of Poland"; and never did Dewey or his foreign policy adviser, John Foster Dulles, entertain the notion that the Russians would "lie down and be nice boys" once the alliance was over. But, having pledged in his acceptance speech to keep "the military conduct of the war . . . completely out of politics," Dewey did not dare to disrupt Allied unity. He therefore chose

---

*The "Four Freedoms"—speech, worship, and freedom from want and fear—were articulated in FDR's 1941 State of the Union Address. They served, along with the Atlantic Charter, as the expressed ideals behind the Allied cause.

not to make Poland or the potential Soviet menace a major campaign theme in 1944.[35]

Although the U.S.S.R. proper was removed as an election issue out of consideration for the ongoing alliance, Dewey did accuse the New Dealers of cynically trying to "insinuate that Americans must love communism or offend our fighting ally, Russia." This was too absurd for "even the gullible" to believe, Dewey said, because "in Russia, a Communist is a man who supports his government," whereas "in America, a Communist is a man who supports the Fourth Term so our form of government may more easily be changed." Even if it was impossible to condemn communism without at least indirectly criticizing the U.S.S.R., Dewey gambled that few voters held the Communists in the same regard that they reserved for, say, the heroic Russians who defended Stalingrad. An article published in the Fall 1944 issue of *Public Opinion Quarterly* predicted that the immediate benefits of the PAC would prove "illusory" for the Democrats in the long run, because "the taint of communism inevitably puts an organization on the defensive" and "alienates more support than can be derived from Communist participation." The Opinion Research Corporation recommended that Dewey "castigate the Hillman group as extremists and radicals," and the challenger, facing an uphill struggle against the man who may have been America's greatest politician, elected to make communism an important issue in his campaign. John D. Hamilton, former chairman of the Republican National Committee, stated the basic question that he hoped "that great group of voters" would ask themselves: "What is it that causes the CIO, the Hillmans, the Communists and the Browders, to be so insistent upon the nomination and reelection of Franklin Delano Roosevelt?"[36]

The syllogism that the Republicans put before the country was simple: The Communists run the PAC; the PAC now dictates Democratic party policy; therefore the Communists control the Democratic party. No patriotic American could give his or her vote to a party in such a state of arrears. Arthur Krock, respected political columnist for the *New York Times,* wrote in his 25 July 1944 column that Roosevelt, before giving final approval to the Truman nomination, had given the Democratic national chairman final instructions to "clear it with Sidney" before making the announcement. In another of its reports the Un-American Activities Committee disclosed that White House telephone records indicated that the administration had forged close ties with Hillman's organization. Robert Stripling, chief investigator for HUAC, bluntly characterized PAC as "not so much a labor political committee as it is the political arm of the New Deal administration." Naturally, Republicans seized upon these allegations as their "proof" that Hillman had gained dictatorial control over the Democratic party. Radio spot announcements purchased by the GOP reiterated the "clear-everything-with-Sidney" slogan throughout the country. The phrase was plastered on billboards everywhere, whereas other signs brandished this question: "Sidney Hillman and Earl Browder's Communists have registered. Have you?" Governors Earl Warren, of California, and Raymond Baldwin, of Connecticut, gave radio speeches in late August charging that the Communist-controlled CIO–PAC was in charge of the Democratic campaign.[37]

In the print media, the Dewey–Bricker ticket had the support of the rabidly anti-Roosevelt Hearst press, the isolationist McCormick–Patterson papers, the influential Scripps–Howard and Gannett chains, and numerous other newspapers around the country. Many were highly critical of the PAC, including, for example, the *Cleveland News,* which asserted that "there is a Communist issue [in this campaign]. It is created, for all to observe, by the support which a handful of American Communistic leaders, zealots working for the Soviet-statist U.S.A., are giving President Roosevelt." Other publications agreed. John Cort, writing in the widely respected *Commonweal,* a Catholic journal, conceded in an otherwise friendly article about the PAC that "the danger of Stalinist penetration" in some local PAC organizations was quite real. A cover story in Republican Henry Luce's *Time* magazine made prominent mention of Hillman's association with well-known Socialists, his foreign birth, and his Jewish faith.[38]

Anti-Semitic attacks were nothing new to Hillman; John L. Lewis once accused him of trying to be the "big Jew in the labor movement." Now, however, he was a truly national figure closely identified with FDR, and the issue was bound to trouble those with bigoted minds. Joseph P. Kennedy, without specifically mentioning Hillman, advised the president in a private memorandum that he was now "surrounded" by "Jews and Communists" who "will write you down in history, if you don't get rid of them, as incompetent, and they will open the way for the Communist line." Hillman tried to neutralize such slurs by saying that "Red baiting and Jew baiting" were twin evils. To their credit, Dewey and Bricker avoided anti-Semitic references in their verbal assaults on Hillman and the PAC. Realistically, though, the fact that Hillman was Jewish probably made it easier for many voters to believe he was peddling "foreign" or "Communistic" ideas, something that Dewey and Bricker did charge. Bricker's stump speeches, in particular, contained references to Hillman's "foreign" ideas and "alien" ideology. The glamorous Mrs. Luce, who frequently raised the Communist issue in her own reelection campaign that year, commented that if her head "rolls in the basket at this election, surely, it's a more American head than Mr. Hillman's."[39]

To be sure, Hillman's PAC was guilty of its own partisan excesses, as when it tried to link its opponents to Nazi-fascist ideology. "Joe Goebbels wasn't listed on the program," read the NC-PAC's *Weekly Report* of 18 October, "but the ideas of Hitler's master propagandist found expression in every major address delivered at the Republican National Convention which nominated

Dewey." A CIO–PAC campaign pamphlet, *A Woman's Guide to Political Action,* claimed that allegedly profascist elements in the United States "wholeheartedly" supported the GOP ticket "because they know that Dewey and Bricker . . . and all of the rest of the people around Dewey-Bricker are their kind." This was exactly the kind of smear tactic the Communists were using in this campaign. Browder, speaking at a Communist rally in Madison Square Garden, charged that Dewey's election would be "an invitation" to civil war in Europe and "a message" to the Soviet Union "that America disapproved in principle of cooperation between the two countries." William Z. Foster called Dewey's effort the "spearhead of post-war world reaction." Vito Marcantonio said that voting for Dewey "may write the induction papers of every male child five years of age today," but a reelected Roosevelt would "preserve his future—his very life" by continuing to cooperate with the U.S.S.R. At its first meeting in May 1944, the Communist Political Association passed a resolution that condemned the "Hoover–Taft–Vandenberg–Dewey machine" for plotting "to bring about a compromise peace with nazism-fascism and [for seeking] to establish a pro-fascist government within the United States."[40]

However, if one may exclude these fringe Communist actors in the Roosevelt camp, the Republican attacks on the incumbent administration and its alleged domination by the Communists were in general sharper and more sustained than comparable Democratic rhetoric that year. Dewey first raised his Reds-in-America issue on 18 September during a campaign appearance in Seattle, Washington. The challenger said that a Dewey administration would work to remove racketeers and Communists from their positions of influence within the labor movement. After Roosevelt kicked off his own campaign with his famous, mocking "Fala" speech to the Teamsters convention, Dewey responded by pledging that he would "not join my opponent in his descent to mud-slinging." Dewey did not keep this promise. On 25 September he directly linked his opponent to the Communists when he said that the supposedly indispensable Roosevelt was indeed "indispensable to Earl Browder, the ex-convict and pardoned Communist leader."[41]

A day later Dewey was in Tulsa, promising a crowd of 10,000 that he would sweep out all the Communists holding political jobs in the federal government. The Republican challenger accused Roosevelt of releasing Earl Browder from prison in 1942 just so the Communist leader could work on behalf of the fourth-term candidacy in 1944. Stung by Dewey's strident red-baiting attacks, FDR pointedly rejected "the support of any person or group committed to communism, or Fascism." When Dewey took his campaign into the Appalachian region, he toughened his anti-Communist attacks even further by strongly implying that Roosevelt's "soft disclaimer" of Communist support was inexcusably late and motivated by sheer political expediency.[42]

In a campaign appearance in Charleston, West Virginia, Dewey stated that the president's reelection was "essential to the aims of the Communists."

According to Dewey's reasoning, the Communists knew that "unemployment and discontent" best serve their interests; therefore, it was only logical for them to support the individual who had been unable for 7 long years to pull the country out of Depression. "They love to fish in troubled waters," Dewey said of the Communists, and Roosevelt was their best candidate for keeping America mired in the sort of economic turmoil that made Communistic appeals more attractive to the general public. Saying that he did not know if the president called his program "communism or National Socialism or Fascism," Dewey contended that the New Deal was surely not "an American system and it's not a free system."[43]

Although Dewey's rhetoric during this campaign reflected his determination to remain always on the attack, his running mate's campaign speeches were often even more forceful and demagogic. The pro-Roosevelt *New Republic* drolly conceded Bricker's "perfect background" for participating in this Republican campaign, saying that he "went to Hoover High School, attended McCormick College and took a post-graduate course at Goebbels University." The last association was a low blow, but throughout the campaign Bricker stuck diligently to a script designed to capitalize on the voters' antiradical fears. In Illinois, he launched a slashing verbal attack at those alleged New Deal radicals "whose contempt for the American way of life is surpassed only by their admiration of foreign philosophies." According to the governor, "The sale of the Democratic party to the Hillmans and the Browders and the radical element in this country" had been conceived not at the 1944 convention but had been "in the making within a few months after the President took office in 1933 and has been in the process of consummation for twelve long years." Bricker also charged that Earl Browder and Hillman "were seeking to tie the noose of communism not only around the New Deal, but around the whole American people."[44]

Other Republicans on the campaign trail in 1944 repeated these themes. New Jersey's Governor Walter Edge decried the "unholy alliance" between Roosevelt and the Communists. Governor Simeon Willis, of Kentucky, compared the New Deal to a three-legged stool, with Roosevelt, city bosses, and Browder–Hillman serving as the three "legs." Taft, running hard for reelection in Ohio, charged that the Democratic campaign was being run principally by the CIO–PAC, meaning that if FDR won another term, Sidney Hillman would "predominate" in "all business and economic policy." Mrs. Luce, appearing in Pittsburgh on 16 October, said that the Communist "plot" to help Roosevelt had been motivated by two concerns: "First, because Russia has come into the war and, second, because they see a way of exchanging their support at the polls for the right to take over the whole CIO union today and tomorrow the whole union movement and the Democratic party." (To dramatize her point, Luce made a six-word speech on the House floor: "Mr. Speaker, clear everything with Sidney.") Clare Hoffman, saying that his old nemesis FDR was no longer the "quarterback" of his own administration, claimed that "Sidney Hillman and Earl Browder are the quarterbacks. The Communists are calling the plays." Styles Bridges, in a speech published in *Congressional Digest,* charged that "four more years of Roosevelt mean four more years of 'I am the law' Hague in New Jersey, of the Kelly-Nash gang in Chicago, of LaGuardia and Marcantonio in New York, and the Communist, Earl Browder."[45]

This was precisely the theme that Dewey touched on during a campaign stop in St. Louis on 16 October. "It's clear to everybody by now that the New Deal has been taken over by a combination of big city bosses, Communists and fellow travelers," the GOP nominee said in this nationally broadcast address. Four days later in Pittsburgh, Dewey said the Republican bandwagon was being joined by those Democrats "who deeply resent the kidnapping of their party by the Communists and the Political Action Committee." In Chicago, Dewey continued to press this line of attack, claiming that the special interests, including the Communists, were "working together to perpetuate my opponent in office."[46]

With many political observers predicting a close election, Dewey's red-baiting tactics seemed to be working. He triumphed in Maine's early election, a victory that was sardonically attributed to Sidney Hillman. Representative Clarence Brown described the rural districts of Ohio as "literally on fire over the Hillman-communism issue. That issue is going to bring out the vote." As early as mid-March, James Farley had believed that Roosevelt was in political trouble because of concerns over Poland and a perception that the president had "gone over" to various interests, including the Soviets, the British, or the Jews. Now, in the midst of the campaign, some Democratic leaders started to worry. In his 8 October column, Arthur Krock reported that the Roosevelt campaign managers were becoming increasingly anxious about the Communists' obvious preference for their candidate. Edwin Johnson, a Democratic Senator from Colorado, suggested that FDR's people "ought to put Earl Browder, Sidney Hillman and Henry Wallace in cold storage along with Eleanor" (the president's wife), until the votes were counted because "they are proving to be a millstone around the President's neck." Senator Josiah Bailey of North Carolina announced that if Hillman "and his CIO and Communists" seized outright control of the party, he would resign.[47]

Acutely aware that he had become a central issue in the campaign, Hillman repeatedly tried to blunt the accusations made against him and his organization. Addressing the United Electrical Workers (which was Communist-dominated) convention in New York City on 28 September, Hillman emphatically denied that the PAC was Communist controlled. At another engagement, Hillman asserted that "the whole record of PAC is anti-Communist" and that he personally had volunteered "many times" to testify before the Dies committee to rebut this smear. The campaign against his organization, Hillman asserted, "is not so much a political war as a class war."[48]

Joseph Gaer, a key PAC staff member, also sought to portray the Communist question as an implied attack on organized labor when he said that "if anyone wishes to accuse Mr. Murray, the members of his Executive Board, and the entire membership of the CIO as being Communists or Communist-inspired, he may do so," though workers would be justified in drawing the conclusion that the accuser was a foe of labor. But Governor Bricker, seeking votes in Indiana, tried to assure American workers that Republican attacks were not directed at the laboring class, proper, by noting that the majority of workers "cherish sacred American rights" and that they know "a radical and communistic labor element will in the end defeat the honorable and legitimate aims of organized labor in this country." Other Republicans made similar statements in an effort to win a respectable portion of the labor vote for the GOP. Republican National Chairman Herbert Brownell, Jr., said that PAC's "arrogance" was driving organized workers away from the Democratic party. Taft, speaking at an AFL meeting in Cleveland, tried to persuade his union audience that the CIO–PAC had "forfeited its right to speak for labor because it is in fact a political party, the original Fourth Term party."[49]

As the campaign drew to a close, the GOP had some last-minute ammunition to use against the administration, courtesy of the House Un-American Activities Committee, which issued a second harshly critical report on the CIO-PAC. HUAC made its final attempt to influence the 1944 election through the hearings process, which, formally speaking, were conducted by a specially empaneled subcommittee of HUAC members Starnes, Costello, and Thomas.* Several CIO members testified to PAC's evil effects on the labor movement and the political process. But the main testimony came from J. B. Matthews, a former Communist himself but now the committee's intrepid staff director, who spoke as an expert witness. This was a convenient means of reading into the record the findings of the committee's investigations. According to Matthews, NC–PAC was "the Communist party's major front organization, its supreme bid for power" in 25 years of operations in the United States. Armed with a battery of charts and lists that detailed the overlap in Communist-front and NC–PAC membership rosters, Matthews concluded that NC–PAC was staffed with people who had formed "the nucleus of the Communist front movement in this country during the past decade." Both groups were "now receiving the active assistance of a number

---

*The retiring Dies took no part in these proceedings, preferring instead to relax in Jasper, Texas. To friendly newsmen, he granted occasional interviews, in which he railed about the Communists' penetration of Hollywood, yet hopefully predicted that the New Deal "nightmare," along with "its Communists and subversive allies . . . and other dictatorial embellishments," would soon be thrown out of power. (*New York Journal-American,* 26 and 28 June 1944.)

of officials of the government." All this, Matthews reasoned, justified the allegation—raised by the Dies committee and picked up by the Dewey campaign—that PAC was "a Communist-front organization, having the ambitious objective of worming the way of the Communists into the Democratic party."[50]

Seizing immediately on these "findings," Bricker said in Detroit that the Dies committee had presented data that "conclusively prove that Franklin Roosevelt and the New Deal are in the hands of the radicals and the Communists." In Boston, Dewey said that Sidney Hillman's PAC and Earl Browder's Communists were the high bidders in the auctioneering of the Democratic party to the special interests. No such attempt at taking over the Republican party could be successful, Dewey claimed, and the Communists knew it. Bricker followed up these attacks by criticizing FDR for not repudiating the Browder–Hillman scheme for redesigning the economy "on European lines"; in Philadelphia the following day, 3 November, Bricker declared that he did not want returning veterans to "find Sidney Hillman with his alien philosophies of government sitting at the right hand of the President, and Earl Browder . . . sitting at the left hand of the President." Meanwhile, Dewey, hoping against hope that this latest news from the Un-American Activities Committee would clinch the Republicans' case against their long-time adversary, extended a final invitation from Madison Square Garden to wavering Democrats to abandon their once-great but now Communist-owned party and return the GOP to power in Washington.[51]

But Roosevelt, who followed his adversary to Boston to deliver some final partisan blows of his own, finally responded directly to Dewey's repeated claims of Communist influence within the administration and the campaign staff. Any candidate, Roosevelt argued, who would imply that the United States could be sold out to the Communists betrayed "a shocking lack of trust in America." Noting that his opponents also had accused him of trying to establish a monarchy, Roosevelt sarcastically asked, "Now, really—which is it—communism or monarchy?"[52]

On election day, FDR emerged triumphant again, handily winning the popular vote and garnering an even more impressive majority in the Electoral College. PAC was credited with having tipped the balance in several key states, especially those with large urban populations. Some contended that PAC was *the* decisive factor in Roosevelt's reelection, but others dispute this, pointing out that Hillman and his controversial organization had to cost the president votes he otherwise would have got. In any event, several well-known congressional conservatives, including Ham Fish, joined Dewey in defeat.[53]

Yet, this electoral setback—like the war itself—failed to bury the "Communists-in-government" issue. Anti-Communists were a hardy, irascible lot. They can be faulted for their divisive and irresponsibly exaggerated accusations, directed at the commander-in-chief in the midst of enormous crisis.

However, these individuals did not act from treasonous or profascist motives. In most cases, their hatred for the New Deal long preceded the war and would long survive it. Although there *were* Communists in the government, the CIO, and PAC at this time, it was a perverse refusal to accept the New Deal that accounts for the extremism of men like Martin Dies. As a Democrat, Dies gained little from his anticommunist crusade except an early retirement in 1944—though he would return to Congress in the 1950s. Governor Dewey's attacks on the administration probably were more partisan than ideological; yet even his most strident rhetoric accurately reflected the views of his party's more conservative wing. Owing largely to wartime conditions, both Dies and Dewey suffered setbacks in 1944. However, for the staunchest anti-Communists of both major parties, better days lay just ahead.

NOTES

1. *Congressional Record*, 78th Congress, 2nd Session, p. A2148 (hereafter *CR*, 78–2, p. A2148); *Chicago Tribune*, 17 February 1944; *CR*, 78–1, p. A3371; *CR*, 77–2, p. 8176; *CR*, 77–2, p. A2354; *CR*, 78–1, p. 6892.
2. *San Francisco Examiner*, 3 March 1943; *CR*, 77–2, p. A2084; *CR*, 78–1, p. 6302; Burton Wheeler and Paul Healy, *Yankee from the West* (Garden City, NY: Doubleday and Company, 1962), p. 390.
3. *Chicago Tribune*, 17 May 1942; *San Francisco Examiner*, 17 May 1942; *New York Times*, 17 May 1942.
4. *New York Times*, 1April, 23 April, 16 May 1942; *New York Teacher News*, 11 April 1942, from clipping in ACLU Papers, Book 2369, p. 102
5. Jack Tenney, *Red Fascism* (New York: Arno Press, 1977), pp. 12–17, 88–92.
6. *CR*, 77–2, p. 408; *Chicago Tribune*, 27 September 1942; *CR*, 77–2, p. 3211.
7. *CR*, 77–1, pp. 10061–62; August Ogden, *The Dies Committee* (Washington, D.C.: Catholic University of America Press, 1945), p. 251; *San Francisco Examiner*, 23 January 1942.
8. Harold Ickes, *The Secret Diary of Harold Ickes* (New York: Simon & Schuster, 1954), p. 529; *CR*, 77–2, p. 409; Walter Goodman, *The Committee* (New York: Farrar, Straus and Giroux, 1968), p. 128.
9. Ogden, p. 260; *CR*, 77–2, pp. 3205–6; *New York Times*, 30 March 1942; Frank Thone to Henry Wallace, 30 March 1942, Henry Wallace Papers (Library of Congress), Reel 23.
10. Francis Biddle, *In Brief Authority* (Garden City, NY: Doubleday and Company, 1962), pp. 296–307; Goodman, pp. 125–7; *CR*, 77–2, p. 7441-2, 7458; U.S. House of Representatives (77– 2) Report No. 833, p. 3; *New York Times*, 18 April 1942; U.S. House of Representatives (77–2), Report No. 2748, pp. 7–8; *CR*, 77–2, pp. 7682–99.
11. U.S. House of Representatives (77–2) Report No. 2277, 2 parts, pp. 8, 12, minority report, p. 5; *CR*, 78–2, p. 2435; *CR*, 78–1, p. 60; Jerry Voorhis, *Confessions of a Congressman* (Garden City, NY: Doubleday and Company, 1947), pp. 207–32; Roger Baldwin to Thomas Eliot, 17 April 1942, ACLU Papers, Book 2369, p. 102
12. *CR*, 77–2, p. 2295; *CR*, 77–2, p. 1430; *CR*, 77–2, p. 2282; *CR*, 77–2, p. 3756; William Gellerman, *Martin Dies* (New York: John Day Company, 1944), p. 257.

13. "The Dies 'Front,'" *Nation*, 3 October 1942, pp. 285–86; "Dies Helps Hitler," *New Republic*, 6 April 1942, p. 445; United Press dispatch, quoted in *CR*, 77–2, p. 2434; *CR*, 77–2, p. 7441.

14. *Daily Worker*, 29 January 1942; William Z. Foster, "The Reactionary Offensive and the War," *The Communist*, April 1943, p. 306; Earl Browder, *Victory—And After* (New York: International Publishers, 1942), p. 65.

15. Ogden, p. 263; Martin Dies, *The Trojan Horse in America* (New York: Dodd, Mead and Company, 1940), pp. 79, 129, 304–46; *CR*, 77–2, p. 1925; *CR*, 77–2, p. 7457; *CR*, 78–1, p. 474; *CR*, 77–2, p. 408.

16. *CR*, 77–2, p. 408; *CR*, 77–2, p. 800.

17. Browder, *Victory—And After*, p. 62; Browder, "Hitler's Secret Weapon—The Bogey of Communism," *The Communist*, March 1943, p. 199.

18. *CR*, 78–1, pp. 474–86; Goodman, pp. 141–143.

19. Roland Young, *Congressional Politics in the Second World War* (New York: Columbia University Press, 1956), pp. 49–51; "The New Red Network," *New Republic*, 2 August 1943, p. 136; *CR*, 78–1, p. 732; U.S. House of Representatives (77–2) Report No. 2748; Ogden, p. 288.

20. James Caldwell Foster, *The Union Politic, The CIO Political Action Committee* (Columbia: University of Missouri Press, 1975), pp. 3–48; *New York Times*, 10 March 1944; *CR*, 78–2, p. 2439.

21. U.S. House of Representatives. (78–2) Report No. 1311, pp. 7, 12.

22. *New York Times*, 13 May 1944; Dies, *Martin Dies' Story*, p. 82; Maurice Isserman, *Which Side Were You On?* (Middletown, CT: Wesleyan University Press, 1982), p. 212.

23. *New York Times*, 29 July 1944; Chicago *Tribune*, 29 July 1944; *Times* 2 April 1944.

24. James Patterson, *Congressional Conservatism and the New Deal* (Lexington: University of Kentucky Press, 1967); *Daily Worker*, 5 November 1942; *CR*, 78–2, p. 8121; Brooklyn *Tablet*, 30 May 1942; *CR*, 78–1, p. 698; Raymond Clapper, *Watching the World* (New York: Whittlesey House, 1944), p. 180; "The Country Turns Republican," *Life*, 15 November 1943, p. 27.

25. Donald Bruce Johnson, *The Republican Party and Wendell Wilkie* (Urbana: University of Illinois Press, 1960), pp. 188–307; Joseph Barnes Papers, Box 10, "Speeches and Articles by Wendell L. Wilkie, 1944"; Wendell Wilkie, *One World* (New York: Simon & Schuster, 1943); *The Communist* (1943), p. 565; Earl Browder, "Wilkie's Growing Stature," Earl Browder Papers, Series 3, Reel 7, No. 131:23; Marvin Stromer, *The Making of a Political Leader, Kenneth S. Wherry and the United States Senate* (Lincoln: University of Nebraska Press, 1969), p. 22; Steve Neal, *Dark Horse, A Biography of Wendell Wilkie* (Garden City, NY: Doubleday and Company, 1984), p. 290; "Wendell Wilkie," *New Republic*, 16 October 1944, p. 479; Selig Adler, *The Isolationist Impulse* (New York: Abelard–Schuman Limited, 1957), p. 344.

26. Richard Norton Smith, *Thomas E. Dewey and His Times* (New York: Simon & Schuster, 1982), pp. 393–437; Geoffrey Perrett, *Days of Sadness, Years of Triumph* (New York: Coward, McCann and Geoghegan, 1973), p. 290; Barry Beyer, *Thomas E. Dewey, 1937–1947* (New York: Garland Publishing, Inc., 1979), pp. 253–58; Karl Pauly, *Bricker of Ohio, The Man and His Record* (New York: G. P. Putnam's Sons, 1944).

27. *Proceedings of the Twenty–Third Republican National Convention* (Chicago, IL, June 26–28, 1944), pp. 138, 140–41.

28. *Ibid.*, pp. 159, 162–63, 165.

29. Torbjorn Sirevag, *The Eclipse of the New Deal* (New York: Garland Publishing, Inc., 1985), pp. 412–22, 416; *Chicago Tribune*, 9 July 1944; *Salute to Our Russian Ally*, (New York: National Council of American–Soviet Friendship, 1942), pp. 116–17; Donald McCoy, *Landon of Kansas* (Lincoln: University of Nebraska Press, 1966), p. 489.

30. Allen Drury, *A Senate Journal, 1943–1945* (New York: McGraw–Hill, 1963), p. 221; *Daily Worker*, 13 July 1944; Norman Markowitz, *The Rise and Fall of the People's Century: Henry A. Wallace and American Liberalism, 1941–1948* (New York: Free Press, 1973), pp. 81–123.

31. Sidney Hillman, "Is the PAC Beneficial to Labor and to the Country?" *Reader's Digest*, November 1944, p. 77; Julius Emspak, Columbia Oral History Project, p. 314; Jean Gould, *Sidney Hillman, Great American* (Boston: Houghton Mifflin Company, 1952), pp. 317–25; James MacGregor Burns, *Roosevelt: The Soldier of Freedom* (New York: Harcourt Brace Jovanovich, 1970), pp. 524–25.

32. Matthew Josephson, *Sidney Hillman, Statesman of American Labor* (Garden City, NY: Doubleday and Company, 1952), p. 605; Charles Madison, *American Labor Leaders* (New York: Frederick Ungar Publishing Co., 1962), pp. 348–50; David Saposs, *Communism in American Politics* (Washington, DC: Public Affairs Press, 1960), p. 73; George Soule, *Sidney Hillman, Labor Statesman* (New York: Amalgamated Clothing Workers of America, 1939), p. 147; *San Francisco Examiner*, 18 July 1944; *Examiner*, 5 May 1944; Earl Browder, "The GOP Against Teheran," Earl Browder Papers, Series 3, Reel 7, No. 131:10; Isserman, p. 208; Richard Rovere, "Labor's Political Machine," *Harper's Magazine*, June 1945, p. 599.

33. Saposs, p. 76; Foster, *The Union Politic*, p. 29; Joseph Gaer, *The First Round* (New York: Duell, Solan and Pearce, 1944), pp. 223–24; *New York Times*, 31 March, 2 November 1944; *Report and Record, Twenty–fifth Convention of the International Ladies' Garment Workers' Union* (29 May–9 June 1944, Boston, MA), p. 229.

34. Smith, *Thomas E. Dewey and His Times*, p. 433; George Mayer, *The Republican Party, 1854–1966* (New York: Oxford University Press, 1967), p. 464; Wallace White Papers, Box 68, "Speeches, Articles, Remarks, 1941–1943"; *Chicago Tribune*, 11 April 1944; *San Francisco Examiner*, 31 October 1944; John Burke to Robert Taft, 27 July 1944, Robert Taft Papers, Box 158, "Miscellaneous Campaign Material" file; R. L. Buell to H. Alexander Smith, Papers of H. Alexander Smith, Box 89, "Republican National Convention–1944"; *New York Times*, 31 May 1944.

35. Stephen Garrett, "Eastern European Ethnic Groups and American Foreign Policy," *Political Science Quarterly*, Summer 1978, p. 314; Richard Norton Smith, *An Uncommon Man, The Triumph of Herbert Hoover* (New York: Simon & Schuster, 1984), p. 334; *New York Times*, 7 October 1944; Papers of Tom Connally, Box 561, "Speeches, Dallas, Houston, Baltimore"; Michael Guhin, *John Foster Dulles, A Statesman and His Times* (New York: Columbia University Press, 1972), pp. 131–32; Thomas Dewey interview, in John Foster Dulles Oral History Project (Princeton University), p. 50; *Public Papers of Thomas E. Dewey, Fifty–first Governor of the State of New York, 1944* (Albany, NY: Williams Press, 1946), p. 760; H. Bradford Westerfield, *Foreign Policy and Party Politics* (New Haven, CT: Yale University Press, 1955), pp. 135–36; Robert Divine, *Foreign Policy and U.S. Presidential Elections, 1940–1948* (New York: New Viewpoints, 1974), p. 141.

36. *New York Times*, 2 November 1944; Joseph Rosenfarb, "Labor's Role in the Election," *Public Opinion Quarterly*, Fall 1944, p. 385; A. Russell Buchanan, *The United States and World War II*, Vol. 2 (New York: Harper & Row, 1964), p. 297; John D. Hamilton Papers, container 26, "Speeches of John D. Hamilton, 1940–1955," p. 3253.

37. *New York Times*, 25 July 1944; Jack Goodman, ed., *While You Were Gone* (New York: Simon & Schuster, 1946), p. 389; Burns, p. 525; Buchanan, p. 297.

38. *Cleveland News* editorial of 25 September 1944, available in Taft papers, Box 158, "Miscellaneous (1944 campaign)"; John Cort, "Hillman, CPA and PAC," *Commonweal*, 20 October 1944, p. 8; "The New Force," *Time*, 24 July 1944, pp. 18–20.

39. *New York Times*, 29 September 1941; Frances Perkins interview, Columbia Oral History Project, p. 424; Arthur Krock Papers, Box 1, Book 1, p. 151; *New York Times*, 20 October 1944.

40. Robert Taft Papers, Box 158, "Labor (CIO and PAC)" File; Gaer, p. 437; Beyer, pp. 254–255; "The War and the Elections," Earl Browder Papers, Series 3, Reel 7, No. 15; William Z. Foster, "Dewey and Teheran," *The Communist*, November 1944, p. 1011; Vito Marcantonio, *Security with FDR* (New York: National Fraternal Committee for the Re–Election of President Roosevelt, 1944), p. 30; *The Communist*, June 1944, p. 503.

41. Dewey, *Public Papers*, pp. 736, 749; Burns, pp. 521–524.

42. *New York Times*, 27 September 1944; *Times*, 6 October 1944; *Times*, 8 October 1944.

43. Dewey, *Public Papers*, p. 753; New York *Times*, 15, 16 October 1944.

44. "The Education of John Bricker," *New Republic*, 30 October 1944, p. 556; *San Francisco Examiner*, 12 October 1944; *New York Times*, 6 October 1944.

45. *New York Times*, 19 October 1944; Radio Broadcast, 23 October 1944, Taft Papers, Box 1299, "Broadcasts, 1944" file; "The New Deal is the Issue," 14 September 1944, Taft Papers, Box 1299, "Addresses, 1944" file; Wilfrid Sheed, *Clare Boothe Luce* (New York: E. P. Dutton, 1982), p. 94; *Times*, 17 October 1942; *CR*, 78–2, p. 7709; *CR*, 78–2, p. 7755; *Congressional Digest*, May 1944, p. 146.

46. Dewey, *Public Papers*, pp. 755, 763, 771–72.

47. Robert Sherwood, *Roosevelt and Hopkins*, Vol. 2 (New York: Harper and Brothers, 1948), p. 465; *CR*, 78–2, p. 8028; *Chicago Tribune*, 13 September 1944; *New York Times*, 21 October 1944; James Farley Papers, Box 45, "Private File, 1944–45"; *Times*, 8 October 1944; *Times*, 14 October 1944; *San Francisco Examiner*, 15 May 1944;

48. *New York Times*, 29 September, 8 October 1944.

49. Gaer, p. 159; *New York Times* 10 September 1944; Robert Taft Papers, Box 158, "Miscellaneous (1944 Campaign)"; "P.A.C.," *Life*, 11 September 1944, p. 91; Robert Taft Papers, Box 158, "Labor (CIO and PAC)" file.

50. *Special Committee on Un–American Activities, Hearings*, Vol. 17, 27–29 September, 3–5 October 1944, pp. 10303, 10339.

51. *New York Times*, 31 October 1944; Dewey, *Public Papers*, pp. 781–85 *Times*, 3 November 1944; *Times*, 4 November, 1944; Dewey, *Public Papers*, p. 792.

52. *New York Times*, 5 November 1944.

53. Divine, p. 162; Foster, *The Union Politic*, pp. 40–44, 48; Josephson, p. 634; Michael Parenti, *The Anti–Communist Impulse* (New York: Random House, 1969), p. 212.

4

The Politics of Anti-Sovietism in
Wartime America

In the true spirit of American democracy, foreign policy continued to provoke sharp political debate during World War II. At one point, a concerned Speaker of the House Sam Rayburn even tried to dissuade his colleagues from engaging in any "dangerous talk" or "dangerous propaganda" that might bring about "wrong thinking in our own country or disunity among us and those allied with us." Rayburn's remark, everyone knew, was directed primarily to those who had set themselves squarely against what Democratic Senator Burton Wheeler, of Montana, described as "the fawning of some prominent Americans on the Russians, who overnight had become advocates of peace and friendship" merely by virtue of the U.S.–U.S.S.R. alliance.[1]

The Soviets' most persistent wartime critics included Wheeler, Robert Reynolds, Styles Bridges, Robert Taft, Arthur Vandenberg, and C. Wayland Brooks in the Senate and Hamilton Fish, John Lesinski, Jessie Sumner, and Clare Boothe Luce in the House. Others in Congress periodically voiced doubts, dismay, or uneasiness over matters involving Soviet–American relations during the war. Collectively, they raised some difficult, disquieting issues, such as whether a "Europe-first" strategy for winning the war—the plan clearly in the Soviets' best interests—was in fact in America's best interests; whether America was conducting an unwise policy of appeasement toward the Soviet Union; whether Stalin—and Roosevelt himself—were genuinely committed to the principles enunciated in the Atlantic Charter; and whether the political and territorial makeup of the postwar world, Eastern Europe in particular, would be just and honorable.

In general, congressional hostility and suspicion toward the U.S.S.R. remained strongest among the isolationist bloc (Bridges and Luce were conspicuous exceptions) that had opposed American involvement in the war in the first place. During the war, these lingering isolationist-bloc suspicions blended perfectly with still-virulent anti-communist attitudes among some congressional figures. Significantly, those raising these sensitive issues came from both major parties, although Republicans were more inclined to personalize the debate by directly attacking President Roosevelt's handling of wartime diplomacy. It probably would exaggerate matters to say there was an anti-Soviet congressional "bloc" during the war, as there was little united action seriously undertaken to impede the president's close cooperation with Joseph Stalin. Nor would any such action have been successful, given the dire circumstances of the time, and the fact that the president's own Democratic party controlled Capitol Hill. Nevertheless, anti-Soviet congressmen—despite the countervailing pressure of the alliance—maintained at least a foothold in the political arena of World War II America.

From the start, it was clear to Roosevelt and most of his military experts that Hitler posed a greater threat than Japan and therefore needed to be defeated first. General George C. Marshall argued for an early second front against Germany, and Roosevelt even assured Soviet Foreign Minister Vyacheslav Molotov, who visited Washington in the spring of 1942, that such a front would be opened later that year. The invasion of North Africa, begun in November 1942, partially fulfilled this pledge, although Stalin, American Communists, and others continued to press for a full-scale second front in Europe right until the eventual D-Day invasion in early June 1944.[2]

Of course, anyone who opposed an immediate second front could expect to be roundly denounced by the Communists (Herbert Hoover did so and was castigated for echoing "the Goebbels line"), but the Communist party, as well as FDR himself, probably was more alarmed about the "Japan-firsters," who offered an even more direct challenge to the administration's war-making strategy. "We have our own war in the Pacific," insisted Representative Jessie Sumner, one of the most extreme of the Japan firsters, "but we have been persuaded that it is to the interest of America to aid in other war." The "Japan-first" argument had a special appeal to isolationists, who well knew that it was the sneak attack on Pearl Harbor—by people of another race—and not any overt act by Germany, that had forced America into the war. Even if it was conceded that Germany was the strongest of the Axis powers, Japan was more capable of mounting an attack directly on the Aleutian Islands, or other American territory. Republican Senator Hiram Johnson, an unrepentant isolationist from California, said that the "worst part of this Japanese war" was that it had taken America into the European conflict; Johnson demanded that the "defense of our shores against invasion" take precedence over all other considerations. Colonel Harold Kay, an aide to the governor of Hawaii, pleaded in April 1943 for more mainland military assistance, claiming that "the danger is so immediate and terrific . . . that its real nature cannot be disclosed until steps have been taken to meet it." Some frustrated "Japan firsters" in Washington went so far as to suggest that the administration, having decided to dispose of Germany first, had misrepresented the real views of Pentagon strategists on this matter. FDR established a Pacific War Council in 1942 to demonstrate that he was not ignoring the Japanese threat, but complaints persisted that America was directing her main resources into the wrong theater of the war.[3]

If there was a single-most important leader of the rear-guard "Japan-first" cause, Senator Albert "Happy" Chandler, a Democrat from Kentucky, best deserves the appellation for two speeches he made in the spring of 1943. In April he called for a strengthening of American forces in Alaska, so that the Japanese could be driven from the American-owned island of Kiska. A month later, in a well-publicized Senate speech, Chandler argued that America should deploy the bulk of its military resources to the Pacific war. If it did not, Japan would have time to strengthen its own defenses, making the eventual invasion of their islands even more difficult and costly. "I want our country to fight Japan while we are strong, and while we are able to deliver the strongest possible blow against them," Chandler insisted. A premature strike against Hitler would cost many more lives than was necessary and would "leave the flower of American manhood and woman-hood on Flander Field, between the channel coast and the Rhine River."[4]

Several of Chandler's Republican colleagues hastened to applaud his "Pacific-first" proposal. Henrik Shipstead, Republican of Minnesota, said Chandler "knew he might be attacked" for his remarks but that "American citizens of the future will give him due credit" for his courage and vision. Arthur Vandenberg said the Kentuckian was "wholly right," that "the interests of the people of the United States" dictated that "we must . . . attack Japan first." Also commending Chandler was C. Wayland Brooks, of Illinois, who claimed "that it is high time for someone to start shouting, louder and louder, for the interests of America." Styles Bridges, New Hampshire's senior Republican Senator, also weighed in with the "Japan-first" cause, arguing that the success of the North African campaign left America "freer now to act in the Pacific than we have ever been before."[5]

Significantly, the Japan firsters also believed their strategy would prove to be in the long-term interests of those countries in the European theater of the world conflict. Their reasoning, simple and rather cynical, was articulated perfectly by Democrat Burton Wheeler. Were the United States to have already defeated Japan, the Senator surmised, "We would be in a much better position to deal with Russia when we came to the peace table, and to protect Poland, for which England went to war." Chandler agreed: "What kind of a peace in Europe shall we be able to establish if we have to turn all of our strength into the war with Japan, and if the Soviet Union is at peace, free to use the pressure of all its strength on Europe?" Should those circumstances materialize, Chandler doubted that the United States would be able to resist any Russian territorial demands on its devastated neighbors. No, the proper course of action, the Senator said, was to hold off on the invasion of Europe, and by so doing "we might be able to set up a Europe of democracy and peace."[6]

These controversial assessments were widely disputed, but no one attacked the Asia-first strategy with more causticity than the American Communist party. Communist propagandists insisted that "The battle of the Pacific cannot be won unless Hitler is destroyed at his base in the Atlantic," preferably by means of a speedy second front. Anyone in a leadership capacity who disagreed with this approach could expect to be skewered in the Communist press. The *Daily Worker* denounced Chandler's call for a Japan-first strategy as a "full-blown defeatist, pro-fascist, imperialist program" put forth "to avert Germany's defeat." Another *Worker* editorial asserted that the "Japan-first" campaign stemmed from a "desperate desire to avert Germany's defeat." Similarly, the procommunist intellectual journal *Amerasia** linked the Japan firsters to those "circles in America ... well-known for their hostility to the United Nations coalition."[7]

There was the ring of truth to this last accusation because most of the Asia firsters had well-deserved reputations as intense anticommunists. Although there is no proof that any of the Pacific-first advocates in Congress actually desired an outright Soviet defeat, they certainly recognized that their plan would result in greater Russian casualties and, perhaps, a weakened U.S.S.R. Still, it was at least possible to construct a case, on purely military grounds, for a Pacific-first strategy—and it was inescapably true that Japan, not Germany, had attacked America first. Ironically, the Communists were guilty of precisely what they accused the Japan firsters of doing. *Their* reason for advocating a Europe-first strategy was dictated entirely by their ideological and emotional commitment to the survival of the U.S.S.R. and not at all from objective military analysis. If anything, the Communists (along with the British) were rather grateful to Tojo for having brought the United States into the war—the war against Hitler. Indeed, just after Pearl Harbor, Communist leader William Z. Foster carelessly referred to the attack as "this tremendous event."[8] In truth, the Communists cared nothing about the Pacific war, except insofar as resources directed against the Japanese could not be shipped to the U.S.S.R. or, better yet, used by American fighting forces to open another European front. Having no quarrel with Japan, the Communists would have raised no objection—indeed they would have been pleased—if the U.S. military had simply conceded the Pacific to the emperor and devoted its exclusive attention and resources to the European front.

Of course, this was impossible, as the American people probably hated the sneak-attacking Japanese even more than the Nazis. As such, the U.S.S.R.'s refusal to renounce its April 1941 neutrality pact with Japan and the fishing

---

*Amerasia was so prepossessed by the U.S.S.R.'s fate that at one point it even said Germany had to be beaten first, in a hurry—before Japan had time to attack Siberia! ("European vs. Pacific Fronts," *Amerasia,* September 1942, p. 308.)

rights treaty concluded between the two countries in April 1943 were sensitive matters. This was especially true for those already unreconciled to the prospects of genuine U.S.–Soviet friendship. Senator Wheeler wondered aloud if the American people would question "the sincerity of some of our Allies when they see American food supplies and equipment being permitted to go through Japanese-controlled waters to Russia." "Happy" Chandler considered the renewal of this trade treaty an unfriendly act on the part of a supposed ally; the senator also hinted darkly—"who knows?", he asked— that perhaps some of the lend lease material that Japan permitted to reach the U.S.S.R. found its way back to the Japanese.[9]

This was unlikely, given the Soviets' own desperate plight. However, any degree of Soviet–Japanese cooperation was certain to stir rumors among those officials whose anti-Soviet opinions had not been softened by the U.S.–Soviet alliance. Representative Richard Welch, a Republican from California, said that the Russo–Japanese treaty gave the enemy access to the Kamchatka weather station, thus giving them a 1-to-6 day advantage in weather forecasting over American meteorologists. The United States was providing food supplies, and other lend lease assistance to the U.S.S.R. in its fight with Germany, so why was the Soviet Union not forthcoming with similar aid in America's struggle in the Pacific against Japan? This was an emotionally loaded question bound to strain the U.S.–Soviet alliance if pressed. "Why shouldn't we demand," Wheeler asked, "that they [the Russians] give us bases to bomb... those Japs that are bombing our boys in the Aleutians, in New Guinea, and the swamps and foxholes of Guadalcanal?" Republican Senator Henry Cabot Lodge, of Massachusetts, conceding that the subject of Russian nonassistance in the war against Japan was "a topic of great delicacy" nevertheless declared that "the whole character of the Pacific war would change if the United States had access to the Pacific coastal area of Russia." Perhaps as many as 6 million American lives might be saved. North Carolina's Democratic Senator Robert Reynolds, dubbed by a *Daily Worker* columnist as "the tarheel fuehrer from Buncombe County," wanted the U.S.S.R. to permit American access to Siberian bases for use against Japan because this would "save the sons and daughters of American fathers and mothers, and I do not think it is asking too much of Russia... in view of all we have done for her."[10]

Because the Russians would not permit American access to their airfields for sorties against Japan, Chinese airfields became even more strategically vital to U.S. air control in the Pacific. The Japan firsters believed that the fate of faraway China impacted on American security interests far more than FDR appreciated. In September 1944, Senator Warren Magnuson, Democrat of Washington, claimed that the United States could have invaded China "cheaply" if the operation had been undertaken 2 years ago, but "it will be horribly expensive now." Representative Melvin Maas, of Minnesota, blamed the president for "not sparing enough from Europe to save China and our own necks there." Though the European theater had received most of the administration's attention, "our real war lies ahead," Maas predicted. Democratic Representative John Lesinski, of Michigan, saw even greater trouble in the postwar period. He raised the possibility of a "clandestine pact between Japan and Russia, to divide China into two spheres of influence," and warned that "Russia has been doing everything possible to communize China."[11]

When Congress learned that the administration had approved the transfer of some American naval vessels to the Soviet navy, the suspicions of some anti-Soviet officials were further aroused. Styles Bridges, a member of the Senate Military Affairs Committee, caustically asked if this maneuver was "part of our patchwork policy of appeasing Russia." Michigans's Clare Hoffman, one of the most conservative and anti-Communist House members, sarcastically said he did not wish to formally criticize this policy as such, though it did seem to him "that as long as Japan is not being assailed by Russia we could use our ships in the Pacific." Senator Edward Robertson, of Wyoming, objected on the same grounds, as did "Happy" Chandler and others on Capitol Hill. Undoubtedly, Chandler spoke the thoughts of other "Japan firsters" when he noted that "it is difficult for me to believe that the Soviet Union will give us any real help against Japan" even after Germany had been subdued, but Representative J. Parnell Thomas, of New Jersey, publicly suggested an even more terrifying scenario. "There is always the danger," he said, "that the Communists in this country will oppose, will do everything they possibly can to interfere with our Military Establishment in the war with Japan, if Russia isn't in the war."[12]

Of course, the suspicions over Soviet intentions in the Pacific could hardly have exceeded the concerns generated by the U.S.S.R.'s potential plans for postwar Europe. Would the Soviets betray the principles for which the Allies supposedly were fighting? These cherished ideals had been most eloquently expressed in the famous Atlantic Charter of August 1941, before the United States even entered the war. A list of Anglo-American war-and-peace aims drafted by Roosevelt and Churchill, the charter proclaimed that the right of political self-determination should be enjoyed by all people. Point 2 of the charter expressed opposition to any "territorial changes that do not accord with the freely expressed wishes of the people concerned." On 1 January 1942, the Soviet Union joined 25 other nations in subscribing to the Declaration of United Nations, which pledged to fulfill the principles of the Atlantic Charter. Yet, throughout the war some doubted the sincerity of this Soviet promise; after all, with the Germans deep in Soviet territory, Stalin probably would have made almost any pledge to placate his major supplier of arms and other materiel. In April 1944, Vandenberg reminded his fellow Senators that all such pledges had been made "at the altar of our common sacrifice." Periodically, Senators and Congressmen who were hostile to the U.S.S.R. would pointedly

remind FDR of the Atlantic Charter and ask him if it remained U.S. policy—
"or is it a thing of the past?", as Styles Bridges cynically queried.[13]

Bridges and other irreconcilable foes of the U.S.S.R. would believe nothing
but the worst about Stalin, who they believed was both a shrewd nationalist
and a Hitlerian dictator who had wound up on the British–American side by
accident and necessity, not choice or ideological compatibility. Although a
useful military ally, Stalin simply could not be trusted: former President
Hoover counted some 40 agreements that the Russian leader had made with
other countries, without honoring any of them. Through even more audacious
treachery, only Hitler had got the better of Stalin in a deal, though it was
suggested by some Soviet haters that the two dictators might again work out an
arrangement and conclude a separate peace between their two countries. If this
happened, Burton Wheeler guessed, Stalin would use his fully mobilized Red
Army forces to overrun all the rest of Europe.[14]

While the anti-Soviet faction in Congress often sounded the alarm against
possible treachery by America's newfound ally, the vice president of the
United States publicly stated, in March 1943, that his government should not
try to "double cross" the U.S.S.R. This remark, which was warmly praised in
many liberal quarters as an example of high-minded statesmanship, was
greatly resented by anti-Soviet Senators and Congressmen. Arthur Vandenberg felt obliged to interrupt a related Senate speech by Tom Connally in order
to make the Texan concede that America had not as of yet double-crossed the
Russians. In the House, Hamilton Fish condemned the vice president's
"unwarranted" and "infamous" statement, which Fish said "challenged the
integrity and the honesty of the Government of the United States." South
Dakota Republican Representative Karl Mundt's wartime criticisms of the
vice president went even further:[15]

> Unless some of our New Deal global star-gazers [Wallace had an interest in
> mysticism and astrology] quickly change their pattern and their practices . . . there is
> grave danger that we shall find the wagon of American destiny hitched to the red
> star of Russia with the stars and stripes folded and hidden under the wagon and with
> no American even included as a welcome guest on the driver's seat.

In the same month that Wallace made his controversial remarks about U.S-
Soviet relations, the American ambassador to the U.S.S.R., Admiral William
Standley, created additional controversy by publicly accusing the Soviet
government of not fully informing the Russian people of the extent of
American lend lease assistance. An annoyed Standley considered this an
indication of bad faith and ingratitude on the part of the Kremlin, but he was
himself widely criticized in America for contributing to an unwanted
atmosphere of suspicion and disunity. Breckenridge Long, an assistant
secretary of state, noted in his diary that Standley had "sown a seed which
will grow resentment." However, the admiral also had his supporters, among
them Hamilton Fish, who in a rare defense of an administration official said

that Standley "has been unjustifiably criticized" without anyone demonstrating that his words had been inaccurate. In the Upper House, Wheeler confessed to some surprise over the ambassador's remarks, yet the senator said he did not have "the slightest doubt that his statement was correct and true."[16]

The flap created by Standley's remarks was not the only controversy involving the strategically vital lend lease policy. The British were criticized by a Senate committee for wasting and misusing some of the aid they had received. However, the attacks leveled at the Soviet beneficiaries of America's productive energies were far more pointed and revealing. Representative William Pittenger, Republican of Minnesota, described lend lease as a "one way road" favoring the Russians. Senator Brooks, toward the end of 1944, said that Europe was "being carved up . . . with tanks, planes, and supplies furnished largely by the American people." More ominous yet were the sporadic claims that lend lease materiel sent to the U.S.S.R. might one day be used to kill Americans. Republican Representative Fred Bradley, of Michigan, suggested that Stalin had been storing away some of the trucks, airplanes, and other lend lease equipment, for possible use after Germany was defeated. Congresswoman Sumner claimed that because no attempt had been made to ascertain how much assistance Stalin really needed to stave off the Nazi invaders, Stalin might be accumulating a surplus, particularly with the policy of "phantasmagorical" appeasement toward the Russians that seemed to be in effect. "Who today can intelligently doubt," Sumner asked rhetorically, "that Stalin is using American men and American money to gain domination not only over Europe but also over China and the Americas?" Money put into Stalin's hands, she said, would be used "to make himself so irrepressibly powerful that soon America will be asked to fight in World War No. three against him."[17]

The best way to prevent "World War III," reasoned President Roosevelt and most other informed opinion makers interested in foreign policy, was to build upon the good relations with the U.S.S.R. that the alliance had created. Roosevelt hoped to solicit Stalin's cooperation in establishing an organization of United Nations, including the U.S.S.R., that would provide an international forum for airing grievances and disputes, while the "big powers"—America, the U.S.S.R., Great Britain, and perhaps China—took on the added role of "policemen" that would curb potential aggressor countries before peace was disrupted. Various plans for meeting these general objectives were widely discussed during the war, but clearly the Soviet Union's full cooperation was implicit in any workable blueprint for constructing a long-term international peace. Although the anti-Soviet minority in Congress firmly believed that Stalin's real intentions were irreconcilable with America's stated objectives for fighting the war, the administration, buoyed by the pro-Soviet spirit that abounded in wartime America, was determined to try.

In October 1943, Secretary of State Cordell Hull traveled to Moscow for discussions with his British and Soviet counterparts, Anthony Eden and Molotov. They pledged not to employ their military forces within the boundaries of other states, except for operations in the war against the Axis. Hull returned to the United States to a chorus of cheers, but some critics suggested that this general mood of triumph was premature or unwarranted. Herbert Hoover warned that American sovereignty and independence should not be bargained away in peace negotiations with the U.S.S.R. or any other country. Alf Landon, another political icon for many conservatives, said the conference had made him "apprehensive" about future dealings with the Russians because he could find no evidence that they "have yielded one inch" in their quest to dominate Eastern Europe. Landon claimed that "it would be disastrous for the country" if Republicans endorsed the administration's attempt to cultivate the friendship of the Soviets through a policy of servility and appeasement. It did not escape the notice of anti-Soviets that the Moscow conferees had made no public declaration concerning the territorial boundaries and political makeup of Finland, the Baltic states, Poland, or the other countries of Eastern Europe. This omission, Representative Sumner said, gave these countries reason to doubt that they would receive "characteristically American" justice from the peace settlement. The Congresswoman expressed her wish that Hull "had contracted writer's cramp and come home without signing anything."[18]

Getting Stalin to meet directly with FDR was not easy because the Soviet leader refused to stray far from the Kremlin. Hoffman, who relished any administration setback, joked that "somebody's been sort of courtin' and coaxin' Stalin for quite a while and he's still staying outside. He don't [sic] even come to call on us." Some Congressmen believed that direct negotiations with Stalin would be pointless at best and possibly disastrous to the United States. "We do not know what Stalin will want," admitted Republican Representative Harold Knutson, of Minnesota, in mid-May 1943, but "he is going to get what he wants, you can be sure of that." This in itself might negate the fruits of an Allied victory, because what Stalin probably wanted was to control Eastern Europe, which would violate the letter and spirit of the Atlantic Charter. "It matters little," commented the ever-caustic Hoffman, "whether Hitler gets us and skins us from the top down or whether our ally, Joe Stalin, gets us and skins us from the heels up."[19]

Roosevelt, of course, had no misgivings about his ability to negotiate with the Soviet leader, whom he finally met, along with British Prime Minister Winston Churchill, in late November 1943, in Teheran, Iran. Immediate war aims received the highest priority at their meetings, but some attention also was paid to the looming question of what the political and territorial complexion of Europe would be after the war. Stalin made it clear that the Baltic States would be reabsorbed by the U.S.S.R., and Churchill and

Roosevelt agreed to this demand, though they did not reveal this concession publicly after the conference. The Polish boundary dispute—that "Pandora's box of infinite trouble" that Cordell Hull had deliberately avoided at the Moscow conference—was an even more nettlesome problem. Roosevelt understood this, yet at Teheran he essentially acquiesed in Stalin's insistence that his country's western frontier be extended to the Polish–Soviet border that had been proposed in 1919—the so-called "Curzon Line"—whereas Poland would be compensated on its western border with German territory. FDR's major concern at Teheran, which he freely admitted to the Soviet leader, was the adverse political consequences he would suffer if Polish–American voters learned of this deal before the 1944 presidential election. After the conference, the Big Three released a vaguely worded pledge of continued Allied cooperation, but the details of their discussions remained secret.[20]

Intended in part to showcase the Big Three's firm commitment to continued cooperation, for the time being the Teheran conference fulfilled this expectation. The meeting may not have been, in Browder's hyperbolic phrase, "history's greatest turning point," but the conference did seem to be a hopeful augury for postwar collaboration among the Allies. However, Teheran did little to ease the suspicions of anti-Soviet congressional figures; if anything, the gathering served to heighten their concerns, by creating more questions than answers. "What, if anything, tangible was accomplished?", Bradley, of Michigan, asked. "What decisions were arrived at? . . . Is it not about time that Mr. Roosevelt gave us the answer to these questions? . . . Why has a report so strangely been withheld from the American people and from the Congress? . . . The American people have a right to know." In the absence of facts, there was open speculation, later confirmed, that FDR had made agreements that he knew would be difficult to explain to the American people. Senator John Danaher, Republican from Connecticut, guessed that "the Atlantic Charter, the terms of which we reasonably thought had been made the basis of our national action, has been relegated to a limbo all its own." Bridges suggested that Roosevelt might have conspired with Stalin to turn Yugoslavia into a Communist regime—and was this "the first expression of a deeper design"? The president needed to know, Bridges said, that the American people did not share his willingness to rely "on the goodwill of Mr. Stalin . . . as their only safeguard against war and the threat of war." But Jessie Sumner feared that Stalin left the Iranian capital convinced of exactly that, thanks to the supine performance of the American delegation:[21]

> At Teheran nobody told him he was not doing all right. They drank his liquor. They laughed at his playful rowdyism. They gave him everything he asked, including upper Europe and a second front filled with American soldiers. He thought he was a hit.

Their suspicions untempered by the bits of information that leaked out from Moscow and Teheran, anti-Soviets in Congress looked on with anxious foreboding as the Red Army first halted the Nazi offensive for good, then slowly began to push the Germans back toward Eastern Europe. Even without knowing of Roosevelt's capitulation to Stalin's Baltic and Polish demands, some in Congress criticized the president's apparent lack of forcefulness in dealing with the Soviet dictator. "This is a sweet time for our Government to turn isolationist!", chided Jessie Sumner. The possibility of the United States standing helplessly by as the U.S.S.R. assumed control of this region was too painful for anti-Soviet politicians like Senator Robert Taft to ignore. Taft claimed that FDR clung to "the delightful theory that Mr. Stalin in the end will turn out to have an angelic nature and do of his own accord the things which we should have insisted upon at the beginning." Failing "even to suggest restraint to Mr. Stalin" would prove disastrous to the country's postwar goals, Taft warned, because a world filled with "sore spots"—small nations yearning for the restoration of their territory and independence—would undermine any United Nations experiment. Taft called for "definite steps" toward "a political settlement which will give freedom to those people who are capable of self-government and desire freedom," though neither he nor the others in the anti-Soviet bloc were able to suggest what these "definite steps" should be.[22]

By early 1944 the ultimate destruction of Hitler's Europe was near certain, but this welcome news inevitably heightened concerns about what would take its place. Clearly, questions concerning the political and territorial makeup of Eastern Europe could not be postponed much longer. The smaller countries were the key: If the final peace treaty was unjust to them, then all the fine talk about establishing a world of free men and women would be exposed as meaningless rhetoric. Senator Brooks, voicing the thoughts of other congressmen hostilely inclined to the Soviet Union, said that these countries had "pinned their faith on the Atlantic Charter and on the United States as a champion of right over might" but were "steadily losing hope" that America would help them attain their freedom in the face of the mounting Soviet threat.[23]

One of these nations was Finland, which continued to attract the sympathy of many anti-Soviet Americans even though the Finnish government technically was aligned with Germany against their mutual adversary, the Soviet Union. In 1939–40, shortly before the German attack on the U.S.S.R., the Soviets invaded Finland; therefore when Hitler launched his attack on Stalin, the Finns were willing to cooperate with the Wehrmacht in this phase of its operations. Taft excused this transgression by saying that Finland's "freedom throughout history has always been threatened by Russia far more than by Germany, and naturally in a war between Russia and Germany it took the German side. But we are not at war with Finland any more than Russia is at war with Japan." Others in Congress were equally sympathetic to the Finns.

Vandenberg called "Free Finland . . . the supreme victim of this cruel ritual." Democratic Representative Philip Philbin, of Massachusetts, insisted that "if the words of the Atlantic Charter are sincerely put," the United States could not "logically take sides" against the brave people of Finland. Bridges described Finland as "a test case," by which he meant two things: If the Soviet Union dealt harshly with the Finns, this would "confirm the already deepening fears of some that Russia has intentions other than have been publicly revealed"; and, "if Finland is 'sold down the river'" by the U.S. government, it would "set a precedent for all nations and all peoples in the future."[24]

To some Congressmen, Roosevelt's handling of the Finnish problem seemed to symbolize his overall policy of weakness toward Stalin. In March 1944, Representative John Bennett, a Republican from Michigan, asked if it was "fair or honest on our part to be silent while the Soviet Union makes a one-sided peace treaty with Finland," a country that the Congressman hailed as an "honest and loyal friend" of the United States. In June 1944, the State Department ordered the Finnish Ambassador to America to leave the country, a decision that led a disgusted Representative Harold Knutson, of Minnesota, to say that he and "millions" of other Americans "feel humiliated over the shabby treatment that this administration has accorded the Finnish people." Bennett, equally frustrated by the apparent abandonment of the Finns, simply because their dilemma was a potential point of friction between America and the U.S.S.R., asked a reasonable question: "If we cannot secure the co-operation of our allies, in peace arrangements which are concluded during the progress of the war, how can it reasonably be expected that we will secure such cooperation when hostilities . . . end?" As it happened, however, the terms of the September 1944 Soviet–Finnish armistice were in some respects not excessively harsh on Finland, although from this point forth the U.S.S.R. would exert indirect but nevertheless substantial influence over Finnish domestic and foreign policy.[25]

Considerably less fortunate were the three Baltic States—Latvia, Estonia, and Lithuania. Nestled between Russia and the east coast of the Baltic Sea, these countries had a complicated history: Various powers controlled this strategic region in the Middle Ages; Russia took control of the Baltic States in the eighteenth century; then, seizing the opportunity handed them by Russia's defeat in World War I, the three states declared their independence in 1918. Although the Soviet–German nonaggression pact was in effect, Stalin dispatched troops of occupation into all three helpless Baltic States. Forced to sign security "treaties" with its mighty neighbor to the east, the Baltic republics ceased to exist as independent sovereignties. Then Germany overran these tiny regions in the course of its headlong invasion of the U.S.S.R. Having lost his conquests so quickly, Stalin was determined to reincorporate the Baltic States into his regime after the expulsion of the Nazis. He never attempted to hide this ambition from his allies (not that FDR ever publicly acknowledged this reality), and indeed even most anti-Soviet public officials realized there was little that could be done once the Red Army reoccupied this region.

Even so, the plight of the Baltic countries was not entirely ignored in wartime Washington. In November 1943, Senator Reynolds offered an amendment to the Connally resolution (for a postwar international organization) that would have given Senate endorsement to a "guaranty of the independence and territorial integrity of the Baltic States," as well as "other subjugated nations" in Europe. In Reynolds's opinion, the United States should assist the Baltic States in their efforts to remain independent from the U.S.S.R. because "civilized nations have never been isolationist in their attitude toward international bandits and robbers."[26]

Reynolds's amendment failed of adoption, but a few congressmen kept the issue alive, if barely. Idaho's Democratic Representative Compton White, in a speech about alleged Soviet atrocities in Latvia, remarked that "for these three countries the question is to be or not to be." White said the Baltic States, hating as they did "both bolshevism and nazism," placed all their hopes on the Atlantic Charter, "and firmly believe that the democratic world will not fail them." Democratic Representative Martin Gorski, of Illinois, speaking on behalf of several Lithuanian–American organizations, called for the restoration of Lithuania as an independent nation, in conformity with the "principles of the Atlantic Charter." The ever-suspicious Styles Bridges suggested—not incorrectly, as it turned out—that the Baltic countries "may be used as pawns in a game called spheres of influence," which would "destroy the prestige of American integrity among the plain people of the world."[27]

Farther south, but also close to Stalin's grasp, lived the "plain people" of the Balkans, historically a tempting target for Russian expansionism. Anti-Soviet political leaders feared that Stalin, in the course of liberating these lands from Nazi control, would use the opportunity to at last bring this region under Russian control. Arthur Vandenberg's diary entry for 4 June 1942—relatively early in the war, but the day the Senate unanimously declared war on Bulgaria, Rumania, and Hungary, "in response to Russia's demand"—records the Senator's concern that America might be conceding effective control of this region to Stalin. This "certainly . . . would reduce the famous 'four freedoms' to a 'scrap of paper,'" Vandenberg privately admitted. As the war continued, the Soviets' capacity for assisting communist insurgencies in the Balkans aroused at least some congressional apprehension. Bridges claimed that Roosevelt's policy for this region was to "sit by" and do nothing, thereby allowing "the swallowing up of the Balkan nations" by the Soviet Union. In March 1944 Representative Roy Woodruff, of Michigan, noted that many of the anti-Nazi but pro-Communist forces in this area were led "by Soviet-trained propagandists and supported by propaganda radio centers located on Soviet territory." Woodruff called it "disgraceful" that the United States had been "induced" to back the Yugoslavian Communist partisans led by Josip Tito, "whose aim is to overthrow by force . . . the loyal forces under General [Draja] Mihailovich . . . ."[28]

The equally aggressive Congresswoman Sumner charged, well before the war was over, that Stalin had opposed an Allied invasion through the Balkan "soft underbelly" of Europe because he knew this route would have placed the Anglo-American forces between the Red Army and the area he coveted. Unlike the wily Churchill (who had first pressed for an invasion by way of the Balkans, then, in an effort to maintain British influence in Greece, cut his infamous "percentages" deal with Stalin in October 1944), Roosevelt had permitted himself to be duped by the Kremlin leader. Senator Reynolds accused Stalin of even worse treachery: The Soviet dictator, the Senator charged, was refusing to permit the distribution of relief supplies to the war-ravaged people of Yugoslavia "unless he and his officials may say who is hungry, who is dying, who needs medical care." A similar state of affairs, Reynolds added, also "exists in Poland."[29]

Among all the countries of Eastern Europe, Poland was, as Vandenberg put it, the "acid test," the one whose fate most aroused the passions of anti-Soviet congressional figures. Poland was the center of their fears for several reasons: because there were so many Americans of Polish descent, because the invasion of Poland had started the war in Europe, and because Stalin's treatment of the Poles would be the clearest indicator of how he intended to treat other powerless people, as well. Ralph Brewster, Republican senator from Maine, expressed the point well by saying that "Poland is the symbol of the world that is to be"—and many agreed. Representative Stephen Day, a very conservative Republican from Illinois, said that Americans "dare not countenance any ravishment of Poland"; whereas Representative Charles Wolverton, a Republican from New Jersey, insisted that an unfree Poland would forever mock "the very rights for which the war was being fought." Clare Boothe Luce, an especially outspoken voice in the cause of Polish freedom, solemnly warned that if Poland were treated unjustly, "we will know what the future holds for all of us. We will not then, if we are wise, ask for whom the bell tolls in Poland. It will toll for all of Europe. And for us."[30]

Having been driven from its homeland by a dual invasion of Germany and the U.S.S.R. in 1939, the London-based Polish government in exile assumed that neither of these countries, if victorious, would grant any mercy to Poland. What the Nazi occupation forces were capable of was only too well known by the Polish people. On the other hand, were Stalin to be victorious, his Red Army would have to march through Poland, where Russian troops might remain to establish a dictatorial, pro-Soviet "buffer state" between the U.S.S.R. and Central Europe. Still, it was not difficult for the "London Poles"—led by Premier Wladyslaw Sikorski, who died in July 1943 and was succeeded by Stanislaw Mikolajczyk—to choose sides. Assuming the Allies won, Poland might be spared from further misery only if the United States took the Atlantic Charter seriously and refused to abandon the Polish people to Stalinist tyranny.

Stalin, in fact, had made little effort to conceal his disdain for the non-Communist Poles in London. Although he agreed to establish diplomatic relations with the exiled government on 30 July 1941, he broke off this arrangement in April 1943, after the London Poles demanded a Red Cross investigation of the Katyn Forest Massacre.* Shortly thereafter, a new organization of Polish Communists, the Committee of National Liberation, was established. This group provided the later framework for the rival, pro-Soviet "Lublin" government of Poland that Stalin formally recognized approximately a year later. Neither the London-based Poles nor their Congressional supporters knew for certain that Roosevelt already had more or less doomed Poland to Soviet domination through his promises at Teheran. Yet, even without this knowledge, some in Congress publicly suggested that Poland's suffering and subjugation would not end with the final cease-fire of World War II—and this in itself, as Senator Taft put it, would mean the war in Europe would conclude as "a grim farce."[31]

Some of the more impractical suggestions for averting the tragedy about to occur included Bridges's demand that America delay its invasion of Europe until her allies reaffirmed their fealty to the Atlantic Charter, and Jessie Sumner's call for a delay in the invasion of Europe until America "had some assurance from Stalin that he would not render our war effort futile."[32] These ideas were rejected, of course, but no one else in Washington offered any better plan for keeping Poland free of eventual Soviet domination. Yet, in the manner of politicians, many wished to go on record as having offered some degree of support for a country with so many kinsmen in America.

Thus it was not surprising that the fifty-third anniversary of the Polish constitution, early May 1944, was an occasion for considerable pro-Polish speechmaking in Congress. Many of these speeches avoided the main dilemma facing Poland, but a few speakers directly acknowledged the Soviet threat. Democratic Representative Philip Philbin, of Massachusetts, noting that many Polish-Americans lived in his district, said that the U.S. government should not be "lulled into any easy-going optimism that these grave developments will take care of themselves." Although the Nazi oppression

---

*This was a tragic and—at least to the Anglo–American component of the alliance—rather embarrassing episode. The Germans, discovering a mass grave of 15,000 slaughtered Polish officers and soldiers, publicized the finding and accused the Russians of having committed the atrocity during their brief occupation of eastern Poland. The denials and counterdenunciations that swiftly followed were not very convincing, even under the unusual circumstances of the time. Today, no doubt exists that responsibility for this beastial crime belongs to the Soviet Union.

from which the Poles were being freed had been "detestable and base," domination by the Soviets would be "no less hateful" and perhaps even more "obnoxious" to Poland, Philbin said. Representative Bennett accused the U.S.S.R. of having "completely ignored and disregarded the Atlantic Charter" in its "dealings thus far with Poland," and Mrs. Luce flatly predicted that a "great crisis of confidence between ourselves and the Russians" was about to crystallize around this one crucial issue.[33]

Events began coming to a head in the last part of 1944. In August, the Polish underground resistance made a bold attempt to expel the German invaders from Warsaw before nearby Soviet troops could occupy the capital city. As the valiant uprising was brutally crushed, the Red Army held its position, just across the Vistula River. Surviving Poles bitterly claimed that promised supplies and other support had been deliberately withheld, so that the soon-to-be victorious Russians would have an even freer hand in Poland than if the resistance forces had remained intact. True or not, in due course the Red Army marched into Poland, Stalin rebuffed the visiting Mikolajczyk, Churchill publicly abandoned the London Poles, and Roosevelt won reelection to a fourth term without being seriously challenged about his plans for Poland. Some in Congress could see what was coming, and their comments reflect a growing sense of anger and desperation. "Is there still hope for Poland?", Sumner asked rhetorically. "Allied indifference to war aims listed in the Atlantic Charter has long since made it obvious that the Atlantic Charter is now a last year's bird nest, apparently never intended for anything but temporary shelter," she said. Fish also asked what had become of the charter—was it "lost, strayed, or possibly stolen by the Communists?" Disgustedly, Fish noted the "incredible" irony of how the country "in whose behalf World War No. Two was started" was now "about to be turned over to the Communists in utter disregard of its terrible sacrifices in fighting the Nazis and the pledges given to the Polish people by the Allies."[34]

As Stalin's ambition to control Eastern Europe became ever clearer with the approach of victory, anti-Soviet politicians felt a sense of what might be called vindicated frustration. "We of the western world are commencing to pay the price," Reynolds said glumly in October 1944, "for Russia's part in this war." The Atlantic Charter had been betrayed, after all: Representative Day claimed that already its promises had been "forgotten"; and Bridges lamented that "the principles which were originally involved in this struggle are being scattered to the four winds," blown away by the advancing might of the Red Army. To be sure, not everyone was so pessimistic; on 15 October Senator Robert LaFollette, Jr., a progressive Republican from Wisconsin, asserted: "It is time for America to show Europe that the choice is not between Communism and chaos." Saying that democracy was superior to either of these alternatives, LaFollette insisted it was time "for American principles to take their place alongside American fighting power."[35]

But many of the more extreme Soviet haters thought this time already had slipped past. Sumner, knowing full well that the action would be futile, introduced a House resolution calling on the administration to abandon an "appeasement policy" that she said was "helping other nations violate the Atlantic Charter" and permitting Joseph Stalin to become "master of the world." Needless to say, President Roosevelt did not ease her frustration when he callously declared, at a 19 December press conference, that "nobody ever signed the Atlantic Charter"; thus "it isn't a formal document." The handwriting on the wall was now much clearer. Representative Fish, saying he did not relish the role of "Cassandra or a Jeremiah," regretfully predicted that communism would spread in both Europe and Asia after the war, whereas Burton Wheeler bluntly stated that "Mr. Stalin is holding the trump card," in Eastern Europe at least. Reynolds contended that the president "has the Russian Bear by the tail, and doesn't quite know how to let go . . . .Something is going to snap soon." Once U.S.–Soviet relations did "snap," Reynolds said, the American people were going to "suffer one of the worst disillusionments they have ever experienced."[36]

For some anti-Soviet politicians, this "worst disillusionment" would commence with Roosevelt's second and final meeting with Churchill and Stalin, in February 1945, at Yalta.[37] This conference heightened their fears for the future while confirming their worst suspicions of the past. At Yalta, Roosevelt and Churchill agreed to redraw Poland's boundaries according to Stalin's demands. Thus a large part of eastern Poland was annexed by the U.S.S.R., with Poland's northern and western borders extended at the expense of Germany. This compensation hardly comforted the millions of Poles who were now subjects of the Soviet Union. Stalin promised that Poland's political future would be determined by "free elections," but with the pro-Communist Lublin Poles now in effective control of the provisional government, the country's eventual domination by the U.S.S.R. was assured. Early congressional reaction to the Yalta agreements was predominantly favorable, as many still wanted to believe the Soviet–American alliance would continue into the postwar period. But some in Washington immediately protested the treatment that Poland had received.

Hugh Butler, a highly partisan Republican senator from Nebraska, bluntly demanded that Roosevelt provide Congress with "a full accounting" of his secret negotiations with Soviet dictator Stalin, so that Americans could know the full sordid story of what their leader had given away on their behalf. Senator Vandenberg, having just adopted an internationalist and bipartisan perspective on foreign policy, tried to soften his displeasure by saying that all decisions "made under pressure of war," including the proposed arrangements for Poland, should be "temporary in fact as well as in name." Noting that "expediency and justice frequently are not even on speaking terms with each other," Vandenberg added that Poland's ultimate fate should "pass in full review at the final peace table." Other Republicans were unwilling to mask their anger even to this limited extent. Mrs. Luce called the Polish settlement a "direct violation of the spirit and the letter of the Atlantic Charter," whereas Representative Alvin O'Konski, of Wisconsin, bitterly concluded that the charter "has been torn up and thrown into the Black Sea."[38]

Before long, Yalta would become a partisan club that Republicans would use against the entire Democratic party. Yet, even in the summit's immediate aftermath some prominent Democrats opposed the Big Three agreements. Senator David Walsh, of Massachusetts, commenting on Poland's fate, said "a frightful injustice" had been done "to a brave people," whereas Burton Wheeler called Yalta "a great victory for Stalin and for Russian imperialism." John Lesinski registered his displeasure by inserting into the *Congressional Record* numerous published articles and other material sympathetic to Poland's plight; one Polish-speaking news release he included was titled "Yalta Agreements Will Result in Third World War." Representative Thaddeus Wasielewski, of Wisconsin, claiming he found it difficult to oppose the president on a foreign-policy issue, lamented that the "dismemberment of our ally Poland" at the Crimea conference "brings only keen disappointment and shame for all of us." Before very long, millions of Americans would come to regard the Yalta accords in precisely this way.[39]

An historical assessment of the various anti-Soviet politicians of World War II elicits a decidedly mixed verdict. Their fundamental integrity seems almost beyond question, as there was little political capital to be earned from criticizing the U.S.S.R. at this time, excluding perhaps the heavily Polish–American districts in the Midwest and elsewhere. No credible evidence exists to suggest that anyone in Congress desired a Nazi victory over the Allies. Those who advocated a Japan-first strategy were not trying to sabotage the war effort. They simply believed that America's interests—as opposed to the U.S.S.R.'s interests, which were all that mattered to the Communists—would be best served by following this route to victory. In retrospect, the Japan firsters probably did not propose the sounder military strategy. Yet, they understood—more clearly than did many of their countrymen—the self-serving and expedient nature of the alliance, as underscored by the Soviets' refusal to enter the war against Japan even as they demanded that America immediately open a second European front. Wartime congressional critics of the U.S.S.R. also correctly predicted that Stalin would dominate postwar Eastern Europe—except for Yugoslavia, whose communist dicator, Tito, proved strong enough to defy the Kremlin. However limited one believes FDR's options to have been, the fact remains that he did not fulfill the promises of the Atlantic Charter, at least not in Eastern Europe. Those who suspected as much during the war were vindicated by history.

However, anti-Soviet political leaders were themselves unable to offer practical solutions for averting the impending disaster. What could they have proposed? No rapid demobilization after the Axis' defeat? A permanent standing army in Europe? War with the Soviet Union? Even those who took it for granted that Stalin's designs on Eastern Europe were no more honorable than Hitler's refused to propose such politically untenable options. Not burdened with the same responsibilities as the president, the anti-Soviet politicians were free to criticize, without having to advance any viable or concrete solutions of their own. Politicians very often prefer to be in this advantageous position! In a broader sense, however, anti-Soviet political figures were in an even more unappealing position than was the ever-optimistic FDR. They could only hope against hope they would be wrong, even as they *knew* that events would slowly but inexorably prove them right.

NOTES

1. Richard Darilek, *A Loyal Opposition in Time of War* (Westport, CT: Greenwood Press, 1976), p. 125; Burton Wheeler and Paul Healy, *Yankee from the West* (Garden City, NY: Doubleday and Company, 1962), p. 389.
2. Stephen Ambrose, *Rise to Globalism* (New York: Penguin Books, 1983), pp. 45–52; Ralph Levering, *American Opinion and the Russian Alliance, 1939–1945* (Chapel Hill: University of North Carolina Press, 1976), pp. 63–96; almost every issue of *The Communist* and the *Daily Worker* from early 1942 on ran impassioned pleas for an immediate second front.
3. Joseph North, "One World—Wendell Wilkie's Challenging Book," *The Communist*, June 1943, p. 568; Earl Browder, "Some Political Problems of the Pacific Front," 18 June 1942, Earl Browder Papers, Series 3, Reel 7, No. 113; James Allen, "The Pacific Front in the Global War," *The Communist*, December 1942, pp. 1012–3220; Robert Dallek, *Franklin D. Roosevelt and American Foreign Policy, 1932–1945* (New York: Oxford University Press, 1979), pp. 331–2; *Congressional Record*, Seventy-eighth Congress, 1st Session, p. 1809 (hereafter *CR*, 78–1, p. 1809; Transcript of radio program "Town Meeting of the Air", 10 December 1942: *Town Meeting* (Columbus, OH: American Education Press, 1942), p. 6; Wayne Cole, *Roosevelt and the Isolationists, 1932–45* (Lincoln: University of Nebraska Press, 1983), p. 503; William Schneiderman, "The California Elections," *The Communist*, August 1942, p. 604; *San Francisco Examiner*, 25 March 1944; *CR*, 78–1 p. 4513; *New York Journal-American*, 30 April 1943; Tom Connally, *My Name is Tom Connally* (New York: Thomas Y. Crowell Company, 1954), p. 260.
4. *CR*, 78–1, pp. 3446–61; *CR*, 78–1, pp. 4503–19.
5. *CR*, 78–1, p. 4511; *CR*, 78–1, p. 4507.
6. *CR*, 78–1, p. 4508; *CR*, 78–1, p. 4512.
7. *Daily Worker*, 4 February 1942; *Worker*, 8 October 1943; *Amerasia*, 3 March 1944, p. 74.
8. *Daily Worker*, 9 December 1941.
9. *Washington Times-Herald*, 1 April 1943; *CR*, 78–1, p. 4508.
10. *Washington Times-Herald*, 1 April 1943; *CR*, 78–1, p. 7923; *New York Journal-American*, 18 October 1943; *Daily Worker*, 12 November 1943; *CR*, 78–2, p. 7092.
11. *New York Journal-American*, 25 September 1944; *CR*, 78–2, pp. 7542, 7546.

12. *San Francisco Examiner*, 24 May 1944; *CR*, 78–2, p. 4913; *Examiner*, 25 May 1944; Special Committee on Un-American Activities, *Hearings*, Vol.17: Sept. 27–29, Oct. 3–5, 1944, p. 10308.
13. *New York Times*, 3 January 1942; *New York Journal-American*, 25 April 1944; *CR,* 78–2, p. 156.
14. Herert Hoover's observation in James Farley Papers, Box 45, "Private File," 1944–45; *Daily Worker*, 26 February 1943.
15. Henry Wallace, *Democracy Reborn* (New York: Reynal and Hitchcock, 1944), p. 229; Papers of Tom Connally, Box 560, "Speech File 1943"; *CR*, 78–1, p. 1823; *CR*, 78–1, p. A4136.
16. William Standley and Arthur Ageton, *Admiral Ambassador to Russia* (Chicago: Henry Regnery Company, 1955), pp. 331–49; Fred Israel, ed., *The War Diary of Breckenridge Long* (Lincoln: University of Nebraska Press, 1966), p. 300; *CR*, 78–1, p. 1822; *CR*, 78–1, p. 1703.
17, *New York Times*, 29 October 1943; *CR*, 78–2, p. A1251; *CR*, 78–2, p. 9309; *CR*, 78–2, p. A1005; *CR*, 78–2, p. 5244; *CR*, 78–2, p. 8949; *CR*, 78–2, p. 5245.
18. Cordell Hull, *The Memoirs of Cordell Hull*, Vol 2 (London: Hodder and Stoughton, 1948), pp. 1247–1318; *New York Times*, 29 October 1943; *Times*, 5 December 1943; *CR*, 78–1, pp. 9156–7.
19. Transcript of radio program "Town Meeting of the Air," 12 August 1943 (*Town Meeting*, Vol. 9, No. 5) p. 18; *CR*, 78–1, p. 4166; *CR*, 77–2, p. 1433.
20. Keith Eubank, *Summit at Teheran* (New York: William Morrow and Company, 1985); Richard Lukas, *The Strange Allies, The United States and Poland* (Knoxville: University of Tennessee Press, 1978), p. 44; Ted Morgan, *FDR* (New York: Simon Schuster, 1985), pp. 693–704.
21. Earl Browder, "Teheran—History's Greatest Turning Point," *The Communist*, January 1944, p. 3; Earl Browder, *Teheran, Our Path in War and Peace* (New York: International Publishers, 1944); *CR*, 78–2, p. A1004; *CR*, 78–2, p. 3898; *CR*, 78–2, p. 186. Also see *Chicago Tribune*, 24 May 1944.
22. *CR*, 78–2, p. 2606; *Chicago Tribune*, 2 April 1944; Robert Taft Papers, Box 1299, "Addresses, 1944 File."
23. *CR*, 78–2, p. 9308.
24. *Chicago Tribune*, 2 April 1944; *CR*, 78–2, p. 6142; *CR*, 78–2, p. A3236; *Tribune*, 8 March 1944; *San Francisco Examiner*, 8 March 1944.
25. *CR*, 78–2, p. A1064; *CR*, 78–2, p. A3080; *CR*, 78–2, p. A1064; C. Leonard Lundin, *Finland in the Second World War* (Bloomington: Indiana University Press, 1957; John Wuorinen, *A History of Finland* (New York: Columbia University Press, 1965), p. 454–57.
26. *CR*, 78–1, p. 9217; I. F. Stone, "F.D.R.'s Victory," *Nation*, 13 November 1943, p. 547.
27. *CR*, 78–2, p. A3675–6; *CR*, 78–1, p. 2272; *CR*, 78–2, p. 188.
28. Arthur Vandenberg, Jr., ed., *The Private Papers of Senator Vandenberg* (Boston: Houghton Mifflin Company, 1952), p. 32; *Chicago Tribune*, 15 January 1944; *CR*, 78–2, p. A1470; *CR*, 78–2, p. 186.
29. *CR*, 78–2, p. 8948–449; Herbert Feis, *Churchill, Roosevelt, Stalin* (Princeton, NJ: Princeton University Press, 1957), pp. 447–49; *CR*, 78–2, p. 9589.
30. *Chicago Tribune*, 20 November 1944; C. David Tompkins, *Senator Arthur H. Vandenberg: The Evolution of a Modern Republican, 1884–1945* (East Lansing: Michigan State University Press, 1970), pp. 228–29; *San Francisco Examiner*, 30 November 1943; *CR*, 78–2, p. A2125; *CR*, 78–2, pp. A4354–5; *CR*, 78–2, p. 3935.

31. "What Foreign Policy Will Promote Peace?" Radio address of 8 June 1944, found in Robert Taft papers, Box 1299, "Addresses, 1944 File."
32. *Chicago Tribune*, 24 May 1944; *CR*, 78–2, pp. 2605–08, 3270.
33. *CR*, 78–2, p. A3230; *CR*, 78–2, p. A2136; *CR*, 78–2, p. 3935.
34. *CR*, 78–2, p. 8466; *CR*, 78–2, p. 9204.
35. *San Francisco Examiner*, 13 October 1944; *CR*, 78–2, p. 9380; *CR*, 78–2, p. 8097; *Examiner*, 16 October 1944.
36. *CR*, 78–2, pp. 8948–50; Samuel Rosenman, ed., *The Public Papers and Addresses of Franklin D. Roosevelt, 1944–45*, Vol. XIII (New York: Harper and Brothers, 1950), pp. 438–39; *CR*, 78–2, p. 9203; *CR*, 78–2, p. 9712; *San Francisco Examiner*, 13 October 1944.
37. For conflicting assessments of this fateful gathering, see the "orthodox" views of Herbert Feis, *Churchill, Roosevelt, Stalin*, pp. 518–29, 561–82, 641–55, and Feis, *From Trust to Terror* (New York: W. W. Norton and Company, 1970), pp. 20– 6; and the "revisionist" account in Diane Shaver Clemens, *Yalta* (New York: Oxford University Press, 1970).
38. *New York Times*, 27 February 1945; *Times*, 9 March 1945; *Times*, 20 February 1945; *Times*, 14 February 1945.
39. *New York Times*, 14 February 1945; *CR*, 79–1, pp. A374, A713, A745, A748, A1833; *CR*, 79–1, p. 2696.

5

Labor: Skepticism and Resistance

During World War II, serious and substantial misgivings attended organized labor's support for the American alliance with its newfound Communist ally, the Soviet Union. This of course was particularly disappointing to American Communists, who took the lead in promoting greater solidarity, selflessness, and commitment to the antifascist struggle. They also hoped the alliance would prompt the American and Soviet labor movements to develop a formal, working relationship. In both instances, however, the self-described true representatives of the laboring class would be frustrated, thanks to the old anti-Red animosities that survived these years of crisis.

In the Congress of Industrial Organizations, American Communists found that the appreciable influence they wielded was at best a mixed blessing. With about a dozen CIO affiliates still under their control, and large pro-Communist factions in the UAW and other member unions, the Communists hoped to mobilize the CIO for an all-out war-production effort in the fight against Hitler. No sacrifice was too great if it would speed factory output and, by way of lend lease, assist in driving the Nazis from Soviet soil. Because of the U.S.–U.S.S.R. alliance, Communists assumed they would be able to couch their demands for total commitment in unassailably patriotic rhetoric, thus forcing the workers to accede to ever-greater levels of sacrifice. This erroneous calculation, carried as usual to its most extreme limits by the Communists, proved disastrous to their reputation as good union men. Their uncompromising stance on the "no strike" pledge helped to undercut their position within the CIO: but the Communists' most serious dilemma arose in 1943 when they attempted to reinstitute unpopular "incentive pay," or peicework, wage formulas in CIO-organized war-production shops. The key battle took place within the United Automobile Workers, the CIO's largest union. Leading the opposition to the Communists was Walter Reuther, who was then rapidly emerging as their most able and determined foe in the entire CIO. The ensuing controversy proved to be the ambitious Reuther's "touchstone,"[1] for it gave him the opportunity to curry favor with the rank and file by claiming that the

Communists' demands for sacrifice—motivated solely by their desire to ensure the survival of Stalin's Russia—were unworthy of broad-based worker support.

In the more conservative American Federation of Labor, the Communists had been purged some years before, though federation leaders continued to worry about what one of them called the "sheer abuse of our goodwill toward Russia" by domestic Communists. But the bulk of the AFL's anti-"Red" efforts were directed at Communists overseas. Although they endorsed "to the limit" all possible assistance to the Soviet Union's Red Army, the AFL's ruling claque of executive council chieftains rejected a British-sponsored proposal to create a new international trade-union confederation because it would have included delegates from the Soviet Union. In the council's view, Soviet trade unions were beguiling illusions created by a repressive, thoroughly dictatorial Russian government. "We would not go into an alliance with an organization which in fact did not exist," explained George Meany. The AFL also suspected that the Russians intended to use any international labor federation as a forum from which to disseminate Communist propaganda to all parts of the world.[2]

Of course, such issues really came into the forefront once the war was over, but the piecework and international trade-union controversies hinted at what would follow—namely that Meany and Reuther would position organized labor squarely behind the "Cold War liberalism" of the 1950s, 1960s, and beyond. Given what they said and stood for during the best years of U.S.–Soviet relations, no other response could reasonably have been expected.

Because the Communists were then a legitimate power group within the CIO, the disposition to avoid raising anti-Soviet and anti-Communist issues was at this time even stronger in the CIO than in the country as a whole. Nevertheless, scattered manifestations of anti-Communist hostility in this body would have been apparent to any careful observer. For example, the *Timber Worker,* the official organ of the International Woodworkers of America (a CIO union recently wrested from Communist control), reaffirmed the union's position that the alliance was one "of sheer military necessity alone, and that Communism and its works had not, or could never have, a place in American life." The 1943 national convention of the International Union of Marine and Shipbuilding Workers upheld an executive board decision to enforce an anti-Communist clause in the union's constitution by expelling one Irvin Nelson, a board member and the president of a Brooklyn local. The Association of Catholic Trade Unionists, an organization peripherally active in CIO affairs and a group that after the war was very helpful to Walter Reuther's drive for control of the UAW, issued periodic reminders that the Communist party was a "cancer" that inevitably would work its "disruptive effect" on American society. All the Communist-orchestrated "yowling" over a second European front, ACTU's main newspaper *The Wage Earner* claimed in 1942, only "puts the enemy on the alert, and sows factionalism among the people." Clearly, not all of the Communists' enemies within the CIO had agreed to forgive and forget in the spirit of national unity and common struggle.[3]

Ironically, the issue that touched off the greatest resentment toward the Communists in the CIO was a product of their own jingoistic demands for total dedication to this war effort, which William Z. Foster said would have to be the workers' "supreme lodestar" for the duration of the conflict. In theory, almost no one in organized labor would have disagreed with Foster, but most non-Communists refused to define patriotism in terms of unlimited self-sacrifice. The Communists did. Indeed, General Secretary Earl Browder went so far as to say that labor would have to bear the "main sacrifice" if victory were to be won. By this, he meant an inflexible ban on strikes, a moratorium on all other manifestations of worker discontent, and a resumption of the vastly unpopular piecework—or to use the more euphemistic term that the Communists then preferred, *incentive* pay—rates in war-work industries. The class struggle had to be put aside. For now, production of war goods was all that mattered, and it was in this spirit that Roy Hudson, chief labor reporter for the *Daily Worker,* exhorted workers to "do your duty like the Wake Island Marines!"[4]

Communist-dominated unions in the CIO, such as the fur-makers and electrical-workers unions, responded to this call by making some considerable sacrifices during the war. In this same spirit, the Communist party only mildly rebuked the 1943 antilabor Smith–Connally Act, Communist-led unions were the last to advocate an adjustment of the so-called "Little Steel" wage formula, and trade-union Communists were alone in endorsing FDR's never-enacted 1944 "labor draft" proposal.* Vice President Henry Wallace, serving also as chairman of the Board of Economic Warfare, noted in a 24 February 1944, diary entry that the Communists "are away over to the right of where most workers and union labor are located." Browder baldly conceded as much, admitting during the war that his party had "completely subordinated its own ideas . . . to the necessity of uniting the entire nation, including the big

---

*The Smith–Connally Act, passed over FDR's veto in 1943, prohibited labor unions from contributing directly to political campaigns. The law also mandated that unions had to wait 30 days before a strike vote could be taken. For the remainder of the war, the National War Labor Board could supervise strike votes; and the president was given the power to seize and operate any strike-bound plant deemed vital to the war effort. The Little Steel formula pegged wage hikes to the cost of living: because living costs had risen 15 percent from January 1941–May 1942, wages were allowed to rise 15 percent above their January 1941 level. A national-service law would have given FDR the power to break strikes simply by drafting the workers into the Army, then assigning them to their old jobs. Organized labor—with no help from the Communists—lobbied successfully to keep Congress from passing this legislation.

capitalist." To this effect, labor–management councils and committees in plants and industries received the Communist party's enthusiastic approval throughout the war.[5]

To facilitate even further the goal of a fully mobilized home front, Browder advocated the increased centralization and planning of the national war economy, as a means not only of improving productivity but of minimizing class conflict, as well. Although the journal *Nation's Business* warned that the Communists were promoting monopoly and state capitalism in order to erode the "popular base" of the system, big business could not help but welcome what *Business Week* called the Communist-led unions' "more conciliatory attitude" in their relations with management during the war. If anything, *Business Week* understated the Communists' new policy toward their theoretical enemies the capitalists. On record as saying that he would work with (an already dead) J. P. Morgan, Browder declared that the no-strike pledge was "absolutely necessary to victory" and that he considered it "the greatest honor" to be "a strikebreaker at this time."[6]

Of course, American Communists advocated a stern no-strike policy as soon as the U.S.S.R. was invaded in June 1941; Pearl Harbor and the resulting "no-strike" pledge made by both the AFL and CIO leadership simply made it easier for the Communists to take an even more militant and unyielding line on this issue. For example, "Red Mike" Quill, leader of the transit workers in New York, emphatically condemned all strikes, regardless of how aggrieved the workers believed themselves to be. "No idle plants, no idle machines— FOR ANY REASONS!" thundered a front-page article in the *Daily Worker*. A few Communists such as Harry Bridges—whose scheduled deportation from the country was repeatedly delayed and indeed never occurred—even favored extending the no-strike pledge for an indeterminate period of time after the war. Not surprisingly, some employers even went so far as to encourage their workers to join Communist-controlled unions, which management now looked upon as model organizations worthy of emulation by the rest of organized labor.[7]

The Communists' hard-line posture on the no-strike issue often put them at odds with the sentiments of the rank and file, many of whom suspected that the much-touted national "equality of sacrifice" policy was in fact biased against labor. CIO President Phil Murray even admitted that "a very substantial portion of the monies collected by each of the international organizations is now being used to enforce the directives of the National War Labor Board," in effect conceding the strength of worker opposition to the official moratorium on strikes. According to labor historian Philip Taft, "Despite the no-strike pledge given by organized labor, labor disputes continued and after 1942 increased in every year of the war"; and a U.S. Senate study revealed that almost two million workers were involved in strikes in 1943. For the 1943–44 period, some 4 million workers were idled by strikes. It is true that most of these were "wildcat" walkouts of short duration, but as Joel Seidman notes in his *American Labor from Defense to Reconversion,* "The figure of 36,000,000 man-days lost during the war because of work stoppages is a sizable one and should not be glossed over."[8]

The most memorable of the war-year strikes were led by John L. Lewis of the United Mine Workers. Four times in 1943, he defiantly took the miners out of the pits, bringing a vital industry to a virtual standstill. Joining numerous labor-baiting newspapers and politicians, as well as much of the general public, Communists denounced their erstwhile ally as Hitler's most effective agent within the ranks of American organized labor. In mid-March 1943, some of Lewis's personal representatives responded with a statement claiming that the only opposition to their leader within the UMW hailed from "the dingy cellars and underground agitation railways of the Communist party." Lewis, the focal point of most national antilabor feeling during the war, nevertheless remained a rather isolated figure in the trade-union movement in this period. His dramatic bid in 1942 to effect an "accouplement" of the AFL and CIO came to naught, with Murray saying that his former mentor was now "hell bent on creating national confusion and national disunity." Lewis next led the UMW out of the CIO in October 1942, but his subsequent bid to reaffiliate with the AFL was refused. Scornfully, Lewis could only red-bait from the sidelines, flaying at Sidney Hillman, the "Russian pants maker," and at the "bug-house 'Commie' finks" who were looking to "hang on to the coattails of the Red Army and [thereby] try to build an ideological bridge between our loyalty to Russia and their own pet scheme." As for Murray, Lewis now charged that he presided over a Communist-dominated CIO, about which "there isn't a blessed thing he can do."[9]

Lewis's anger clouded his judgment. In fact, Murray never was a servile dupe of the Communists. At one point during the war, he even criticized their single-minded determination to stifle all dissent within labor as amounting to "excessive appeasement of anti-labor forces." But Murray was in a difficult position. He was properly concerned that he might precipitate harmful disunity at a critical hour should he break publicly with the "Reds," as he called them in private. Lewis also exaggerated the Communist party's strength in the CIO. The Communists were not preeminent there, as they discovered when they pushed hard for the reimposition of piecework, a system whose virtual elimination in favor of the hourly wage system in the 1930s had been considered one of the great victories of the trade-union movement.[10]

The purpose of piecework, or incentive-pay, systems is always the same: increased production. This was a worthy objective, particularly in time of war; yet, as the authoritative *Monthly Labor Review* stated, few policies "have aroused as much opposition" among the labor force as piecework and "incentive" wage formulas.[11] It is not hard to see why. Although workers receive extra pay for their increased productivity, they usually oppose piecework because whenever employers "cut" the piecework rates (something they are always wont to do) as their work force becomes more proficient, profits get bigger but the workers' paychecks do not. Some "incentive" plans actually can be even worse than straight piecework. For example, if a man received as his base wage 10 dollars a day for building two auto engines, he would not necessarily earn 20 dollars for building four engines. The employee might only get 15 dollars, depending on the wage/production "incentive" scale that had been established, with the employer keeping the other 5 dollars as profit.

For assembly-line workers, incentive-pay/piecework plans also meant the inevitable reimposition of the dreaded "speedup," which made an already monotonous and difficult job unbearable for many workers. One contributor to *Aero-Notes,* a UAW house organ, likened speedup to Hitler's "machine guns and concentration camps." But Harry Bridges, the tough, Australian-born Communist and leader of the CIO's National Maritime Union, understood this problem perfectly. More than most Communists, he addressed the issue with laudable candor:[12]

> The majority of the time of officers, of grievance committeemen, of the unions as a whole must go to winning the war. How? Production. I'd rather say speed-up, and I mean speed-up. The term production covers the boss, government and so on. But speed-up covers the workers—the people who suffer from speed-up are the workers. . . . I mean your unions today must become instruments of speed-up of the working class of America.

Earl Browder's instincts for diplomacy were a shade better than Bridges's*; the party leader at least called for governmental oversight and other protections to ensure that management would not exploit the workers under a renewed piecework system. At the same time, Browder's position—and therefore the position of the Communist party—on speedup was in practical terms no less militant or unequivocal. In early 1943 he declared, with characteristic assuredness, that the workers' desire for wage increases and the national need for stepped-up production "go hand in hand and must be solved together." Browder's solution was to echo those executives on the government's War Production Board who had advocated a resumption of incentive-pay wage systems in America's war-production industries. As soon as his suggestion that "it is patriotic to demand increased earnings based on increased production" appeared in the *Daily Worker,* prominent labor men linked to the Communist party began lobbying for piecework in their customarily disciplined and determined fashion. In short order, the Communists in control of the United Electrical Workers extended the use of

---

*Bridges worked his men as hard as he could, but there were limits to his authority. For example, the stevedores rebuffed his efforts to raise the sling-load limit for bags of cement being loaded onto lend lease ships bound for the U.S.S.R.

piecework-pay rates, despite some rank-and-file displeasure within this important union.[13]

Naturally, the Communists relied on high-minded "win-the-war" appeals as their best means of selling piecework, though their real reason for embracing the idea was to spur production in order to help the Soviet military cause. In an effort, perhaps, to obscure this motive, Browder periodically sought to defend the despised system on its own merits. He tried, for example, to peddle the piecework initiative as a scheme "to take advantage of everything that was permissible under the government freeze order." He also claimed that "the question of incentive wage[s] is the question of unifying the economic interests of the workers and the economic needs of the war, so that they act . . . to help and supplement one another." Management, no doubt appreciating the irony, welcomed this Communist-sponsored reversal of long-standing trade-union policy. But those who "disagreed with Browder's assessment, or any worker who objected to the "minor element" of speedup inherent in incentive pay, was in his view simply "against the war, that's all." In one instance, the Communist party sent a letter to J. Edgar Hoover,* demanding that the FBI "discover and expose" the parties responsible for distributing antipiecework leaflets at war-work factories in the Detroit area.[14]

As it happened, many union men were enough opposed to piecework to risk General Secretary Browder's castigations of their patriotism. The AFL continued its traditional opposition to piecework throughout the war. The CIO's executive board rejected a motion in support of incentive pay, and the issue was never directly addressed at any of the annual CIO conventions held during the war. When the Communists tried to claim that Phil Murray supported their proposal, the CIO president avoided the issue as best he could by declaring the overall organization "neutral" on incentive pay.[15]

Undaunted, the Communists tried to install piecework in other war-production industries, in particular the vital United Auto Workers union, where the Communists had a strong, growing faction (of maybe 1,200 members), plus a like number of followers willing to go along with them on most important policy matters. In addition, UAW Secretary-Treasurer George Addes, though not a party member himself, joined the Communist faction on the piecework issue and immediately became the main official sponsor and spokesman for incentive-pay wages in the auto workers' union. Richard Frankensteen, a UAW vice president and organizer with a well-deserved reputation for political opportunism, also worked closely with Addes and the

---

*No doubt with great difficulty, Hoover did not often publicly criticize the Communists during the war. While commemorating the thirty-fifth anniversary of the FBI, however, Hoover praised the American people for their strong faith in democracy, which was why "Fascism, Nazism and Communism have never been able to get a real foothold" in the United States. The *Daily Worker* promptly inquired: "Does G-Man Hoover Know U.S. is Fighting Fascism?" (*Worker,* 30 July 1943).

Communists in their bid to restore piecework. These seasoned factionalists were motivated chiefly by political calculations, not by ideological commitment. By supporting the Communists on this issue, they hoped to consolidate those elements within the union opposed to the ambitions of a rival high-ranking UAW official, Walter Reuther, whose so-called "atomic spirit of action" and consuming desire to succeed to the UAW presidency were well known in auto-union political circles.[16]

During the first year of the war, an uneasy "unity" truce had prevailed in the contentious UAW, but the piecework issue was a major factor in the resumption of factionalism-as-usual in this union. Reuther perceived that the Communists, along with their cohorts Addes and Frankensteen, had crossed the rank-and-file's threshold of toleration on this issue. Early on, it was obvious that he was right: Though they undoubtedly considered themselves as patriotic as all other Americans, most non-Communist UAW members flatly rejected the argument that the war emergency obliged them to resume working under the odious piecework system. Reuther was eager to turn their aroused sentiments to his own advantage. He persuaded his colleagues on the UAW executive council, in a March 1943 meeting, to reject the Browder–Addes incentive-pay scheme. Browder responded by taking out a half-page advertisement in a Detroit newspaper to denounce Reuther's "use of the most unprincipled demagogy and lying propaganda" in his efforts against incentive pay. Reuther probably welcomed this attack because it sharpened the distinction between his position and the one advanced by the Communists. Thanks to them, he had become, in the words of one labor observer, "the fair-haired boy of the [UAW] rank and file . . . principally for his stand against the introduction of the incentive pay-system in the automobile industry."[17]

In April 1943, Richard Frankensteen reintroduced the piecework issue before the UAW executive board. As the director of the union's aviation department, Frankensteen had an additional reason to support incentive pay: It was the only means by which the below-average paychecks of his aviation workers could be raised while President Roosevelt's "hold-the-line" order on wages was in effect. Frankensteen also suggested that the War Production Board might mandate incentive-pay schemes unless the unions voluntarily established them in consultation with management. These arguments may have partially impressed some members of the board because this time a motion in favor of incentive pay was simply tabled by these UAW officials. Shortly thereafter, however, regional auto workers' conferences in Detroit and New York City soundly rejected the various piecework proposals that came before them.[18]

Throughout the controversy, Reuther remained on the attack, hammering against piecework. He called this "crusade to put across incentive pay" a scheme "cooked up jointly by the Communist party and those employers who yearn for the 'good old days' of piece-work and slave-driving." These were effective arguments. At a conference of General Motors locals on 30 April in Detroit, Reuther charged that the Communists supported piecework "because they think, mistakenly, that that is the best way to help Russia win the war and because they don't give a tinker's damn what happens to the American labor movement." In May 1943 a conference of Michigan UAW locals passed a resolution calling upon the international union to "aid any local union which desires to rid itself" of incentive-pay systems. This conference also called on the executive board to request the resignations of all union members involved in studying piecework systems for the government. Addes, who had the responsiblity of carrying out decisions of the UAW's executive board, tried to minimize the differences of opinion among board members on piecework in his correspondence with the locals. In other forums, though, he continued to lobby for the adoption of incentive pay.[19]

Nor did the official Communist propaganda effort lose any momentum because of these early setbacks. Reuther, the acknowledged leader of the antipiecework forces, continued to be the principal target of their attacks. Because Reuther had extended some public support to the UMW during one of the miners' walkouts, the *Daily Worker* accused its foe of helping to "spread the infections of disunity and defeatism." Browder tried to link Reuther as closely as possible to the unpopular and supposedly traitorous John L. Lewis. "The difference between [them] is not so great as it appears," Browder declared. "Lewis comes out in the open and Walter Reuther has a hypocritical mask on his face." Browder also accused Reuther of consciously seeking to foment strikes, presumably to weaken the Allied effort and thereby assist the Axis in achieving victory. By forestalling the sort of just wage settlement that would have made the workers "immune to the strike moods," Browder said in denouncing Reuther, "you can keep them stirred up, you can get them excited over all the current issues of the day, you can get them desperate in feeling the only way out is strike." This was why, continued Browder, "Walter Reuther is fighting against the incentive wage in the airplane and automotive industry."[20]

The issue was finally resolved at the UAW's national convention, held in October 1943 in Buffalo, New York. This tumultuous gathering has been described as "an exercise of democracy hardly matched in any other large organization"; and a contemporary observer writing for the Socialist newspaper *The Call* characterized the 1943 convention as one that would determine "the future influence of the reactionary Communist group in the union." Reuther, having seen delegates to the July 1943 Michigan CIO convention recommend that the national CIO rescind its no-strike pledge, was determined to take advantage of what he recognized as the spirit of workers' insurgency in the air, notwithstanding the ongoing war. Victor Reuther, chairman of the resolutions committee and a key member of his brother's faction, drafted a majority resolution opposing piecework in factories where it was not currently in use. The Addes–Frankensteen–Communists forces countered with a proposal giving local unions the power to accept or reject incentive pay in their own shops. Refusing to be outflanked, Reuther cuttingly ridiculed this attempt to convert the issue into a kind of referendum on democracy.[21]

The Reuther faction also sought to portray the incentive-pay advocates as untrustworthy union men who were more concerned with the survival of the U.S.S.R. than with the welfare of the auto workers. Reuther's forces lampooned their opponents with a derisive jingle, sung to the tune of "Reuben and Rachel," whose first stanza went:

> Who are the boys who take their orders Straight from the office of Joe Sta-leen? No one else but the gruesome twosome George F. Addes and Frankensteen.

The purpose of this "Ballad of the Gruesome Twosome" was to brand the propiecework forces as the servile clients of a foreign dictator. Several Addes delegates protested that the song was disrespectful to Marshal Stalin, "one of the greatest of our allies," and tended to "cast slurs" upon the U.S.S.R. But the Reuther group had made its point. Victor Reuther's resolution calling for "guarantees of democracy" for "all" nations in Eastern Europe may have been another indirect "slur" intended to arouse whatever latent suspicions of Soviet intentions existed among the workers.[22]

Reporting on these proceedings, the *Daily Worker* charged that "delegates to the Auto Workers Union convention are getting a first-hand taste of the fascist technique." Convention delegates were kept well supplied with red-baiting literature by the Reuther group, the *Worker* reported. According to the *Worker,* the Reutherites were "trying to disguise their opposition to the anti-Axis struggle by an orgy of red-baiting in the well-known manner of Goebbels and Martin Dies." This was typical Communist hyperbole. The Reuthers were no more opposed to the "anti-Axis struggle" than were the Communists— though Victor Reuther did prevent through parliamentary maneuver a resolution calling for the opening of a "second front" against the Nazis, in a possible bid to forestall any effort at making the convention proceedings a referendum of the UAW's commitment to Allied victory.[23]

No one, however, could have prevented a vote on the bitter incentive-pay issue. Delegate after delegate rose to speak against the Communist party-backed proposal. "We fought nine years to eliminate piecework," one worker stated. "You put it up now and, by God, our children's children won't eliminate it!" One propiecework delegate, Fred Williams of Local 208, claimed that it would be an easy matter to "kick the incentive system out the plant . . . damned quick" after the war, but the majority of his fellow auto workers in Buffalo were unwilling to take that chance. "Vote down piece-work!", Walter Reuther cried to tremendous applause, and by a two-thirds majority the assembled delegates did precisely that. "UAW Kills Piece Work" read the banner headline of the *United Automobile Worker.* As a reward for his support of their immediate interests, the rank and file elected Reuther first vice president over his main competitor Frankensteen. (R. J. Thomas, who cynically opposed both of the resolutions, held onto his job as president.) Addes narrowly avoided losing his post as secretary-treasurer, mainly because black workers appreciated the support he had given to their efforts to have a representative on the executive board. Nevertheless, the convention was properly regarded as a tremendous success for the up-and-coming Reuther.[24]

In his reminiscences many years later, Earl Browder claimed that his support for piecework during the war had been a sound decision. Others have in various ways also tried to defend the policy. Communist party member Len DeCaux has argued that the Communist party "incurred much factional disadvantage by making its pledges with uncrossed fingers." This of course is a self-serving attempt to cast the Communists in as noble and patriotic light as possible. The historian Joel Prickett has claimed that because Reuther favored other measures—the no-strike pledge, restrictions on premium pay, and in-house reprisals against wildcat strikers—that subordinated the workers' interests to the war effort, the piecework debate was "hardly the stuff of which principled philosophical differences are made." (George Addes made the same point in his account of the 1943 convention.) Wyndham Mortimer, a UAW Communist who wrote an interesting memoir, *Organize!*, chipped in with what he called "the lack of principle that has animated Walter Reuther all throughout his life."[25]

These arguments seem to overlook the key points. Unquestionably, Reuther was an opportunist: For example, he tried to avoid taking a clear position on the sensitive no-strike pledge,* a maneuver that was as cyncial as any the Communists tried during the war. Nevertheless, Reuther's stance against piecework was in harmony with majority rank-and-file opinion, whereas the Communists supported a wage system that the workers had long regarded as injurious to their interests. For this simple reason, most historians have concluded that the piecework proposal was disastrous for its sponsors. Bert Cochran has called it "an evil hour" for the Communist party; Harvey Levenstein writes that Browder's incentive-wage idea plunged Communist union men "into scalding water"; and Maurice Isserman notes that the Communists, having made a "fateful error" on this issue, were forced "to pay a political price on the shop floor" for even the few short-term victories, as in the electrical workers' union, that they achieved.[26]

---

*He proposed that the no-strike pledge be maintained in war-manufacturing plants for the duration but lifted in those factories producing civilian goods as soon as the war in Europe was over. Opponents complained that companies would keep up a little war production in every plant to avoid strikes, even as they shifted to predominantly nondefense manufacturing. Reuther's obvious straddle was decisively rejected at the 1944 UAW convention.

Even if one concedes—as Carl Haessler, a UAW press-relations worker, does in his oral-history memoirs—that the Communists wanted to raise workers' wages through piecework, their chief desire was "to help the Soviet Union." Historian Nelson Lichtenstein has addressed the point squarely in one of his publications on this subject: "The ultimate commitment of domestic Communist leaders . . . was less to the defense of the American working class in its day-to-day struggles than to the political/military success of the Russian regime." Joel Seidman agrees: Changes in party policy came fast in this period—embracing piecework was an important but hardly the most dramatic one—and these changes "can best be explained by reference to the real or supposed needs of the Soviet Union."[27]

This always-embarrassing connection, which the piecework controversy underscored in a way certain to attract rank-and-file attention, would prove ruinous for the Communists. Some workers believed that the Communists were prepared to convert "the UAW into a Russian type labor organization—a glorified, compulsory company union," as charged by Frank Marquart, a long-time official engaged in the UAW's labor education work. Even if this was an exaggeraton, Reuther clearly was on the mark as to the true motive behind the Communists' sudden clamor for an idea as widely unpopular as incentive pay. Nat Ganley, a Communist functionary in the UAW, later conceded that the "down-with-Browder's-piecework" campaign had served Reuther well, just as similar tactics brought him to the UAW presidency shortly after the war. As two observers sympathetic to Reuther wrote after this far greater triumph, Reuther won because he "had gambled on the idea that the Communist party could be defeated . . . by showing the totalitarian strings to which the Communist party danced."[28]

In the American Federation of Labor, anticommunism per se posed no internal problems because virtually all of the AFL's power brokers believed that communism was irredeemably evil. For example, in his 1943 Labor Day address, AFL President William Green indirectly likened the U.S.S.R. to Nazi Germany, just as he might have done in a similar speech before the war. "Grave as the post-war readjustments may be, we must solve our problems by democratic methods," Green said. "We must reject Fascist, Nazi and Communistic shortcuts that only lead to despair." Green also refused to join the CIO's leaders in calling for a second European front in 1942, an issue that the Communists regarded as a litmus test of genuine solidarity with the U.S.S.R. The AFL president neatly sidestepped the issue by saying that "we must leave that to the military experts of the United Nations who are planning their strategy on a world-wide scale."[29]

Green's views were in perfect accord with those of his fellow executive council members. Teamsters President Dan Tobin believed that supporting the U.S.S.R. was sound policy "not because we hate Communism less, but because we hate Hitlerism more"—a remark that hardly bespoke much enthusiasm for the new Soviet–American alliance. In February 1943 Tobin wrote an editorial in his union's main publication, *The Teamster,* that argued that "if the sprinkling of Communists still in our country keeps on holding meetings behind screens and allowing their disturbers to endeavor to control or destroy the labor movement in America they are doing the greatest possible injury that could be done to the Russian people today." William Hutcheson, of the Carpenters Union, also held fast to old prejudices: In October 1942 he told Vice President Henry Wallace that the CIO was nothing but "a bunch of Communists." John Frey, head of the AFL's Metal Trades Department, did not alter his prewar opinion that the New Deal was badly tainted with communism: he still railed on against "the theorists, the thinkers, the pinkish-hued and the outright radicals who have saturated the National Labor Relations Board." David Dubinsky, who brought the garment workers' back into the AFL fold in 1940 and who had had more direct experience with the Communist party than did most of his colleagues, also continued his crusade against Communists. "They are a danger," Dubinsky insisted. "They are a menace. They are not loyal. They are not faithful. They have their feet on our ground, on our soil, but their hearts belong elsewhere. Beware of them!"[30]

Nor did Matthew Woll, head of the Photo-Engravers Union and the AFL's acknowledged in-house expert on foreign affairs, see any reason to change his deeply anti-Communist, anti-Soviet convictions. After he was criticized in "War and the Working Class," the official organ of Soviet trade unionism, Woll declared that "the American Federation of Labor and its spokesmen have never made a secret of their opposition to Communism, its practices and policies." Woll insisted that military collaboration with the U.S.S.R. "does not require that we abandon our trade union principles and jeopardize the security and integrity of our labor movement to help promote the Communist conception of social and labor cooperation." And his reaction to the dissolution of the Comintern, if unusually dramatic and colorful, was totally in keeping with a federation policy for which Woll had been largely responsible: "International Communism will continue to speak with the voice of Jacob," Woll declared, "but the hand will be and remain, as always, the hand of Esau."[31]

This hostility to the Soviet Union remained potent enough to forestall an ambitious plan to establish formal ties between the British and Russian unions and the largest trade-union organization in the United States. In May 1942 Sir Walter Citrine, president of the IFTU and the general secretary of TUC, suggested that the American Federation of Labor partake in a new Soviet–Anglo–American labor alliance to maximize Allied cooperation in the war effort. The common emergency already had strengthened ties between the British and Russian labor movements. For years, the AFL had maintained friendly relations with its English counterpart, the British Trades Union Congress, but no such relationship existed with the Russian labor movement.

With the United States now in the war, Citrine assumed that American labor would want to make the final link, through some kind of affiliation with the Russian trade unions.

To his surprise and disappointment, the AFL executive council politely but firmly rejected his appeal—made also by other visiting British labor leaders—for greater American cooperation with Soviet organized labor. In the AFL's view, the Grand Alliance with Britain and the Russians did not oblige American labor to treat each ally equally. Green bluntly told Citrine that "we have a different situation here, a different state of mind, and a different psychology; therefore, it would be difficult to explain to our workers why we would join with Soviet Russia. . . ." Green's second in command, Secretary–Treasurer George Meany, shared his boss' uncompromising view. The purported Soviet labor movement was controlled by a dictatorial, repressive Soviet government, Meany believed, and because "there were no [free] Russian trade unions," the AFL had no choice but to reject the Citrine proposal.[32]

Appeals from the British and American governments for the AFL to reconsider its position on this issue came to no avail. However, in recognition of the alliance, the AFL did not widely publicize its refusal of Citrine's grand design for Allied labor unity. (Woll, speaking before the 1942 AFL convention on the proposal, cryptically suggested that "there are many things which perhaps might be said on this question that might better be left unsaid at this time.") In fact, the first "official" announcement of AFL policy on this sensitive issue was published in the July 1942 issue of *The Carpenter*, the house organ for the union led by the very conservative William Hutcheson. The announcement stated that because

> the so-called Trade Union movement of Russia is dominated, controlled, and directed by the Soviet Communist Government, and is, therefore, not a free Trade Union Movement, we cannot endorse or participate in any such procedure . . . .The United Brotherhood of Carpenters and Joiners of America can in no way cooperate or collaborate with the Communist Trade Union Movement of Russia.

At about the same time, an editorial appeared in *The Elevator Constructor*, another AFL house organ, which made very much the same point. After ritualistically paying tribute to the "long-abused workers in the U.S.S.R. now bravely fighting Hitler," the editorial noted that "the Soviet labor movement, of course, is State dominated, and has never had the freedom of conduct heretofore enjoyed by independent labor movements." Federation policy had been clearly laid down: The AFL would have no direct relations with the so-called trade unions of the U.S.S.R.[33]

In its formal reply to Citrine, the executive council softened its position slightly by offering a counterproposal to the Englishman's idea: that an Anglo-American Trade Union Committee be established for the purpose of "carrying on current war activities and requirements." Thus the British, who in 1942 also joined in an Anglo–Soviet Trade Union Committee, could "act as a liaison with the trade unions of the U.S.S.R. on any matter of direct concern to the trade unions which may arise." Citrine reluctantly agreed to this compromise arrangement (which if anything served to underscore the AFL's disinclination to work with the Soviets), and the Anglo-American Trade Union Committee began operations in July 1942.[34]

As far as the persevering Citrine was concerned, this half-way measure did not satisfactorily establish the principles or process he was eager to advance, and in 1943 he resumed his efforts to entice the AFL to work directly with its Russian counterparts. Once again he would discover that the war and the alliance had not shaken the AFL's resolve to remain apart from the trade-union affairs of America's battlefield ally, the Soviet Union. Responding to this second request with a carefully prepared statement, the executive council insisted that "our unwillingness to recognize the Soviet trade unions other than as governmental agencies and our refusal to cooperate with them . . . [because] they are unlike our free trade unions" would in no way "detract or lessen" the federation's "zeal" for providing "every possible aid, support and help" to the Russians in their hour of greatest need. But the council held firm in its belief that the proposed association would only "result in friction and confusion here at home, and at a time when elements of discord are to be discouraged."[35]

To no one's surprise, delegates to the 1943 AFL convention in Boston soundly defeated a proposed resolution calling upon the federation to reverse itself and "consider the possibilities of joining with the British and Russian Trade Unions in the Anglo-Soviet Trade Union Council." Instead the convention overwhelmingly approved an executive council report that restated at length its disdain for collaborating with Soviet trade unions:[36]

> Our desire to support our Government in pursuance of its laudable national and international objectives does not impose upon us any obligation or necessity to recognize or cooperate with the Russian labor organizations, which are not trade unions in the sense that American workers understand the term. The fundamental differences between the federation and the government-controlled Russian unions are so glaring that no liaison between the two is now remotely possible.
>
> Russian Labor organizations are the instruments of policy of the Russian Government. They are not free and voluntary associations of workers in the sense that characterizes American and British unions. They constitute a department of the Russian state, so to speak, and enjoy no more autonomy than do the various agencies in any totalitarian government. . . . Also, experience teaches us that approachment between American organizations and their Russian counterparts immediately becomes an instrument to aid in domestic Communist infiltration.

In emphatical terms, this policy reflected the anti-Communist and anti-Soviet sentiments that had remained predominant in AFL circles, notwithstanding the U.S.–Soviet alliance. *The American Photo-Engraver,* the house organ for Matthew Woll's union, reminded its readers that

> Unlike the American unions, which feel themselves free to differ with their respective governments at all times, the Russian "unions" act like so many automatons of the Communist policymakers in the Kremlin. Insofar as independence of action is concerned, the Russian unions are on the same level as Hitler's Labor Front.

In addition, the Association of Catholic Trade Unionists, which had some supporters in the AFL as well as in the CIO, praised the federation's "sound position" on Soviet trade unions. George Meany added the argument that the Soviet labor movement ought to be recognized "for what it is—a government-controlled, government-fostered, and government-dominated labor front that denies to the workers of Soviet Russia the basic human freedoms."[37]

The handful of Socialists active in AFL affairs—principally David Dubinsky and his associates in the International Ladies' Garment Workers' Union—also reaffirmed the federation's animus toward the U.S.S.R. and its labor movement. Isidore Nagler, an ILG official and an AFL delegate sent to confer with the British Trade Union Council, said that any direct dealings between the AFL and the Soviet trade unions "would only accentuate already existing ideological differences and conflicts and would carry division into the ranks of [American] labor." Nagler added some harsh words for the American Communists, who, he said, "under the cloak of our military alliance with Soviet Russia ... [claim that] we ought to embrace as well its political, its economic, its social philosophy." Similarly, the garment-workers' union's committee on national and international relations held that "there are certain basic principles that must be common to all trade unions, and one of the principles is freedom of action and freedom from state domination. Such basic freedoms the Russian unions still do not possess." The committee also stated, though, that in its view—and Dan Tobin of the Teamsters happened to concur—the federation's policy need be "neither static nor frozen." Should the Soviet labor movement ever receive its emancipation from state control, then the ILG, and no doubt the rest of the AFL, "will be happy to welcome the Russian unions into its councils on a basis of fundamental equality."[38]

Unfortunately for Sir Walter Citrine, such a welcome was unlikely to be tendered at any time in the near future. Under continued pressure from his unions to arrange direct communications between American and Soviet trade-union leaders, Citrine decided to bypass the AFL, which had now twice rebuffed him, and to take his plans to the federation's main rival, the Congress of Industrial Organizations. Still a very young organization, the CIO hungered for the sort of legitimacy and recognition that affiliation in an international society of unions might bring. The CIO had been shut out of the now-moribund International Federation of Trade Unions because in this body each country was allowed representation by only one organization, and the

AFL already claimed America's place on the IFTU roster. The Federation also had jealously excluded the CIO, which protested to no avail, from even participating in the Anglo–American Trade Union Committee. Now, however, Citrine envisioned a conference to organize a new World Federation of Trade Unions, to absorb and supplant the broken, war-ravaged, IFTU. The CIO readily agreed to join this new organization, thus stealing a march on its elder rival.[39]

From the outset, it was understood by all concerned parties, including the AFL executive council, that this new group would include trade-union representatives from the U.S.S.R. This was no problem for the CIO. Pro-Communist elements in the organization had been calling for such a show of solidarity since the attack on Pearl Harbor. The ever-militant Harry Bridges contended that international labor unity was of paramount significance because "we won't win the war until we get it." At the CIO's national convention in November 1942—hailed in the Communist press as the "win-the-war conven-tion"—delegates with ties to the party voiced strong support for direct Soviet–American trade-union cooperation. Reid Robinson, president of the Mine, Mill and Smelters Union, wrote that "Anglo–Soviet–American trade-union unity is a logical extension of the unity of governments and armed forces" among the Allies. Irving Potash of the Fur and Leather Workers insisted that "the only contamination we may have as a result of collaboration with such a trade union movement is that we may be contaminated with their courage and their determination." Jack Lawrenson of the National Maritime Union said that the Soviets did not need the American unions, but "we need the Soviet trade unions to help us write the common peace of the world."[40]

Non-Communist CIO officials were not inclined to quarrel the point. In November 1942, R. J. Thomas, president of the UAW–CIO, declared that "We must begin at once to forge this solidarity of the labor movements of our own nation with the workers of the British Commonwealth of Nations, Russia, China and the other allies in our struggle for freedom." "If we are United Nations in fact," Philip Murray said in March 1943, "we must be so in practice—not only in the relations between governments but in the relations between the trade unions of the United Nations." At this juncture, Murray was not about to divide his organization over a painless and essentially symbolic gesture that could easily be promoted as serving the interests of "Allied unity."[41]

The CIO's willingness to join the proposed WFTU was warmly applauded by the Communist party, which had predictably condemned the AFL for its alleged sabotage of Allied unity. Rose Wortis, writing in the *Daily Worker*, claimed that the executive council's "psychic fear" of associating with Soviet unions "is the effect that such an association will have in stimulating the already developing progressive trends in the AFL itself." According to the *Worker*, the AFL leaders, determined "to put across their defeatist line," brazenly flouted rank-and-file opinion by rejecting Citrine's overtures. An article in the November 1942 issue of *The Communist* also accused the AFL's executive council members of blundering, perhaps ignorantly, into treason:

> They do not realize that in opposing labor unity they are following in the footsteps of the Municheers who are ready to sell our country to Hitler for fear of the Soviet Union. Such policies give grist to the mill of the defeatists and the Fifth Column, who play on outmoded fears and prejudices against the Soviet Union.

As the AFL maintained its hostile stance toward the Soviet labor movement, *The Communist* sharpened its criticism accordingly. Accusing the AFL of attempting to surround the U.S.S.R.'s union with a labor "cordon sanitaire," the principal intellectual journal of the American Communist movement insisted that world trade-union unity was "the paramount issue now confronting the A.F. of L." As such, *The Communist* again lashed out at the federation's obstreperous posture toward the Soviets:[42]

> The efforts to undermine the United Nations Coalition, to sabotage the Moscow Conference, to convert the A.F. of L. into a center of anti-Soviet intrigue, to advance the political objectives of the Hutcheson-Lewis-Woll conspiracy on the home front, to disrupt national unity and the growing political unity of labor—all these objectives became concentrated in the attack upon international labor unity. . . .

With somewhat less hyperbole, others who were currently sympathetic to the Communists joined this propaganda offensive against the AFL. *The New Statesman and Nation,* a left-wing British journal, criticized what it termed the "reactionary attitude of the A.F. of L. towards Russia." In October 1943, George F. Addes of the UAW said that the AFL power brokers "have succeeded in sabotaging the establishment of sound relations among the labor movements of the United Nations." And even Walter Reuther, speaking on behalf of an "international labor unity" resolution at the 1943 CIO convention, said that American labor had to overlook "the shortcomings" ("yes, there are many of them," he admitted) in trade-union movements across the seas.[43]

Having taken upon itself the task of repairing this "sabotage" as best it could, the CIO avoided the questions raised by the AFL about the nature of the Soviet labor movement. Bridges admitted, for example, that he was "no expert on the Soviet trade unions" because he had "never been there." Sidney Hillman, of the Amalgamated Clothing Workers, addressing his union's 1944 convention in Chicago, told the delegates it was impossible to "organize labor internationally and have Russia out." President Roosevelt's main supporter in the U.S. labor movement, Hillman, had no qualms about permitting the administration to take the lead on all policy matters regarding the U.S.S.R. "It will be well for us not to jump in and take a position on every controversy," Hillman suggested. Honest misunderstandings would crop up, of course, but Hillman advised "that in many cases, yes, in most cases, we withhold judgment. . . ."[44]

But in 1944 the AFL again refused to suspend its judgments about either the nature of the Soviet government or the likelihood of substantial changes occurring within that regime any time soon. Dan Tobin, at times a bit hopeful about future U.S.–Soviet relations, flatly stated in February 1944 that "Russia will never give up its present form of government at the ending of this war." More ominously, the AFL hierarchy—especially Woll—suspected that the Soviets would try to extend communism beyond Russian borders as the Red Army drove into Europe. For some time, Woll had believed that the U.S.S.R. wanted to control the Balkans, either directly or through "alliances" with Communist-controlled home governments. This would put Stalin in a strong position to dominate all of Europe. In his *American Photo-Engraver* editorials, Woll expressed the fear that America "might well lose the war after having achieved military victory in Europe." He bitterly criticized the cynical "realism" of those who argued that the Atlantic Charter had to be abandoned because there was no way of stopping Stalin's armies. In Woll's view, this perspective "disregards utterly the rights of small people." Above all, Woll did not want the Balkan people and other Europeans driven by "disillusion and desperation" over misguided U.S. policies "into the outstretched arms of Stalin." As such, he and his AFL colleagues remained certain that their agreeing to collaborate with the Russian unions would be a contribution to such policy because their doing so likely would lead to situations in which "sections of the American labor movement might be used as pawns in Soviet political adventures."[45]

As a further caution against this eventuality, the federation set up a postwar planning committee, which included those executive council members most interested in foreign policy—Woll, Dubinsky, and George Meany. This committee was established to "begin immediate preparation of a program designed to give reality to the ideals for which America is now fighting," and staffed principally by Dubinsky's associates from the ILG, many of whom were Socialists knowledgeable about European labor conditions. Resisting what Dubinsky called the prevailing "unfortunate and dangerous tendency to confuse ruthlessness with realism" would be a major task of this committee. It was Woll, however, who delivered what amounted to a keynote address for this committee during a mid-April 1944 labor forum in New York City. He charged that "one of our allies on the continent is altering the face of Europe to suit itself, by its own means and to its own pleasure, without any relation to the principles accepted by all of the United Nations as the basis for the new world." No one was in the dark as to which country Woll meant. Although the bulk of the postwar planning committee's efforts would be undertaken after the war, even before this the committee published several issues of the journal

International Postwar Problems, to make clear its view that "Soviet Russia is upholding her prewar political regime of rigid dictatorship and is, in addition, developing trends toward nationalistic and militaristic expansion." As such, "the main objective of labor in the struggle ahead of us should be not the magic formula of security but the understanding that security without justice is neither realizable nor desirable."[46]

Given these attitudes, it was inevitable that the Communist press would accuse the AFL during the war of engaging in "anti-Soviet intrigue internationally." However, as the European conflict neared an end, it seemed as though it was the federation, not the Communists and their colleagues in the CIO, which had become isolated in the world labor community. The World Federation of Trade Unions was about to become a reality, though not before Citrine's grand scheme for Allied labor unity was beset with further organizational difficulties. The first meeting was to be held in London and was scheduled, quite by coincidence, for 6 June 1944. James Carey, selected as a CIO delegate to this as-yet unorganized body, was called into the Oval Office shortly before he was to leave for England. The president told Carey he wanted this first WFTU meeting delayed, though of course FDR could not divulge the fact that Carey and his colleagues had inadvertently created a schedule conflict with D-Day. "He advised me that in giving reason for postponing the first conference of the World Federation of Trade Unions," Carey later recalled, "it might be desirable to have a reason somewhat like the real reason but not the real reason." Citrine received the same message from Churchill and of course he also complied.[47]

Additional war-related delays prevented the meeting from getting under way until February 1945, at which time a conference in London created the World Federation of Trade Unions. This organization included delegations from the CIO, Great Britain, the Soviet Union, and some 32 other countries. AFL observers were certain of heavy Communist influence in the WFTU's formation, though of course the federation would have been enthusiastically admitted, along with the CIO. Indeed, the AFL was the only major labor organization from a non-Communist country to remain outside the WFTU. Fearing that both the CIO and the U.S.S.R. had succeeded in undermining their international credibility, the AFL leadership decided to "go public" with its reasons for refusing to join the WFTU. In a speech to the New York Central Trades and Labor Council on 5 April 1945, Meany lashed out at the U.S.S.R. and its Communist system. With biting rhetoric, Meany posed a series of questions to his listeners:[48]

> What common ground could we find in cooperation with those who pretend to speak for the workers but in reality represent the government? What could we talk about? The latest innovations being used by the secret police to ensnare those who think in opposition to the group in power? Or, perhaps, bigger and better concentration camps for political prisoners?

With Germany's surrender still a month away, the U.S. government naturally wanted to hold the already-weakening Grand Alliance together for as long as possible—and Meany's strident words hardly were helpful to this endeavor. To limit the damage, officials in Washington apparently were able to prevail upon the New York City newspapers to ignore the secretary–treasurer's harshly anti-Soviet speech.[49] This allegation remains unproven, though it is indeed difficult to think of other reasons why all the major metropolitan dailies did not report on such a seemingly newsworthy story. In retrospect, of course, Meany's words are enormously significant, because they proved to be the opening salvo in the AFL's participation in the Cold War crusade against the Soviet Union.

Despite the many substantial differences between the AFL and CIO, the anti-Communist credo remained viable in both organizations during the war/ alliance period. In the AFL, it was on anti-Communist principle alone that the autocratically run executive council declined to work with Soviet trade unions in an international body. During the war, it would have been a simple matter for the federation to have put aside this principle, at least to the point of sending representatives to a few pro-forma meetings with Soviet trade-union representatives. Yet, the executive council adamantly refused to do so. Principle was less of a factor in Walter Reuther's fierce struggle with the UAW's Communist faction, which was then promoting an "everything-for-the-war" line, including a wage system that subordinated workers' interests to the immediate needs of the U.S.S.R. At the free-wheeling 1943 UAW convention, the workers themselves repudiated the Communists' piecework proposal, but Reuther helped make their essentially selfish decision more palatable by his artful appeals to their latent suspicions that the Communist party was controlled by the Soviet dictatorship. To that extent, the perceptions of the pro-Reuther forces in the UAW-CIO dovetailed with those of Woll, Meany, and the other AFL chieftains who sat on the executive council. After the war, Reuther and the AFL hierarchy would unite their respective organizations into one mighty AFL-CIO. To no one's surprise, this politically formidable organization would bring its full strength to bear in support of the anti-Communist Cold War struggle of the postwar generation.

NOTES

1. Eldorous Dayton, *Walter Reuther, The Aristocrat of the Bargaining Table* (New York: Devin-Adair, 1958), p. 146.
2. *United Construction Worker News*, 1 March 1944, p. 8; Archie Robinson, *George Meany and His Times* (New York: Simon & Schuster, 1981), p. 131; "Support for Russia," *The Carpenter*, February 1942, p. 21.
3. *Timber Worker*, 25 February 1942, p. 13; *The Wage Earner*, 1 October 1943, p. 13; *The Wage Earner*, 16 October 1942; Richard Ward, "The Role of the

Association of Catholic Trade Unionists in the American Labor Movement''
(unpublished Ph.D. dissertation, University of Michigan, 1958), pp. 133–52.

4. Sidney Lens, *Left, Right and Center* (Hinsdale, IL: Henry Regnery Company,
1949), p. 344; Daniel Guerin, *100 Years of Labor in the USA* (London: Ink Links,
1979), p. 121; Clayton Fountain, *Union Guy* (New York: Viking Press, 1949), p.
162; *Daily Worker*, 3 March 1942.

5. John Morton Blum, ed., *The Price of Vision, The Diary of Henry Wallace,
1942–1946* (Boston: Houghton Mifflin Company, 1973), p. 305; Earl Browder,
Victory—And After (New York: International Publishers, 1942), pp. 112–13;
Browder, "Production for Victory," *The Communist*, January 1943, pp. 24–5.

6. Lawrence Drake, "Our Communists' New Line," *Nation's Business*, July 1944,
p. 36; "Bridges' Setback," *Business Week*, 18 March 1944, pp. 83–84; Earl
Browder, "Teheran—History's Greatest Turning Point," *The Communist*, January 1944, p. 8; *Daily Worker*, 8 May 1943; Browder, "The Strike Wave
Conspiracy," *The Communist*, June 1943, p. 490.

7. David Shannon, *The Decline of American Communism* (Chatham, NJ: Chatham
Bookseller, 1971), p. 6; L. H. Whittemore *The Man Who Ran the Subways, The
Story of Mike Quill* (New York: Holt, Rinehart & Winston, 1968), pp. 111, 113);
Daily Worker, 3 March 1942; Howe and Coser, *The American Communist Party,
A Critical History* (New York: DaCapo Press, 1974), pp. 400, 411–12; "Party of
the Right," *Common Sense*, February 1944, p. 43; Guerin, p. 122.

8. Bert Cochran, *Labor and Communism* (Princeton, NJ: Princeton University Press,
1977), p. 201; Philip Taft, *Organized Labor in American History* (New York:
Harper and Row, 1964), pp. 553–54; Lens, p. 341; A. A. Hoehling, *Home Front,
U.S.A.* (New York: Thomas Y. Crowell Company, 1966), p. 121; Arthur
McClure, *The Truman Administration and the Problems of Postwar Labor,
1945–1948* (Cranbury, NJ: Associated University Presses, Inc., 1969), p. 32; Joel
Seidman, *American Labor from Defense to Reconversion* (Chicago: University of
Chicago Press, 1953), p. 150.

9. *PM*, 16 March 1942; William Z. Foster, "John L. Lewis and the War," *The
Communist*, July 1943, pp. 497–506; Foster, "The Coal Miners' Strike," *The
Communist*, June 1943, p. 532; Earl Browder, "Hold the Home Front," *The
Communist*, July 1943, pp. 582–83; *PM*, 14 March 1942; Melvyn Dubofsky and
Warren Van Tine, *John L. Lewis, A Biography* (New York: Quadrangle, 1977),
pp. 447–49; Saul Alinsky, *John L. Lewis, An Unauthorized Biography* (New
York: Vintage Books, 1970), p. 302; Joseph Rayback, *A History of American
Labor* (New York: Macmillan, 1959), p. 383; *Proceedings of the Constitutional
Convention of the United Mine Workers of America*, Vol. I, 12–20 September
1944, p. 14; *United Mine Workers Journal*, 15 June 1944, p. 11; *New York Times*,
29 February 1944; *United Construction Worker News*, 1 March 1944, p. 8.

10. Lens, p. 344; *The Call*, 27 November 1942; Cochran, p. 211; Roger Keeran, *The
Communist Party and the Auto Workers Union* (Bloomington: Indiana University
Press, 1980), p. 238; Walter Galenson, *The CIO Challenge to the AFL*
(Cambridge, MA: Harvard University Press, 1960), p. 191.

11. "Incentive-Wage Plans and Collective Bargaining," *Monthly Labor Review*, July
1942, p. 1.

12. *Aero-Notes*, 12 July, 29 September 1943, p. 5; Cochran, p. 214.

13. Earl Browder, *Production for Victory* (New York: Workers Library, 1942), p. 23;
Browder, "Production for Victory," *The Communist*, January 1943, pp. 10–29;
Daily Worker, 25 February 1943; Nelson Lichtenstein, *Labor's War at Home, The
CIO in World War II* (New York: Cambridge University Press, 1982), p. 74.

14. Earl Browder interview, Columbia Oral History Project, p. 392; Gould and Hickok, p. 213; Browder, "Hold the Home Front," *The Communist*, July 1943, p. 587; Browder, "The Strike Wave Conspiracy," *The Communist*, June 1943, p. 489; Art Preis, *Labor's Giant Step*, p. 186.
15. "Incentive Wage Schemes," *American Federationist*, October 1943, p. 4; Cochran, p. 213; Preis, p. 186; Lichtenstein, p. 147.
16. Lichtenstein, p. 144; Jean Gould and Lorena Hickok, *Walter Reuther, Labor's Rugged Individualist* (New York: Dodd, Mead and Company, 1972), p. 204.
17. Keeran, pp. 238–39; Fountain, p. 162; *Detroit News*, 9 and 14 May 1943.
18. Richard Frankensteen interview, Wayne State University Oral History Collection, pp. 97–99; Cochran, p. 216; Keeran, p. 238.
19. Walter Reuther, "Incentive Pay Conflicts with Union Goals and Principles," Walter P. Reuther Papers, Box 9, Folder 3; Speech by Walter Reuther in Detroit, 30 April 1943, Reuther Papers, Box 540, Folder 10; "Incentive Pay Again," *The Call*, 14 May 1943; *United Auto Worker*, 1 September 1943, p. 6A.
20. *Daily Worker*, 4 May 1943; *The Communist*, June 1943, pp. 490–91.
21. Irving Howe and B. J. Widick, *The UAW and Walter Reuther* (New York: Random House, 1949), p. 117; *The Call*, 1 October 1943; *Proceedings of the Eighth Convention of the United Automobile, Aircraft and Agricultural Implement Workers of America (UAW-CIO)*, 4–10 October 1943, in Buffalo, NY, pp. 170–72, 181–82; for the entire piecework debate, see pp. 169–233.
22. John Barnard, *Walter Reuther and the Rise of the Auto Workers* (Boston: Little, Brown and Company, 1983), p. 83; *Proceedings*, 1943 UAW convention, pp. 132–33, 158–59.
23. *Daily Worker*, 7 October, 8 October 1943; *Proceedings*, 1943 UAW convention, pp. 92, 94, 132, 134.
24. *CIO News*, 11 October 1943; *Proceedings*, 1943 UAW convention, pp. 182, 207, 215; *United Automobile Worker*, 15 October 1943, p. 2-A; Keeran, pp. 233–34; Walter Reuther, "How to Beat the Communists," published in *Walter P. Reuther, Selected Papers* (New York: The Macmillan Company, 1961), p. 34; Victor Reuther, *The Brothers Reuther* (Boston: Houghton Mifflin Company, 1976), pp. 235–37.
25. Earl Browder interview, Columbia Oral History Collection, Part II, p. 389; Len DeCaux, *Labor Radical, From the Wobblies to CIO* (Boston: Beacon Press, 1970), p. 434; James Prickett, "Communism and Factionalism in the United Automobile Workers, 1939–1947," *Science and Society*, Summer 1968, p. 267; George F. Addes interview, Wayne State University Oral History Collection, p. 34; Wyndham Mortimer, *Organize!* (Boston: Beacon Press, 1971), p. 198.
26. Howe and Widick, pp. 118–24; Keeran, pp. 244–45; Cochran, p. 209; Harvey Levenstein, *Communism, Anticommunism, and the CIO* (Westport, CT: Greenwood Press, 1981), p. 162; Maurice Isserman, *Which Side Were You On?* (Middletown, CT: Wesleyan University Press, 1982), pp. 140, 163.
27. Carl Haessler interview, Wayne State University Oral History Collection, p. 146; Nelson Lichtenstein, "Defending the No-Strike Pledge: CIO Politics During World War II," *Radical America*, July–August 1975, p. 63; Joel Seidman, "Labor Policy of the Communist Party During World War II," *Industrial and Labor Relations Review*, October 1950, p. 55.
28. Frank Marquart, *An Auto Worker's Journal* (University Park: Pennsylvania State University Press, 1975), p. 157; Nat Ganley interview, Wayne State University Oral History Collection, p. 40; Howe and Widick, p. 171.

29. *The Union Leader*, 11 September 1943. Press release (9 November 1942) of Green's speech to Congress of American–Soviet Friendship found in American Federation of Labor Papers (Wisconsin State Historical Society), Box 19 "Russia".

30. *International Teamster*, January 1942, p. 38, and February 1943, pp. 11–12; Blum, ed., *Diary of Henry Wallace*, p. 128; *Portland Journal*, 10 April 1943, from clipping found in John Frey Papers, Box 5, Container No. 27; *Report and Record, Twenty-fifth Convention of the International Ladies' Garment Workers' Union* (29 May–9 June 1944, Boston, MA), p. 514.

31. *American Federation of Labor Weekly News Service*, 2 June 1943, and 28 December 1943.

32. Colston Warne, *Yearbook of American Labor*, Vol. I (New York: Philosophical Library, 1945), p. 508; Goulden, p. 125; Archie Robinson, *George Meany and His Times* (New York: Simon & Schuster, 1981), p. 131.

33. Goulden, p. 125; *Report of the Proceedings of the Sixty-second Annual Convention of the American Federation of Labor*, held in Toronto, Ontario, Canada, 5–14, October 1942, p. 630; *The Carpenter*, July 1942, p. 3; *The Elevator Constructor*, July 1942, p. 32.

34. *Proceedings*, 1942 AFL Convention, p. 231.

35. Report of the *Proceedings of the Sixty-third Annual Convention of the American Federation of Labor*, Boston, MA., 4–14 October 1943, p. 149.

36. *Ibid.*, pp. 568, 574.

37. "What About the Balkans?" *The American Photo Engraver*, December 1943, p. 883; *The Wage Earner*, 19 February 1943; Goulden, p. 122.

38. *Proceedings*, 1943 AFL Convention, pp. 571–72; *Proceedings*, 1944 ILGWU Convention, pp. 494–95; *The Teamster*, February 1944, p. 5.

39. Levenstein, p. 209; DeCaux, p. 437.

40. Text of Bridges speech found in AFL Papers, Box 19 "Russia"; Roy Hudson, "The C.I.O. Convention," *The Communist*, December 1942, p. 985; *New Masses*, 23 June 1942, p. 9; *Proceedings of the Fifth Constitutional Convention of the Congress of Industrial Organizations*, 9–13 November 1942, Boston, MA, pp. 365, 367.

41. Press release (8 November 1942) of Thomas speech to Congress of American–Soviet Friendship found in AFL Papers, Box 19 "Russia"; *CIO News*, 29 March 1943.

42. *Daily Worker*, 28 October 1943; Rose Wortis, "Trends in the A.F. of L.," *The Communist*, November 1942, pp. 934–35; William Z. Foster, "The C.I.O. Convention," *The Communist*, December 1943, pp. 1152–53; J. K. Morton, "The A.F. of L. Convention," *The Communist*, December 1943, pp. 1161–62.

43. "The A.F. of L. is Still Obstructing," *The New Statesman and Nation*, 20 March 1943, p. 182; *Foreign-Born Americans and the War* (New York: American Committee for Protection of Foreign Born, 1943), p. 19; *Proceedings of the Sixth Constitutional Convention of the Congress of Industrial Organizations*, 1–5 November 1943, Philadelphia, PA, p. 195.

44. Text of Bridges speech available in AFL Papers, Box 19 "Russia"; *Proceedings of the Fourteenth Biennial Convention of the Amalgamated Clothing Workers of America*, 15–19 May 1944, in Chicago, Illinois, pp. 17, 155.

45. *Report of the Executive Council of the American Federation of Labor to the Sixty-fourth AFL Convention*, 20 November 1944, New Orleans, LA, pp. 177–78; Dan Tobin, "Tobin Looks at Russian Labor," *The International Teamster*, February 1944, p. 4.

46. *American Federation of Labor Weekly News Service,* 28 December 1942; "AFL
    Forum Adopts Sweeping Post-War Program," *Railway Carmen's Journal,* June
    1944, p. 127; Text of Woll's speech "Labor in the Post War World," found in
    AFL Papers, Box 30 "Post War Planning Committee"; *New York Times,* 13 April
    1944; Raphael Abramovitch, "The Strategy of European Labor," *International
    Postwar Problems,* June 1944, p. 304; Oscar Jaszi, "Labor's Stake in the Postwar
    World," *International Postwar Problems,* September 1944, p. 497.
47. *The Communist,* December 1943, p. 1161; James Carey interview, Columbia Oral
    History Project, p. 260.
48. Minutes of 11 April 1945, meeting of the AFL International Labor Relations
    Committee, found in AFL Papers, Box I8 "International Labor Relations";
    Meany quoted in Arch Puddington, "Business, Labor, and the Anti-Communist
    Struggle," *National Review,* 27 January 1984, p. 35.
49. Goulden, p. 126.

6

The Right-Wing Press, Uncensored

It is to America's credit that the freedom of its press has for the most part been honored,* even in time of war. Except for necessary military censorship and the prohibition of blatantly seditious publications from the U.S. mail, during World War II America's newspapers maintained all their customary prerogatives to criticize the commander-in-chief and his domestic and foreign policies. Many papers continued to exercise these rights yet refused to reproach the chief executive to the point where national unity might be jeopardized. But FDR's most virulent press critics—the McCormick–Patterson and Hearst newspaper chains, and syndicated columnists Westbrook Pegler and George Sokolsky—practiced no such self-restraint.[1] They continued to assault the president without quarter, especially with respect to his policies regarding communism and the Soviet Union.

These right-wing newspapers and commentators** maintained that the Roosevelt administration was using the crisis to acquire dictatorial control over citizens at home, even as American forces were struggling against dictatorships abroad. FDR's press enemies also claimed that the still-dangerous Communist party was supporting the president's efforts, partly because his totalitarian ideas were similar to its own, and partly because this avenue seemed the Communists' only route to real power. Of course, these conservative journalists opposed the president's "Communist-supported" bid for a fourth term, which they regarded as the most audacious assault yet on American democracy.

---

*There have been notable exceptions, particularly during the Civil War, and during World War I, when Socialist publications were unlawfully censored and repressed.
***Right wing* is an inherently inexact and controversial term. Used here, the expression refers to the rabid and inflexibly anti-Communist, anti-New Deal opinions that were a hallmark of the newspapers and commentators we shall discuss in this chapter. They were not anti-Semitic, however—unlike many others who are routinely labeled *right wing*. I use the term throughout the chapter to distinguish my subjects from the hundreds of Republican-conservative newspapers which opposed FDR but did not regard him as a communist, a would-be dictator, or an enemy of America.

Given their views on FDR's relationship with domestic communism, the right-wing press suspected that Roosevelt's war policies were being unduly influenced by the needs and demands of Joseph Stalin's evil regime. This explained his decision to concentrate on the European theater first, even though it was the Japanese who had forced America into the war. Roosevelt's press critics also predicted he would betray his own Atlantic Charter by sacrificing Eastern Europe to international communism. This would subvert the very ideals for which the war supposedly was being fought, with grave consequences for the long-term survival of U.S. democracy. These were serious, divisive charges, repeated incessantly by an important segment of the American press.*

The potential ability of these commentators to sway public opinion and hurt the president was considerable. The McCormick–Patterson news chain boasted a huge readership: the *New York Daily News'* circulation of 2 million was the largest in the country, the *Chicago Tribune* had the second-largest with about 1 million, and the *Washington Times-Herald* enjoyed the largest circulation in the nation's capital. Both Pegler and Sokolsky were widely syndicated. The Hearst empire, which included the *San Francisco Examiner, New York Journal-American,* and organs in other major cities, reached about 8 million readers. These figures explain the ferocity with which the administration, its left-liberal and progressive supporters, and the Communists themselves attempted to discredit these newspapers, usually with the charge that they were pro-Nazi, and seeking to undermine morale and national unity through their attacks on both the commander-in-chief and America's most important ally.

Critics of these anti-Communist editorialists frequently condemned them "en masse," implying that they were engaged in a conspiracy against the Allied cause. This was clearly not the case.** What *would* be accurate to say is that most of Hearst's opinions could as easily have appeared in one of Pegler's columns or on the editorial pages of the McCormick–Patterson trio of papers.

---

*Of course, anti-Communist/anti-Soviet commentary, of one degree or another, did not disappear from all other newspapers and magazines during the war. The Scripps-Howard papers were anti-Communist, and the *Wall Street Journal* remained generally hostile to the U.S.S.R. The *New York Times* occasionally irritated the Communist party with its editorials. *Reader's Digest* did not exclude anti-Soviet material from its wartime issues. Even *Life* magazine, which gushed over the Russians in March 1943, later published a defiantly anti-Soviet piece by former Ambassador William C. Bullitt (see "The World From Rome," *Life*, 4 September 1944, pp. 94–96). However, none of these publications matched the intensity or sheer volume that marked the right-wing press' attention to anti-Communist/anti-Soviet issues.

**This is not to say there was *no* professional interrelationship among some of these figures. Pegler's and Sokolsky's columns ran for a time in the Hearst papers, and Eleanor Patterson routinely printed her brother Joe Patterson's *Daily News* editorials in her *Times-Herald*.

Differences in tone, style, and emphasis aside, these right-wing commentators articulated generally similar views that were feverishly anti-Roosevelt, anti-Communist, and anti-Soviet. Clearly, such arguments were in the minority at this time. Nevertheless they are historically significant, for they rapidly emerged as the core issues in the ensuing Cold War and McCarthy crises.

Throughout the war, FDR's most implacable press antagonists contended that the struggle to preserve freedom could be lost on the home front, unless Americans were alerted to what its own government was doing in the name of maintaining that freedom. The *Chicago Tribune,* Roosevelt's long-time Midwestern nemesis, said the administration was encroaching upon "every phase" of citizens' lives, in "the same evil pattern" as "communism, or fascism, or Nazism, or New Dealism." Linking Roosevelt's policies to these totalitarian ideologies also remained a staple of Hearst's commentaries: "the New Dealers," growled the *Journal-American,* "are threatening the very war morale of millions of Americans by their Commufascist decrees." It did not matter that most of these "decrees"—rationing, high taxation, bureaucratic planning, and the "communistic device" of wage and salary controls—were necessary aspects of modern war. Hardliners like Hearst and McCormick suspected that the New Dealers were planning to use the crisis as an excuse to nationalize industries and erect an ever-larger, permanently more intrusive federal government. FDR's long-standing goal of supplanting free enterprise with a classless, collectivist state was nearing completion. "The American war economy," lamented the *Tribune,* "is in essential outline that socialized dream world that the heavy thinkers in the New Deal have envisioned as the inevitable outcome of the processes set in train in 1933." According to the *Tribune,* the "leftists in the New Deal" were "borrowing Stalin's laws" and plotting to use the inevitable "postwar confusion in employment, finance and production" as an excuse to seize even greater power. Only by exposing this scheme could American democracy be saved. Otherwise, as Joe Patterson of the *Daily News* warned, America would continue "moving toward a total-itarian form of government, in a war which we say we are fighting to overthrow totalitarianism."[2]

Another frustrating irony to conservative newsmen was the credibility and patriotic cover the Communists derived from basking in the Red Army's glory. The right-wing press was certain this was a self-serving sham. The Commu-nist party remained committed, as the *Tribune* put it, "to destroy[ing] the kind of government that Americans want." As early as January 1942 the *Tribune* warned that "the Communists are no less dangerous to America today than they were two months ago or two years ago." The *Examiner* agreed, saying that communism's basic challenge to the American way of life could not be denied or ignored, merely because of the present "shotgun alliance." This was why Westbrook Pegler remained committed to "proving up the practical identity of Hitlerism and Stalinism." The *Journal-American* went even further: Nazism was less dangerous domestically, for it arrived "later on the scene" and thus lacked "the prepared ground in which communism has incubated and grown."[3]

As had been their custom before the war, right-wing newspapers and commentators exaggerated the strength and influence of the American Communist party. For example the Hearst press blamed juvenile delinquency, a matter of growing concern in the 1940s, on the "ideological poisons" of Communist teachers. (The *Journal-American* and *Daily News* strongly endorsed State Senator Frederic Coudert's reelection because of his role in investigating Communist activities in New York's schools and universities.) Similarly, the *Tribune* provided no evidence for its charge that Communists were responsible for the race riots that erupted in 1943 in Detroit. Nor was there much validity to the *Journal-American*'s contention that party propagandists were still spattering patriotic American industrialists with "abuse and venom." Actually, big business' relations with Communist-directed unions were never more cordial than during World War II. Even more far-fetched were the *Tribune*'s claims that Communist officials in various CIO unions were encouraging workers to gamble and malinger while on the job. Sabotage, too, supposedly remained a tactic of Communist-run unions—and of course the administration condoned this criminality because it "would rather lose the war than alienate its Communist supporters." At this time such charges made no sense, because the Communists strove harder than anyone to maximize war-goods production and the availability of lend lease supplies.[4]

Other criticisms leveled by the anticommunist press were more on target. The party's frequent gyrations on important policies, including their support for the Nazi–Soviet Pact of 1939, were not forgotten by the hardliners. Nor did these individuals pretend—as did so many during the war—that communism's fundamental hostility to organized religion or the capitalist system had substantively changed. Such reminders were intended to embarrass the Communists, to confront them with their hypocrisy, and to brand them as the real long-range threat to national unity. "Now the American Communists say American democracy and American industry are wonderful," conceded the *Tribune;* yet "as soon as the war is over, if not before, the agitators will be back at the old stand, seeking once more to destroy both." The slightest word from Moscow would remobilize the movement in America or anywhere else, despite the formal dissolution of the Comintern in May 1943—an initiative that impressed the *Examiner* as another worthless Soviet pledge that further proved Stalin's contempt for his allies' "lack of intelligence in world politics." George Sokolsky believed that the Communists still would "propagate Russian interests and attitudes," if only by "habit and instinct." Similarly, when Communist party members changed their group's name to Communist Political Association, the *Times-Herald* scoffed that this was the only change contemplated. Whatever its name, the organization "still hopes to bring the

Communist form of totalitarianism to this country, [and] is still boring away inside American institutions."[5]

Nothing disturbed anti-Communist conservatives more than what West-brook Pegler described as the "important aid and comfort" the Communist movement supposedly was receiving "from the New Deal administration." As proof that American Communists had influential friends in the government, conservative journalists frequently cited the commutation of Earl Browder's prison term and the repeated delays in Harry Bridges's deportation proceedings. Even worse, the Communists themselves had infiltrated the federal government's executive branch; in February 1942 the *Times-Herald* charged that "every other week or so" a "Communist, near-Communist or recently retired Communist gets a well-paid Government job." The *Examiner* estimated that "several thousand" people composed this "strong revolutionary machine" in Washington. Because of their efforts, the country was "traveling . . . at considerable speed" toward a Soviet–style dictatorship. The right-wing press devoted considerable news and editorial space to alleged Communist activities in the Office of War Information, Federal Communications Commission, and Office of Price administration. This last agency had to endure a Hearst campaign against its administrator, John Kenneth Galbraith, and his grade labeling program, which Hearst regarded as a "Communistic device . . . to undermine public confidence in American industry and business."[6]

Of course, the greatest villain was the president himself. With his vast powers, FDR had apparently done far more than Earl Browder ever had for the Communist movement. As the *Tribune* noted, "It was only when Roosevelt opened the door to them and put them in positions of power in his administration" that they grew into "a force to be reckoned with in American politics." The Roosevelt–Communist relationship now was "of the utmost intimacy," for "he gives them jobs in the government not only because he either likes them and their ideas but also in return for political support received and . . . other favors to come." The Hearst press acknowledged that FDR was too smart to admit being a Communist, even as he "secures Communist support," accepts "Communist money," and relies upon "Communist methods" to remain in power atop an administration rife with Communists. It was small wonder the Reds regarded him as "our friend."[7]

Harsh as they were, at least these characterizations gave FDR some backhanded credit for having enough sense to demand compensation for his generosity. At other times the Right portrayed him as a dupe of the radicals. Said Paul Mallon of the *Journal-American:* "Like ants the Commies have swarmed over the democratic bandwagon and are now trying to drive it . . . telling Mr. Roosevelt what he should do here and internationally." The *Examiner* added that the Communists' latest line had been "swallowed hook, line and sinker" by a gullible administration. This conflicted somewhat with the notion that FDR and the Communists were pursuing the same evil goals, but it is unlikely the accusers were much troubled by the inconsistency. They regarded both the president and the Communist party as utterly ruthless totalitarianists, with ambitions equally inimical to the American way of life. For now at least, they were working together. Should the Communists turn against their current benefactor at some point—the *Tribune* questioned whether the Democrats "have read the little poem about the lady from Niger"—this would be par for the course, as well.[8]

Except for FDR, Vice president Henry Wallace was the administration figure most abused in the conservative press. The *Chicago Tribune* called him an advocate of Communist totalitarianism and one of America's "enemies"; Hearst's ultraconservative columnist Benjamin deCasseres called Wallace an "ever-present danger to our way of life"; and Pegler branded the vice president as one of America's "leading pro-Communists." First Lady Eleanor Roosevelt, Secretary of the Interior Harold Ickes, and Senator Claude Pepper, of Florida, were among the other leading New Dealers subjected to red-baiting attacks. Even if these individuals were not Communists as such—a point by no means conceded by the right-wing press—their sympathetic tolerance for Communists was just as unforgivable. "Anyone," intoned the *Tribune*, "who aids them in advancing their program is a traitor to America." For good measure, the *Tribune*'s Anglophobic Colonel McCormick found room on his lengthy traitors' list for the New York millionaire snobs whose goal was "to return us to the status of a colony of the British crown." Because their first allegiance also was to a foreign power, these Park Avenue "cookie pushers" had joined in a conspiracy with the Communists and New Dealers to destroy their common adversary, the United States of America.[9]

Ironically, one of the right-wing press' greatest heroes belonged to the president's own Democratic party. This was Representative Martin Dies, of Texas, chairman of the House Un-American Activities Committee. He, too, took pride in refusing to curtail his demagogic anti-Communist crusade during the alliance. Dies's sweeping attacks and unflattering "reports" on the administration were always front-page news in the *Tribune,* which lauded his having "found hundreds of Communists on the government payroll." The Hearst press, also a big champion of Dies and his committee, exclaimed that "the Republic is safer and sounder because of their labors." The *Examiner* credited HUAC with giving "the plain, inarticulate people of America" an "education in the tricks and treacheries of subversion." And Sokolsky credited the often-embattled chairman with having "served his country well."[10]

The more-acerbic Pegler correctly described Dies as "uncouth" and "a bit of a bumpkin" but gladly acknowledged that "most of his material has never been refuted." Although many of Dies's critics wondered why he was less successful in exposing Nazis, his press supporters insisted that this merely reflected the much greater magnitude of the Communist danger. In 1942, the *Journal-American* estimated there were "about one thousand revolutionary Reds to be smoked out to every Nazi"; by mid-1944 Hearst's *New York Daily Mirror* put the ratio at "ten thousand subversive Kremlinites, of all litters and breeds, in the U.S.A. to every single Fascist or Nazi." Roosevelt did not seem to object to this imposing Communist presence, which explained his hostility to HUAC's operations.[11]

Believing that Congress alone had sufficient authority to check the administration's pro-Communist policies, conservative commentators regarded the 1942 elections as especially important. They gave all-out editorial support to Republicans and anti-administration Southern Democrats. The *Tribune,* virtually a GOP house organ, was especially supportive of Republican candidates, the more conservative the better. The Hearst press supported anti-New Deal candidates of both parties. As expected, the right-wing press contended that the countervailing efforts of the Union for Democratic Action and other liberal groups were somehow immoral or subversive of the democratic process. According to the *Tribune,* their "aim was to kill the free republic and replace it with a tyranny of blood." Translated into specifics, they were trying to defeat Martin Dies and other committed opponents of the New Deal. Should the "smear brigade" succeed in their attempted "purge," the independence of the legislative branch would be destroyed and all power would belong to the president and his Communist allies.[12]

When the key primary contests went against the administration, a pleased Sokolsky observed that "the tide flows in a manner wondrous to behold." Even so, on election day the *Daily News* worried that the Communists might "maintain their present power in Washington," and this "may indeed be the last free and undilutedly democratic election in this country." Sokolsky was the better prognosticator. Republicans scored impressive gains, and very few of the candidates targeted by proadministration activists were defeated. A jubilant *New York Journal-American* bragged that this "series of public rebukes" to the UDA and other left-wing "vendettists" had been "a demonstration of real 'democratic action' in America." This Republican rout, exulted a front-page *Tribune* editorial, "was a victory of religion over atheism, of morality and conscience over licentiousness, of patriotism over foreign interference and colonialism." The country had survived. Yet, president Roosevelt remained in the White House, dispensing favors, jobs, and political power to the Communists. Putting a stop to that would have to wait until 1944.[13]

During this campaign, the president's supporters tried to portray him as the "indispensable man," whose great leadership was desperately needed if America were to triumph over the Axis, then establish a postwar world of international cooperation and peace. The right-wing press regarded it as "indispensable" that voters deny him a fourth term. To the *Times-Herald* the choice would be "the most important one which this country has made since it became one country." Speaking on behalf of all three McCormick–Patterson papers, the *Times-Herald* affirmed that "a fourth term for president Roosevelt would mean the end of the Republic." The choice, echoed the *Daily News,* was between "our democratic form of government" or "monarchy" and "one-man rule." The Hearst press framed the election in the same apocalyptic way: FDR was looking toward a "life tenure"; the middle class was "in the process of elimination from American life"; Supreme Court Justices would be wearing "red robes"; and the New Deal's "tyrannical lawlessness" would continue unabated unless the voters put a new leader in the White House.[14]

Early on, the right-wing press expressed hope that Roosevelt might not stand for a fourth term, after all. In August 1942, the *Tribune* predicted that a Southerner would be the Democratic nominee. Hopefully, the right-wing press raised the delicate age and health issue well before the campaign season.* However, once it became clear that FDR intended to keep his job, conservatives had to pin their hopes exclusively on the GOP. Although the *Chicago Tribune* would have supported almost any Republican against Roosevelt, the paper much preferred a true-blue conservative like General Douglas Mac-Arthur or Ohio's Governor John Bricker. Wendell Wilkie was too much "the New Deal's stooge," too friendly to the U.S.S.R., and too internationalist in outlook to receive any editorial support from the bastion of Midwestern isolationism. The other McCormick–Patterson papers expressed less personal animosity to Wilkie but agreed with their sister paper that a Roosevelt–Wilkie contest would not provide a clear choice to the American people.[15]

When New York's Governor Thomas Dewey captured the GOP nomination, the *Times-Herald* credited the party's "political sagacity" in having chosen "their best proved New York vote-getter." The *Tribune* feared that Dewey would cut all ties with America's isolationist tradition, but once he obtained the nomination, the paper accepted him as a preferable alternative to the incumbent. Ironically, the Hearst press, less closely identified to the Republican party, was far more enthusiastic about its 1944 standard-bearer. In contrast to "the candidate of communism," Dewey was "an able and worthy American candidate," who along with his running mate Bricker stood for a program that "can be summed up in two words—Fundamental Americanism." Said the *Examiner:* "That they are not liked by Red Russia, the London dailies, by General De Gaulle, by New Deal Reds and other enemies of our American institutions ought to insure their election." Perhaps so, but what the *Tribune* referred to as the "covenant" between FDR and the Communists[16] could not be underestimated by right-thinking Americans.

---

*Eventually the *Tribune* would bluntly say that "a vote for Roosevelt is very likely to be a vote for Truman for president." (*Tribune,* 28 October 1944.)

In fairness, there was some basis to the charge of a link between FDR's fourth-term drive and the Communists. They had endorsed him and were working hard for his reelection, the more so since Stalin made no secret of his preference for FDR over Dewey. But the *Journal-American,* for one, was wrong to characterize Roosevelt as "agreeable to being the Communistic candidate," as this unfairly implied that he was in philosophical harmony with the Communist party. When an embarrassed FDR formally disavowed the Communists' support, Hearst's *Milwaukee Sentinel* simply accused him of uttering "weasel words" to trick the patriotic majority. Careful listeners, the paper said, could still hear the "Communist 'party line' propaganda" in his speeches.[17]

Equally unfair was the contention that the Communists were the major power brokers in this election and that FDR had to appease them if he wanted to keep his job. Yet, according to the *Tribune,* this explained why the president gave scant attention to the Pacific theater and appeased Stalin at every diplomatic turn. No wonder the *Times-Herald* found it "easy to see why the Communists and fellow travelers are so hot in their support of Roosevelt." No other American had done so much for the Communist cause.[18]

Evidence to the contrary, such as FDR's refusal to support his "Communist" vice president for another term, was easily explained. The *Examiner* said Wallace was an embarrassment to Roosevelt and that FDR's presence on the ticket was enough to ensure the Communists' support. The *Tribune* was even more cynical: "Mr. Wallace was too much of everything Mr. Roosevelt intends to forget, for the duration of the campaign, and, if he can, revive later. He feared that his alter ego, an outspoken prophet, would cost him votes."[19]

Interestingly, Wallace's removal from the ticket prompted the ever-suspicious *Tribune* to speculate that even those master tricksters the Communists might be betrayed by the "Great Deceiver" Roosevelt. More typically, the *Tribune* and the other right-wing organs suggested that the Communists would be the big winners in a fourth term. Not only would they have pleased Stalin, but their prospects for taking over the Democratic party—and eventually the country itself—would be enhanced, especially if the *Times-Herald*'s prediction that the war and the New Deal would unleash "confusion and chaos" came true. Communists thrived amidst such conditions. But first, FDR had to be reelected.[20]

To that end, Communists participated in the CIO's Political Action Committee, an organization set up to reelect Roosevelt, defeat anti-New Deal Democrats and Republicans, and strengthen organized labor's electoral clout in general. Allowing known Communists into the organization was the decision of PAC president Sidney Hillman, who admired their energy and dedication to causes in which they believed. But Hillman's decision also allowed the opposition to focus their traditional red-baiting rhetoric on this group. Dewey raised the issue repeatedly while on the stump, but the right-wing press conducted an even more vicious and sustained campaign against the PAC.

The *Tribune* was typically extreme, arguing that PAC—"stiffened by the fanaticism of the Communists"—had made FDR "Sidney's political prisoner." The Communists, evil but not stupid, knew that a reelected FDR would "continue to put the government of the United States at their service, at home and abroad." As a result, the poor "Democratic donkey, under whip and spur, is meekly taking the road to communism and atheism." John O'Donnell, political columnist for the *Daily News,* observed that "old-line Democratic leaders" deeply resented having to "clear everything with Sidney." The *News,* applauding Dewey's effort to keep the "searchlight" on the dangerous Hillman, predicted that the Communist party's chances of taking over the Democratic party would be "greatly brightened" during a fourth term.[21]

Others in the right-wing press advanced similarly florid arguments. To the Hearst press, PAC had "made a Communistic rubber stamp out of the Democratic National Convention"; Roosevelt "knows perfectly well that his campaign is in Communist hands"; PAC was "not above having prison gates opened and immigration barriers lowered" if Roosevelt needed the votes; and "The Hillman–CIO–PAC–Communist alliance" also was using its "immense 'slush fund' and bulldozing methods" to "elect the next Congress." In a lighter vein, Hearst offered cash prizes to readers who mailed in clever limericks that ended with the infamous "clear-everything-with-Sidney" line. George Sokolsky found nothing humorous about PAC, which he called a sinister power play by the Communists, and "the foreruner of revolution." Pegler, whose hatred for organized labor was extreme even by arch-conservative standards, took a somewhat different tack. He regarded the PAC, or "Hillman front," as Roosevelt's "own Communist wing" of the CIO. This suggested that FDR's relationship with the Communists might not be as one-sided as some of his enemies seemed to believe. After all, in an immediate sense, it was his personal and political interests that would be served by a successful fourth-term campaign.[22]

Throughout, the Roosevelt haters clung to the prospect that he might yet be denied that ultimate prize. In July, Sokolsky pinned his faith on the "Southern Democrats and northern Republicans" who would unite in opposing "a Socialist United States." In mid-September, the *Journal-American* hailed "the intention and determination to wash out the New Deal and its Communist Political Action Committee" wherever people still had "the instrument of free choice." *News* columnist John O'Donnell wrote on 3 October that "Dewey should be the betting favorite for November." The *Tribune,* putting hope before reason, predicted the GOP would capture the House, underestimated the breadth of the New Deal coalition, and overestimated any report of a rupture within the Democratic ranks. As the election neared, the *Tribune* found 30 of the 48 states too close to call, meaning that three critical states—

New York, Pennsylvania, and Massachusetts—would determine the outcome. On voting day the great daily stopped arguing and simply pleaded with its readers: "If you love your country, if you value your rights as an American citizen, if you cherish your religion, whatever it may be, help to get other Republican voters to the polls."[23]

Once again, what followed was a shocking comeupance for the right-wing press. No one hurt more than Colonel McCormick of the *Tribune*. If only for that reason, one must credit McCormick for swallowing at least some of his great bitterness. Having written for 12 years that the country was about to fall into dictatorship and having predicted for months that the Communists were about to seize control of said dictatorship, the Colonel obviously had to insist that "great perils in our path" remained ahead. Yet, "no course of folly" (by which he meant the voters' verdict) was capable of destroying this blessed nation "within two years, or four. It is too rich, too strong, too glorious for that. It will live."[24]

Such optimistic commentary was even rarer when the right-wing press turned to FDR's management of wartime foreign policy. Editorials on this subject had a recurrent theme: Unlike the other Allied leaders—Stalin especially—Roosevelt did not make decisions based solely on national needs and self-interest. The most immediate example of this concerned the basic choice of which enemy, Germany or Japan, to concentrate upon first. FDR decided upon Germany, a decision that as we have seen, was roundly criticized in conservative political circles. The right-wing press believed even more fervently that a "Japan-first" policy was correct for America—the Communists be damned. "It is this Asiatic war," Sokolsky said, "that we dare not lose."[25] But lose it we might, unless America's war planners abandoned the strategy that appeased Stalin and adopted the one it said put the interests of America first.

Ever belligerent, the *Tribune* moved into the forefront of the "Japan-first" cause in a deliberate effort to counteract "the official propaganda . . . seeking to concentrate all interest on the European war." Like other isolationists, Colonel McCormick had a particular resentment against the "insane clique of Japanese militarists" who had forced the United States into the war. McCormick's opposition to an early second front was unequivocal, and he accused its advocates of "speaking not as Americans but as Russians." As a constant reminder that the "real war" was in the Pacific, McCormick inserted the battle cry "We're Going Back to Bataan" just below the *Tribune*'s editorial masthead. To hasten that glorious event, General Douglas MacArthur—already the conservatives' favorite war hero—should be "given a free hand to run the war." According to the *Tribune*, the Pacific war qualified as a second front against the Axis, because it prevented Japan from invading the U.S.S.R. More reasonably, Colonel McCormick noted that the shrillest "second fronters" (he meant the Communists) were implicitly criticizing the administration's handling of the war, so why was this not as inimical to national unity as when conservatives attacked the president?[26]

Interestingly, Joe and "Cissy" Patterson, whose wartime editorials almost never disagreed with those of their uncle, were initially supportive of an early second front. However, this did not mean that America should slacken its efforts to "Hold Hawaii" and support MacArthur as much as possible. What the *News* and *Times-Herald* wanted was for the British to provide most of the invasion manpower in Europe. America could lend a few men and the brilliance of General MacArthur. Time was of the essence; on 16 July 1942, the *Times-Herald* said if the Allies "pass up this chance . . . we may pass up our chances of winning the war." The next day's editorial accused the British of stalling so that Americans would do the job, even if the delay handed "victory in Europe, Africa, and the Middle East to Hitler." In other words, America was being used by a selfish ally. No doubt this helped the Pattersons realize their uncle Colonel McCormick had been right on this issue all along. In August, the *News* decided that invasion plans should be determined by "military men," not "mass meetings, letters to your Congressman or editorials in newspapers." (Sokolsky agreed that "the technicians" should set the invasion table—especially since the U.S.S.R. "faces such dire possibilities"!) But the *News* soon adopted an even tougher line, cautioning against "a premature second front adventure" just to satisfy "the urgings of Stalin." By early 1943, the *Times-Herald* was so concerned that the government would concentrate exclusively on the Atlantic war that it proposed moving the nation's capital to the Midwest, "maybe on one of the many beautiful Minnesota or Wisconsin lakes."[27]

For once, not even Hearst suggested something this extreme, but his newspapers clearly supported the "Japan-first" strategy for winning the war. Hearst's 8 December 1941, editorial called for total victory against Japan, whereupon a vindicated America could turn to Europe to "straighten things out there." When the second-front demands surfaced, the *Examiner* was unsympathetic; it was not something for "Browder to decide" because he favored it exclusively as an "aid to Russia." Not surprisingly, this was exactly how Pegler felt; why should Americans listen to those "who would have had us helpless now if they could have had their way"? By mid-1943 the Hearst press was hinting that unless the United States moved against Japan in earnest the task might become impossible; exclaimed an impatient Examiner editorial: "The Time to Beat Japan Is Now!" Revelations in 1944 about Japanese atrocities committed against prisoners of war injected new vigor into Hearst's demands for a primary assault against Japan. "The people we should really get mad at," the *Examiner* argued, "are our own governmental authorities who have restricted the flow of men and supplies to the Pacific war to a dribble."[28]

Hearst also found it instructive that Japan's mistreatment of American prisoners had not prompted even "a whisper from Moscow." The Russians had done nothing to assist American captives who were suffering "torture, starvation and death" at the hands of the Japanese, yet the U.S.S.R. did conclude a fishing-rights agreement with Japan that was, according to Hearst, "vital" to Japan's ability to remain in the war. This deal triggered an even sharper editorial comment from the *Tribune,* which said that "for practical purposes" it constituted an "alliance against the United States," and was an example of "international double dealing" that was "more monstrous" than any in history. Even as America was acting as "Russia's benefactor," the Soviets "are found dealing on terms of friendship with our most menacing enemy." The possiblity even remained that the U.S.S.R. would "ultimately join up with the Japanese"—after all, what Hearst called "the Oriental mind" was common to both countries.[29]

Soviet duplicity was one thing, but how was the administration responding to Stalin's challenge? Badly, concluded the right-wing press. For one thing, Chiang Kai-shek's fragile regime was being menaced by Communist insurgents who, Sokolsky said, dutifully followed "the policy of Soviet Russia." As the *Tribune* noted, the U.S.S.R.'s designs on its southern neighbor were "of long standing," and not to be taken lightly. Unfortunately, "Present Allied strategy and Russian treachery doom China," Hearst warned. His *Examiner* demanded to know why "our American statesmen" were not "pressing our present and obvious" advantages—especially lend lease—while negotitating with the Soviets. The *Daily News* advised Roosevelt to seek "some Russian cooperation" as payment for the "husky favors received from us"; Stalin needed to be informed "in friendly but firm tones" that "Lend-Lease ought to work both ways." Calling for a "quid pro quo" from "our one-way ally," the *Times-Herald* said that "serious requests" should be "repeated until some satisfactory answer is had." But the paper doubted such demands would be forthcoming because "this administration has so many Russia-lovers near its top that pleas for some Russian return of our aid are howled down."[30]

Specifically, the right-wing press demanded exactly what some conservative politicians were calling upon the Russians to provide: access to air bases on Soviet territory, from which American fliers could more easily bomb Japan. The *Journal-American* noted that "Soviet Russia . . . receives nothing but benefits from us" and should be willing "to extend the minimum collateral benefit which will enable us to accelerate and win our war." Some "Siberian bases" qualified as that minimum. Failing to obtain these bases, the *Tribune* calculated, could mean the death "of a million American soldiers." The *Times-Herald* suggested hopefully in a February 1943 editorial that Washington officials would "press this proposition on Russia, and press it now." Given the high stakes, FDR simply had to take a tougher diplomatic line against the U.S.S.R.'s insistence upon neutrality in the Pacific war. But the *Tribune* predicted that would not happen "unless public opinion demands it" because "Mr. Roosevelt and his entourage are not interested in America's welfare."[31]

The right-wing press was just as critical of FDR's management of the Soviet Union with respect to the European conflict. Here, the basic complaint was that the president would permit the U.S.S.R. to tyrannize postwar Europe, negating the whole basis for American involvement in the war. The president's press critics accused him of deceiving the American people about Europe's future, which was true, and of gross naivete in his diplomacy with Stalin, which was probably true. At times, the right-wing press even implied that FDR *wanted* the Soviets to force others to live under communism, perhaps in some sort of "one-world" dictatorship, just as he was doing in America with his New Deal. The *Times-Herald* said this definitely was a "Roosevelt war aim"; and such events as the World Food Conference, the Bretton Woods economic summit, and the planning for a United Nations exacerbated conservative paranoia that America would be reduced to "an atom in an international axis."[32] Such charges were typical of the right-wing press' general anti-Communist fixation. Yet they also stemmed from legitimate frustration over the inevitable expansion of Soviet influence after the war. Because these committed Soviet haters could not come to terms with their own forebodings, they required a scapegoat, someone to blame for what they regarded as an impending catastrophe. That Roosevelt would be their man was probably inevitable, as well.

One weapon used against the president—the Atlantic Charter—was of his own making, with help from coauthor Winston Churchill. As a proclamation of the high-minded values, such as the right of self-determination, for which the Allies supposedly were fighting, the charter was excellent propaganda. Signed by the two leaders shortly before America's entry into the war, the charter lent moral authority to FDR's decision to aid the British against Germany. As a blueprint of specific war aims, however, the Atlantic Charter was badly out of step with reality, particularly with the Soviet Union in the Allied camp. As such, FDR's domestic adversaries made excellent use of the document in their various attacks on Roosevelt. The *Times-Herald* disliked FDR's charter because under its terms "we are to get nothing material out of this war for ourselves." The *Examiner* darkly noted that "free enterprise" had not been guaranteed in the charter; and the *Journal-American* expressed concern that the lordly Roosevelt might think his "so-called Atlantic Charter is an official and binding instrument, which, of course, it is not." The *Tribune* understood the charter's implications a bit more clearly. It noted that FDR might find the charter "too hot to sit on" because Stalin's undisguised intentions to absorb the Baltic States already made "hash" of the president's promises. In truth, his charter was "a hoax," a cynical promise that Churchill, at least, knew would not be honored. He and Stalin were not interested in

Roosevelt's alleged war aims; thus, thanks to the president the American people had been made the "dupes" in the Allied cause.[33]

Although the right-wing press vacillated between condemning Roosevelt for ruthless cunning in one editorial, and blind stupidity in the next, Stalin was a figure about whom they had no doubts. He was still the blood-drenched Bolshevik whose pact with Adolf Hitler had helped launch the war. Now, thanks to Hitler's doublecross, "Pal Joey," as the News cynically called him during the war, was on America's side. Still, he could be expected to pretend to have reformed, to break solemn promises, and to disregard American interests whenever it suited his needs. The right-wing press frequently suggested the possibility that Stalin might conclude another agreement—a "separate peace"—with Germany. After Stalin refused to permit U.S. pilots on a bombing mission in Rumania to use nearby Soviet airfields, the *Journal-American* said he had made the operation more dangerous and was therefore partly responsible for the American casualties. Stalin was cruel but hardly stupid; the *Examiner* credited him with understanding perfectly that after the war his country and America "shall remain far apart—for economic and political reasons." Indeed, the Hearst papers accused him of planning "to install in every country in Europe a Red Regime, which means more torture-chambers, concentration camps, massacres, atheism and a continuous reign of terror." Yet he demanded, the *Tribune* said, "complete compliance of his allies with Russian foreign policy." As the *Daily News* grudgingly admitted, Stalin was a "Russia Firster" in every respect.[34]

This was in sharp contrast to the president of the United States, whose diplomacy consisted of dispensing billions of dollars of lend lease to the U.S.S.R., in return for nothing—not even, the *Times-Herald* said, "Russian lip service." The *Journal-American* suggested that FDR had established "a most intimate relationship" with Stalin's dictatorship and that "Uncle Sam" had been made over into "Uncle Patsy." The *Tribune* accused the president of sending "mash notes" to Stalin, and of standing "under the Kremlin balcony with a mandolin since 1933." In other words, FDR was not merely subservient to the Russian dictator, he admired Stalin and sought out opportunities to serve the Soviet cause.[35]

The right-wing press found this especially alarming at a time when it believed the Soviets were positioning themselves to play a domineering role in postwar European affairs. Midway through the war, the *Times-Herald* predicted that Stalin would attempt to "accomplish what Hitler tried to do—dominate all Europe." The Hearst press reported that bolshevism might finally "crash through" the "gate of western civilization," repainting the "map of Europe" an indelible "Communist red." Indeed, Hearst named virtually every country in Europe as a likely target for a Communist takeover. His papers incorrectly insisted that General Charles De Gaulle was "Stalin's man" and would assist in a Communist takeover of France. The threat was everywhere:

Communists might triumph in Spain, they were resorting to "violent" actions in Greece, Czechoslovakia was imperiled, and Soviet diplomacists were about "to pick up the fruit" in war-ravaged Italy. One Hearst columnist even hinted that the U.S. government might "help Russia communize Switzerland." Germany, too, would be communized, if Stalin so desired. The *Tribune* conceded that such a development "would be the shock of all shockers," yet who would be able to prevent it? Finland, now formally allied with Nazi Germany against the U.S.S.R., retained the sympathy of the right-wing press. This tiny nation, lamented the *Daily Mirror*, was caught "between two totalitarian nation-eaters." After a Finnish diplomat was expelled from the United States, the *Times-Herald* called it "the Roosevelt Administration's latest move to oblige Russia." Obviously Finland's sovereignty was in grave jeopardy, and perhaps the rest of Scandinavia would be next. The *Examiner* warned that "the great Bear has an outstretched paw on Finland and gazes— his jaws adrip—on Sweden and Norway." As for the Balkans, the *Tribune* said the U.S.S.R. would be able "to bear down on the Romanians and Bulgars"; and a front-page, October 1944 *Examiner* editorial condemned those Americans trying to ensure that "Yugoslavia would be thrown to the Communist wolves." And throughout the war, the right-wing press recalled the "terror," the "infamy," and desperate "fight for freedom" in the Baltic States.[36]

Poland, of course, was a special case. The war in Europe started because of Germany's invasion of Poland, so what would the implications be if the Soviets extended their dictatorial control over the Poles immediately after the war, as seemed so probable. It was enough to make the *Daily News* wonder "what our boys are fighting for" in Europe. "The Polish situation is Mr. Roosevelt's baby," the *Tribune* insisted, implying of course that the crisis was entirely Roosevelt's fault. This was the Hearst line, too—the impending betrayal of Poland best revealed FDR's "lack of moral wisdom." Of course, Poland was only one country on the list. After the Teheran conference, Hearst's *New York Mirror* suggested this meeting may have been "a Red Munich," where Stalin was "given the green light to overrun Europe." This was strong rhetoric, but unfortunately Hearst offered no blueprint for designing a workable red light. In contrast, the *News* and *Times-Herald* did offer a plan, but not one offering any hope to Europeans. These papers suggested that FDR adopt a classic "spheres of influence" policy. The United States would control the Americas and dominate the skies with the world's best air force; but the U.S.S.R. would dominate most of the European land mass. "We'd best concede Russia's claims," a *Daily News* editorial suggested in September 1943 because "we must be realistic" and admit the Atlantic Charter "is a pretty misty and dreamy document, anyway." The United States needed to ensure that it always would be "the most powerful nation on this side of the world, even as Russia will be the most powerful on its side." In short, the *News* and *Times-Herald* were themselves willing to sacrifice Eastern

Europe, at least, to Stalin. Yet they continued to criticize FDR for being "neither as potent nor as persuasive at Teheran as he has been" elsewhere, and for dispatching "a lot of roving New Deal gladhanders" to distribute "postwar gifts . . . all over the world."[37]

The *Tribune* was just as hypocritical. Not only did it concede the "physical impossibility" of interfering "in eastern European complications," it added that this "may be our great good luck." Clearly, the *Tribune* still clung to its isolationist heritage; as late as March 1944 it held out hope that America would not have to invade Europe! Although the *Tribune* did claim that Americans had a duty to arrange "honest plebiscites" in postwar Europe, it is hard to imagine how such a policy could have been enforced without accepting the kind of long-term obligation unacceptable to most war-weary Americans, the isolationists in particular. The *Tribune* did not grapple with the inconsistency in its thinking about the European theater. It was much easier, and more satisfying, to attack the president: He was "giving the world a demonstration that it is possible to pay the fiddler without calling the tune"; he was "taken for a ride" at Teheran; and he had "molded his foreign policy so completely to Stalin's wishes." In short, the *Tribune* was telling its readers to hold Roosevelt strictly accountable for the impending crisis in Eastern Europe.[38]

Had the *Tribune* and its ideological brethren not been so blinded by hatred of FDR, they might have better appreciated his dilemma in Eastern Europe. Roosevelt did not want a Communist Europe any more than did his conservative critics, and no one desired a war with the Soviet Union. Unfortunately, at least part of postwar Europe *was* going to be Soviet-dominated, unless U.S. forces were somehow used to prevent it, as many editorials in the right-wing press essentially conceded. The obvious difference between McCormick or Hearst and Roosevelt was responsibility. Editorial writers, through careful selection or omission of facts, can finesse inconsistencies in their daily arguments rather easily. In his own way, FDR tried much the same thing, avoiding the full implications of the situation facing Eastern Europe as best he could. But for him the deception was less easy because as the man on the spot he stood to be blamed when things went awry, even if sensible observers realized they were not his fault. In this instance the critics were only partly sensible because the right-wing press understood more clearly than most that a victorious Stalin would be powerful enough to dominate Eastern Europe whether the U.S. government approved or not. Yet, their attacks against Roosevelt's foreign policy never abated throughout these years of high stakes and great crisis.

Predictably, Yalta was an immediate disillusionment to the right-wing press—though the *Tribune* did not fail to note that the decisions announced at the gathering "prove we were right" all along about FDR. Benjamin deCasseres described the "confab" as "one of the most uproariously tragi-comic failures in history from the standpoint of democracy." In the *Times-*

Herald, columnist George Rothwell Brown predicted that the "proposed partition of Poland . . . would become one of the most provocative causes of war ever invented," and America would become a belligerent in that war, as well. Stalin, conceded the *Times-Herald,* had earned himself a place in Russian history "equal to that of Peter the Great." Pegler said that Moscow, not Washington, was now "the moral and political capital of the world"; Sokolsky declared that "we are now in a new European era—the Era of Stalin" because he had succeeded at Yalta in unifying "Europe under the rule of Moscow." But the most despairing commentary appeared in the *Tribune.* It was bad enough that "the brave new world that was to bring everlasting peace" had been "ushered in with the gasp of death" from "dispossessed" Poland. But far worse was the the the fact that it had been America, the great hope of the democratic cause, which had sent "its president to Yalta to sell a small nation into bondage" to the Soviet Union. It was Munich revisited, with the world treated anew to the spectacle of a victim nation "passing into slavery."[39]

Under any circumstances, Roosevelt's supporters could not have ignored such a sustained and vicious press attack against their great leader; the war simply made their vigorous response all the more imperative. From a coldly political standpoint, the war had handed the proadministration forces a new weapon to use against the right-wing press. Now, their enemies could be accused of hurting the national war effort with their private battle against the commander-in-chief, around whom all patriotic Americans were rallying. By making this argument, opponents of the right-wing commentators obviously hoped to discredit them with their readers. Even if this did not silence conservative arguments altogether, at least it might render the right an ineffective force in the struggle to influence public opinion.

The Communists, now in a proadministration phase and still second to none in their capacity for slanderous vituperation, accused the right-wing press of contributing to the propaganda campaign being waged by the Axis. The charge was explicit. The McCormick–Patterson and Hearst newspapers were the most powerful elements in what the *Daily Worker* called the "copperhead press," a reference to Civil War-era traitors. These papers, the *Worker* claimed, pushed the Axis line "in a more sly and therefore more dangerous way" than overt fascists like William Dudley Pelley. Hearst, "the snake that walks like a man," was just as bad. Said the *Worker:* "Hearst, Hitler's helper," was directing "a monstrous conspiracy against the information and intelligence of millions of unsuspecting citizens who read his paper." His advocacy of the "Japan-first" strategy proved how eager he was to come to "Hitler's aid." As for "Poison Pen" Pegler, he was simply the "American Goebbels." *The Communist,* written for a somewhat more intellectual readership, accused Sokolsky of desiring "a negotiated peace a la Petain, on the ground that it is impossible to defeat Hitler." George Seldes, author of numerous pro-Communist polemics, called Sokolsky an "agent" of "fascist" business interests, Pegler a "mental hoodlum," and Hearst "America's No. 1 enemy." Another prominent Communist, Joseph Starobin, labeled the *Tribune* the "outstanding pro-Hitler paper in the country." And Stalin himself ordered his state-controlled press to call Hearst a "gangster journalist."[40]

Many non-Communist progressives were just as unsparing in attacking the right-wing press. Congressman Elmer Holland, a Pennsylvania Democrat, branded Joe and Cissy Patterson as "America's No. 1 and No. 2 exponents of the Nazi propaganda line." The Union for Democratic Action said the *Tribune* gave "lip service to the national cause" even as it tried "to destroy confidence and morale and impede the winning of the war." The left-leaning Newspaper Guild unsuccessfully tried to have Pegler's material dropped from *Stars and Stripes,* the Army newspaper. According to Freda Kirchwey, of *Nation,* Colonel McCormick wanted "a limited, nationalist war instead of the total war to which this nation is committed." *New Republic* said that the *Daily News* could hardly be more harmful to the war effort if it "were intentionally grinding out quotations for the Axis propaganda." Indeed, all the McCormick–Patterson papers were "doing the best they can to spread . . . doubt and disaffection as to the motives and competence of the leaders of this country and our allies." The *New Republic*—a low-circulation journal whose views were often well to the left of mass opinion—even called for stronger sedition laws for use against the right-wing press.[41]

Several administration figures also denounced the right-wing press. When Archibald MacLeish, the so-called "poet laureate" of the New Deal, called upon the American Society of Newspaper Editors to "police" the "divisionists and defeatists" within its own ranks, everyone knew which papers he had in mind. Interior Secretary Harold Ickes said Hearst and McCormick hated Stalin and FDR so much they "would rather see Hitler win the war, if the alternative is his defeat by a leadership shared by the great Russian and the great American." Ickes also said that Pegler's lengthy list of "Communists" was made up of those "whom he does not like personally or with whose political views he is not in accord." In April 1942, Roosevelt personally got into the act, insisting that the war effort "must not be impeded by a few bogus patriots who use the sacred freedom of the press to echo the sentiments of the propagandists in Tokyo and Berlin." McCormick and the Patterson siblings, FDR said, were afflicted with "unbalanced mentalities."[42]

The *Chicago Tribune,* probably Roosevelt's single-most implacable enemy in the print media, was subjected to more than verbal intimidation. The administration seriously considered prosecuting McCormick for publishing, a few days before the Pearl Harbor attack, details of a secret contingency plan for a U.S. invasion of Europe, should this prove necessary. The declaration of war on December 8 killed this controversy in its cradle, but the administration's rancor remained. McCormick's tax returns and paper supply received unusually close official inspection throughout the war. Moreover, when

Marshall Field, owner of the fledgling *Chicago Sun,* applied for an all-important AP wire-service franchise, Roosevelt asked Attorney General Francis Biddle to assist McCormick's rival with this request. The AP directors soon learned they would be charged in federal court with violating antitrust laws unless Field's application was approved. When this ham-fisted tactic failed to intimidate the directors, the Justice Department followed through on its threat and succeeded in breaking the AP monopoly.[43]

Even more serious was the trouble that arose when the *Tribune* printed a detailed identification of Japanese ships involved in the Battle of Midway. The U.S. Navy feared that Japanese spies, by reading the *Tribune's* account of the battle, would somehow guess that American cryptographers had broken their naval code. With Roosevelt's blessing, the Justice Department moved to indict Tribune officials for violating the nation's espionage laws. But the government could not accuse the paper of having indirectly revealed America's top-secret advantage without directly acknowledging it themselves. As such, no case could be made, and the indictment was dismissed by a Chicago grand jury. This was just as well, because a conviction would have been almost impossible: After all, the story had been cleared by Navy censors, McCormick knew nothing about Navy Intelligence's big achievement, and neither did the Japanese—who proved as much by making no changes in their code.[44]

This campaign to discredit the *Tribune* in particular, and the right-wing press in general, was not especially successful—nor did it deserve to be. First, the right-wing press had no sympathy, latent or otherwise, for Nazi Germany. This scurrilous charge was every bit as inaccurate as the claim that FDR was a Communist. The McCormick–Patterson chain called for all-out victory against all the Axis powers, gave strong backing to war loan drives, and applauded the execution of captured Nazi saboteurs. Sokolsky and Pegler also despised Hitlerism. Hearst's case, however, was a bit more complicated. On a visit to Europe in 1934, he interviewed Adolf Hitler and came away impressed by Germany's economic recovery and by the new chancellor's energy and oratorical ability. But Hearst always condemned Hitler's anti-Semitic policies, and well before the war he had reappraised any positive opinions he briefly may have entertained of the Nazi government.[45] His support for the war against Germany, once declared, was unequivocal.

It also should be remembered that Americans were fighting Hitler to preserve basic human freedoms, including the constitutional right to a free press. Times of adversity are precisely when such values are put to their greatest test. No one of course would dispute the need for military censorship during a war. But restrictions on political and ideological commentary, no matter how disagreeable to an overburdened commander-in-chief, raise doubts about a government's commitment to freedom of speech and press. Beyond question, the right-wing press misused its freedom by grossly exaggerating communism's power in America, then claiming that FDR was part of this vast conspiracy. But such is the price that sometimes must be paid for an unfettered press. Moreover, this most political of presidents hardly was innocent of all published charges leveled against him. For example, he did conceal his abandonment of Poland from the American people, principally to avoid the furor that such an announcement would have caused. The right-wing press suspected as much, wrote about it, and was proved right. Similarly, FDR was more than willing to accept Communist support and services when it served his purposes, such as during the 1944 campaign; but of course, the less discussion of this arrangement the better. In short, he wanted it both ways. The right-wing press loudly demurred, as should always be the case in a vibrant democracy. As Hearst correctly noted during the war, Stalin did not tolerate any press dissent; an unfriendly journalist like Hearst would soon be conducting his "last interview" in the U.S.S.R.[46] In the last analysis, this was *the* fundamental difference between the two allies, between democracy and totalitarianism. That the Communists did not appreciate this at all is understandable; that Roosevlet and other liberals did not better appreciate this during the war is unfortunate.

NOTES

Note: Because the *Deseret News*, the Mormons' official newspaper, carried both the Sokolsky and Pegler columns, for convenience I generally cite this paper when quoting these men. This should not obscure the fact that both columnists appeared in major metropolitan dailies. In New York City, for example, the *World-Telegram* carried Pegler, the *Sun* featured Sokolsky.

1. Among the secondary works consulted for this chapter are John Winkler, *William Randolph Hearst* (New York: Hastings House, 1955); Edmond Coblentz, ed., *William Randolph Hearst, A Portrait in His Own Words* (New York: Simon & Schuster, 1952; W.A. Swanberg, *Citizen Hearst* (New York: Charles Scribner's Sons, 1961); John Tebbel, *The Life and Good Times of William Randolph Hearst* (New York: E.P. Dutton and Company, 1952); Tebbel, *An American Dynasty, the Story of the McCormicks, Medills, and Pattersons* (New York: Doubleday, 1947); Leo McGivena, *The News* (New York: News Syndicate Company, 1969); Alice Hoge, *Cissy Patterson* (New York: Random House, 1966); Walter Trohan, *Political Animals* (Garden City, NY: Doubleday and Company, 1975); Frank Waldrop, *McCormick of Chicago* (Englewood Cliffs, NJ: Prentice-Hall, Inc., 1966); Joseph Gies, *The Colonel of Chicago* (New York: E.P. Dutton, 1979); Lloyd Wendt, *Chicago Tribune, The Rise of a Great American Newspaper* (Chicago: Rand McNally and Company, 1979); Oliver Pilat, *Pegler, Angry Man of the Press* (Boston: Beacon Press, 1963); Warren Cohen, *The Chinese Connection* (New York: Columbia Unversity Press, 1978), pp.71–87.
2. "Candidates and Policies," *Chicago Tribune*, 21 June 1944; "New Deal Communism," *New York Journal-American*, 16 December 1942; "The Maxon Resignation," *San Francisco Examiner*, 21 July 1943; "Planning Gone Haywire," *Chicago Tribune*, 8 August 1942; "Mr. Davies in Moscow and Hollywood," *Chicago Tribune* editorial printed in *San Francisco Examiner*, 27 May

1943; "The Comintern Says Its Dead," *Chicago Tribune*, 25 May 1943; "Toward Totalitarianism," *New York Daily News*, 3 November 1942.

3. "A Basis for Friendship with Russia," *Chicago Tribune*, 13 June 1944; "Jobs and the Party Line," *Chicago Tribune*, 16 January 1942; "Stalin's Worthless Pledges," *San Francisco Examiner*, 27 May 1943; Deseret *News*, 15 November 1943; "Official Facts," *New York Journal-American*, 28 May 1942.

4. "The Trojan Snake," *Milwaukee Sentinel*, 7 September 1944; "Retribution," *New York Journal-American*, 3 September 1942; "Why There is a Labor Shortage," *Chicago Tribune*, 19 November 1943.

5. "These Cockeyed Communists," *Chicago Tribune*, 18 May 1942; "Stalin's Worthless Pledges," *San Francisco Examiner*, 27 May 1943; Deseret *News*, 18 October 1943; "A Red by Any Other Name Would Smell as Sweet," *Washington Times-Herald*, 23 May 1944.

6. Deseret *News*, 23 July 1943; "OFF-OFM-OCD," *Washington Times-Herald*, 23 February 1942; "Who's Who!" *San Francisco Examiner*, 17 April 1942; "Backbone Needed to Crush Red Influences Here," *San Francisco Examiner*, 20 April 1942; "Moving Toward Totalitarianism?" *Washington Times-Herald*, 25 January 1942; "The Maxom Resignation," *San Francisco Examiner*, 21 July 1943.

7. "The Communists and Their Candidate," *Chicago Tribune*, 19 July 1944; "Godless Communism," *Chicago Tribune*, 4 October 1942; "The Communist Vote in New York," *Chicago Tribune*, 30 January 1944; "The Communists and Their Friend," Milwaukee *Sentinel*, 16 October 1944.

8. *New York Journal-American*, 1 June 1942; "Backbone Needed to Crush Red Influences Here," *San Francisco Examiner*, 20 April 1942; "The Plot Revealed," *Chicago Tribune*, 3 November 1942.

9. "The Republic and Its Enemies," *Chicago Tribune*, 14 February 1943; *San Francisco Examiner*, 4 January 1943; Deseret *News*, 15 November 1943; "Jobs and the Party Line," *Chicago Tribune*, 16 January 1942; "Browder's Candor," *Chicago Tribune*, 30 September 1943; "The Queer Bedfellows," *Chicago Tribune*, 30 September 1942.

10. "The Bridges Inquiry," *Chicago Tribune*, 18 January 1942; "Martin Dies," *San Francisco Examiner*, 22 May 1944; Deseret *News*, 12 June 1944.

11. Deseret *News*, 9 May 1942; "The Nazi Net," *New York Journal-American*, 25 August 1942; "A Vicious Smear," *New York Daily Mirror*, 30 June 1944.

12. "Out of the Depths," *Chicago Tribune*, 5 November 1942; "The Smear Defeated," *Chicago Tribune*, 6 August 1942.

13. Deseret *News*, 19 August 1942; "Toward Totalitarianism," *New York Daily News*, 3 November 1942; "Sustained," *New York Journal-American*, 11 August 1942; "Out of the Depths," *Chicago Tribune*, 5 November 1942.

14. "Making It Clear about Sidney," *Chicago Tribune*, 3 November 1944; "Main Issue," *Washington Times-Herald*, 18 April 1943; "Why This Popularity?" *Washington Times-Herald*, 19 May 1944; "The Fourth Term is the Issue," *New York Daily News*, 13 August 1944; "The Big Issue," *New York Daily Mirror*, 22 July 1944; "That America May Live," Milwaukee *Sentinel*, 3 November 1944; "Red Robes on Our Supreme Justices?" *New York Daily Mirror*, 18 September 1944; "A Political Audit," *New York Journal-American*, 19 April 1944.

15. "The Day of Decision," *Chicago Tribune*, 12 January 1944.

16. "Dewey on the First Ballot," *Washington Times-Herald*, 29 June 1944; "An American Flag Bearer," *San Francisco Examiner*, 3 October 1944; "The

Candidates,'' *New York Daily Mirror*, 29 June 1944; *San Francisco Examiner*, 22 July 1944; ''Mr. Busbey is Right,'' *Chicago Tribune*, 1 December 1943.

17. ''The 'Unwilling' Candidate,'' *New York Journal-American*, 5 August 1944; ''Squaring It with Sidney,'' Milwaukee *Sentinel*, 9 October 1944.
18. ''The Issue is the Republic,'' *Washington Times-Herald*, 24 June 1944.
19. ''Fourth Term Purges,'' *Chicago Tribune*, 25 July 1944.
20. ''The Great Deceiver,'' *Chicago Tribune*, 22 July 1944; ''The Issue is the Republic,'' *Washington Times-Herald*, 24 June 1944.
21. ''Making It Clear About Sidney,'' *Chicago Tribune*, 3 November 1944; ''CIO in the Saddle,'' *Chicago Tribune*, 20 July 1944; *New York Daily News*, 3 October 1944; ''The Fourth Term is the Issue,'' *New York Daily News*, 3 November 1944.
22. ''The Communist Origin of CIO-PAC,'' *San Francisco Examiner*, 4 November 1944; ''The Roosevelt Speech,'' *New York Journal-American*, 30 September 1944; ''CIO-PAC Threat,'' *New York Daily Mirror*, 8 September 1944; *New York Journal-American*, 27 September 1944; *San Francisco Examiner*, 27 October 1944; Deseret *News*, 26 July 1944.
23. Deseret *News*, 27 July 1944; ''Clearance Through Sidney,'' *New York Journal-American*, 18 September 1944; *New York Daily News*, 3 October 1944; ''Your Job Tomorrow,'' *Chicago Tribune*, 6 November 1944.
24. ''Look At America,'' *Chicago Tribune*, 9 November 1944.
25. New York *Sun*, 23 February 1942.
26. *A Century of Tribune Editorials, 1847–1947* (Chicago: *Chicago Tribune*, 1947), p.131; ''We All Have Only One Task,'' *Chicago Tribune*, 8 December 1941; ''Our Second Front,'' *Chicago Tribune*, 23 October 1942''; ''The Beasts of the Pacific,'' *Chicago Tribune*, 29 January 1944; ''Put Gen. MacArthur in Command,'' *Chicago Tribune*, 28 October 1942; ''The Second Front is The Pacific,'' *Chicago Tribune*, 2 July 1942; Our Second Front,'' *Chicago Tribune*, 23 October 1942.
27. ''Raids on Dutch Harbor,'' *New York Daily News*, 5 June 1942; ''Second Front Now, Or Maybe Never,'' *Washington Times-Herald*, 16 July 1942; ''What Are They Waiting For?'' *Washington Times-Herald*, 17 July 1942; ''Second Front Possibilities,'' *New York Daily News*, 22 August 1942; Deseret *News*, 3 August 1942; ''Stalin Can't Quit,'' *New York Daily News*, 8 October 1942; ''Move The Capital,'' *Washington Times-Herald*, 30 January 1943.
28. *San Francisco Examiner*, 8 December 1941; ''Second Front,'' *San Francisco Examiner*, 8 October 1942; New York *World-Telegram*, 7 October 1942; ''The Time to Beat Japan Is Now!'' *San Francisco Examiner*, 27 July 1943; ''The Japanese Atrocities,'' *San Francisco Examiner*, 31 January 1944.
29. ''Our Partial Ally,'' *San Francisco Examiner*, 17 February 1944; ''Russia Keeps Japan In The War,'' *New York Journal-American*, 5 April 1944; ''A Russo-Jap Alliance,'' *Chicago Tribune*, 27 March 1943; ''The Oriental Mind,'' *San Francisco Examiner*, 14 February 1944.
30. Deseret *News*, 22 December 1941; ''Russia Outward Bound,'' *Chicago Tribune*, 27 July 1944; ''War Can Be Lost in China,'' *San Francisco Examiner*, 23 May 1944; ''An Opportunity For Lend-Lease in Reverse,'' *San Francisco Examiner*, 12 January 1944; ''Davies Goes Back To Moscow,'' *New York Daily News*, 6 May 1943; ''Some Islands And Some Air Bases,'' *New York Daily News*, 8 October 1943; ''Our One-Way Ally,'' *Washington Times-Herald*, 27 December 1942.
31. ''Lend-Lease' for America,'' *New York Journal-American*, 2 June 1943; ''Confirmation,'' *Chicago Tribune*, 9 October 1943; ''Pierce the Heart The Limbs

Perish,'' *Washington Times-Herald*, 11 February 1943; "The One Hope,'' *Chicago Tribune*, 12 October 1943.

32. "What Are Our War Aims?'' *Washington Times-Herald*, 13 June 1943; "The Anti-American Conspiracy,'' *San Francisco Examiner*, 17 July 1943.

33. "Fighting for the Status Quo Ante,'' *Washington Times-Herald*, 30 April 1944; "Free Enterprise,'' *San Francisco Examiner*, 4 May 1943; "The Atlantic Charter,'' *New York Journal-American*, 19 August 1943; "Churchill, Stalin, And The Freedoms,'' *Chicago Tribune*, 23 March 1943; "The Great Scandal of the Peace Fraud,'' *Chicago Tribune*, 2 April 1944; "America and the Next War,'' *Chicago Tribune*, 17 April 1944.

34. "Pal Joey,'' *New York Daily News*, 13 June 1942; "The Moscow Conference,'' *New York Journal-American*, 29 October 1943; "Stalin Deserts Americans,'' *New York Journal-American*, 18 August 1943; "Stalin's Truth,'' *San Francisco Examiner*, 18 November 1942; "Russia's 'Stake' in Italy,'' *New York Journal-American*, 4 August 1943; "Stalin's Plans For Our Soldiers,'' *Chicago Tribune*, 29 August 1943; "Stalin Fights For Russia,'' *New York Daily News*, 16 November 1943.

35. "Moscow Sleighride,'' *Washington Times-Herald*, 4 February 1944; "The Press at Teheran,'' *New York Journal-American*, 21 December 1943; "Uncle Sam, for America or Uncle Patsy, for the World,'' *New York Journal-American*, 9 December 1943; "Russian Political Morality,'' *Chicago Tribune*, 18 January 1944; "Stalin Benches Max Litvinov,'' *Chicago Tribune*, 24 August 1943.

36. "The Battle of Stalingrad,'' *Washington Times-Herald*, 5 February 1943; *San Francisco Examiner*, 18 February 1944; "DeGaulle Is Stalin's Man,'' *New York Journal-American*, 4 April 1944; "The True Pattern Takes Shape,'' *New York Journal-American*, 11 December 1944; "Russia Picking the Fruit,'' *New York Journal-American*, 18 April 1944; *San Francisco Examiner*, 9 February 1945; "The Herrenvolk And Tovarich,'' *Chicago Tribune*, 6 March 1943; "Finland's Tragedy,'' *New York Daily Mirror*, 3 July 1944; "Finland and Japan,'' *Washington Times-Herald*, 20 June 1944; "Editorial,'' *San Francisco Examiner*, 20 January 1944; "Russia In The Balkans,'' *Chicago Tribune*, 8 September 1944; "Who Here Speaks For Treachery,'' *San Francisco Examiner*, 23 October 1944; "The Baltic Terror,'' *Chicago Tribune*, 22 December 1943; "Infamy in the Baltics,'' *New York Journal-American*, 21 August 1943; *San Francisco Examiner*, 24 January 1944.

37. "The Mystery Of Warsaw,'' *New York Daily News*, 7 October 1944; "Paying The Fiddler For Stalin's Tune,'' *Chicago Tribune*, 1 August 1944; "Gangster Morality,'' *New York Journal-American*, 29 December 1944; "Was Teheran a Red Munich,'' *New York Daily Mirror*, 5 August 1944; "Keep Russia In It,'' *New York Daily News*, 16 September 1943; "The Strongest Nation After The War,'' *New York Daily News*, 15 August 1943; "Four Freedoms Taking Pasting,'' *Washington Times-Herald*, 19 January 1944; "Steering Lodge Into Prominence,'' *New York Daily News*, 14 October 1943.

38. "This Looks Like Lady Luck,'' *Chicago Tribune*, 23 February 1944; "A Fateful Decision,'' *Chicago Tribune*, 31 March 1944; "Kings and Communists,'' *Chicago Tribune*, 15 March 1944; "Paying the Fiddler for Stalin's Tune,'' *Chicago Tribune*, 1 August 1944; *Chicago Tribune*, 23 May 1944; "The Communists and Their Candidate,'' *Chicago Tribune*, 19 July 1944.

39. "MacLeish on Poland,'' *Chicago Tribune*, 27 February 1945; *San Francisco Examiner*, 23 February 1945; *Washington Times-Herald*, 17 February 1945; "The 'Big Three' Meets Again,'' *Washington Times-Herald*, 14 February 1945; *Trenton*

Evening Times, 16 March 1945; *Philadelphia Inquirer*, 16 February 1945; "History Repeats," *Chicago Tribune*, 19 February 1945.

40. William Z. Foster, "The War and Labor Unity," *The Communist*, September 1942, p.709; *Daily Worker*, 6 August 1942; *Daily Worker*, 23 July 1943; *Daily Worker*, 29 February 1944; *Daily Worker*, 3 February 1942; George Seldes, *Facts and Fascism* (New York: In Fact, Inc., 1943), p.229; *Daily Worker*, 19 July 1943; "To the Offensive!" *The Communist*, October 1942, p.774; Seldes, pp.167, 233–34; *Daily Worker*, 28 June 1944; "A Statement," *San Francisco Examiner*, 27 February 1944.

41. Gies, p.199; *The People vs. the Chicago Tribune* (Chicago: Union for Democratic Action, 1942), p.71; Pilat, p.181; Freda Kirchwey, "McCormick's Gas Attack," *Nation*, 23 May 1942, p.590; "Patterson's *Daily News*," *New Republic*, 30 March 1942, pp.423–25; "Free Speech in Wartime," *New Republic*, 27 April 1942, pp.559–60; "Hitler's Guerillas Over Here," *New Republic*, 13 April 1942, pp.481–83.

42. *New York Times*, 21 April 1942; "Fourth Term Smear Tactics," *New York Daily News*, 10 November 1943; Seldes, p.240; Samuel Rosenman, ed., *The Public Papers and Addresses of Franklin D. Roosevelt*, Vol. 11 (New York: Harper and Brothers, 1950), p.234; Hoge, p.191.

43. Wendt, pp.617–23; Waldrop, pp.255–60; Gies, pp.179–97, 203–05.

44. Wendt, pp.627–36; Gies, pp.205–11; Francis Biddle, *In Brief Authority* (Garden City, NY: Doubleday and Company, 1962), pp.248–51.

45. Coblentz, p.110; Tebbel, *Life and Good Times of William Randolph Hearst* p.256; Swanberg, p.446.

46. "A Statement," *San Francisco Examiner*, 27 February 1944.

7

Catholics, Fundamentalists,
and the Red Devil-Ally

Shortly after the attack on Pearl Harbor, President Roosevelt gratefully acknowledged a letter from the U.S. Catholic bishops, who pledged their full support in safeguarding "our God-given blessings of freedom." However, this affirmation of Catholic patriotism did not include a disavowal of the Church's traditional hostility to America's Communist ally, the Soviet Union. Basic Catholic dogma, which condemned communism as a mortal threat to all the religious, ethical, cultural, and moral values of Christian civilization, could not be set aside or reappraised merely because of the military alliance with the U.S.S.R. "A fact is a fact before, during and after an alliance," declared Father James Gillis of *Catholic World*. "I do not believe in the elasticity of truth." He and other Catholic-American opinion makers regarded it as a religious and patriotic duty to remind their countrymen that the Soviet Union was only a limited military partner, not a genuine friend of the United States. Moreover, "as long as the tyranny of communism is the guiding principle of the Soviet State," the Denver *Catholic Register* asserted, "not only Catholics but all men of sound judgment will be against 'Russia.' "[1]

Catholics also feared the Soviet–American alliance would blur the politico-ideological lines and confuse Americans into accepting communism as a respectable, even benign philosophy. This was why the U.S. Catholic press, with a circulation of well over 9 million,[2] persisted in assailing communism as vigorously as it criticized nazism and fascism. Among the dictatorial features they shared was a hostility for religion, a sensitive issue that the Catholic press refused to downplay even as the Kremlin was receiving widespread praise for relaxing religious intolerance in the U.S.S.R. Unimpressed Catholics contended that the Soviet rulers, having nearly extinguished free religious worship, were now cynically manipulating Allied opinion by only temporarily easing official religious persecution.

The inherent antipathy between communism and organized religion was one reason why many Catholics regarded communism as an even greater long--

term threat than nazism. Another factor was the continued presence of the American Communist party, now reaping certain advantages from the ongoing alliance. Catholic opinion makers insisted that this organization had only shelved—not abandoned—its long-term intention of overthrowing the U.S. government. Even if this final catastrophe did not occur, there was a good possibility that the alliance with Stalin's regime would lead Americans to compromise their basic values and best instincts. A betrayal of the Atlantic Charter was what Catholic leaders most feared. They well knew that Catholic Poland's fate hung on whether the United States insisted that its Soviet ally abide by the charter's "self-determination" principle.

As they pressed their concerns about Poland and related issues, Catholic–American leaders were criticized by left-liberal elements eager to suppress anti-Soviet commentary within the United States. Although the American Communist party avoided criticizing Catholics during the war (probably fearing this would recall the party's antireligious reputation), fellow-traveling journals such as *Nation* and *New Republic* frequently criticized the Vatican and the American diocesan newspapers for being latently profascist and irrationally opposed to continued good relations between the United States and Soviet Union. More significantly, in 1944 the Soviet government launched several propaganda broadsides at the Holy See, prompting heated counterattacks from the American Catholic press.

On a more provincial level, Christian fundamentalists also remained hostile to what *Moody Monthly,* a fundamentalist publication associated with the Moody Bible Institute in Chicago, called the "God-denying, Bible-destroying religion" of communism, and to what the Reverend Gerald L. K. Smith called the prevailing tendency "to assume that Russia is a democracy; that Stalin is Sir Gallahad [sic]; and that everything is lovely in the land of the Big Brown Bear."[3] Smith, the most prominent fundamentalist preacher–activist of this period, carried on his anti-Communist mission by running for governor of Michigan in 1942 and president of the United States in 1944, and by editing his far-right newspaper, *The Cross and the Flag.* Smith's anti-Communist screeds were laced with virulent attacks on Jews and President Roosevelt, who Reverend Smith believed were in league with the Communists in a diabolical plot to enslave the world. *The Moody Monthly,* the National Association of Evangelicals, and the American Council of Christian Churches did not share Smith's more deranged views, but they did continue to preach vigorously against the evils of communism, to a rather insular audience of true believers. Smith's antics aside, the Protestant fundamentalist cause was as yet unmobilized for effective political action. Yet, the fundamentalists' resistance to the wartime rapprochement with the U.S.S.R. is an instructive prelude to the powerful Christian-Right involvement—at times in harmony with Catholics—in American politics today.

Those with misgivings about the Soviet ally always believed they were the ones who had America's best interests at heart. The Catholic press' reaction to the "second front" controversy is a good example of how "pro-American" and anti-Soviet arguments could be meshed together, even during the alliance. Almost unanimously, Catholic opinion makers refused to join the Communist-supported clamor for an immediate Allied attack in Western Europe. The Jesuit weekly *America* called the second-front crusade "half-cocked," "un-reasoned public emotionalism," and "Party Line" propaganda deserving of "a sound rebuke." San Francisco's diocesan paper, *The Monitor,* observed that "Russia has done nothing that directly benefited us," so it was not entitled to any special consideration from American military planners. More bluntly, Philadelphia's *Catholic Standard and Times* said in March 1942 that the Soviets "should not be considered an ally"; later that year, a contributor to *Catholic World* wrote that the second-front agitation was intended "not to achieve victory for the united Nations but to divert pressure from the Russian front." Several Catholic journals criticized Wendell Wilkie for his effusive campaigning for a second front in Europe, which was not necessarily in America's best interests. "Our first duty," insisted the *Catholic Herald Citizen* of Milwaukee, "is to this country and its own fronts, to Guadalcanal before Stalingrad."[4]

As for the Asian theater, the Catholic press noted that the Soviet Union had no plans for opening a second front against "the little slant-eyed people," as the very conservative Brooklyn *Tablet* referred to the Japanese. Why were Americans obliged to assist the Red Army, when the reverse was apparently not true? Catholics were not afraid to raise this troubling question. In March 1942, Father Edward Curran of the International Catholic Truth Society exclaimed, "Why, we are sending help to cousin Joey, while Joey doesn't even give us a nod . . . .He is defending Russian soil, while we are galloping around the world scattering our forces and leaving our coasts defenseless." As late as March 1944, the *Catholic Herald Citizen* claimed that lend lease materiel shipped to the Red Army "might have prevented our own disastrous and humiliating defeats in the Pacific." Some Catholic commentators also hinted that the U.S.S.R. would betray the United States in the Asian theater, by cooperating with Japan or by encouraging the Communist forces in northern China to overthrow the country's Christian leader, Chiang Kai-shek.[5]

Such remarks aside, the Catholic press generally showed far more interest in the European theater of the war, a trait shared with the Communists. But to the chagrin of American Catholics, Pope Pius XII adopted a strict policy of neutrality, refusing to condemn the Nazi atrocities against the Jews and other victims. To put it mildly, his stance was difficult to explain, yet it did not

prevent other prominent Catholics from condemning the German aggressors.*
"The Nazi god imposes no restraint on the brutal and degenerate murderers
who follow him," declared the *Catholic Telegraph-Register* of Cincinnati.
"The course of his followers is godlessness in conquest, in government, in
everything." "He who abandoned the Catholic Church has sought to have the
youth of Germany abandon God," Baltimore's *Catholic Review* said of Adolf
Hitler. Repeatedly, Catholic leaders expressed outrage over Nazi persecutions
in Poland and other occupied countries. The Denver *Catholic Register* spoke
for nearly all Catholics when it noted that "The Nazis have deliberately
devastated huge sections of Europe," and "it is not to be expected that their
postwar treatment would be any less harsh."[6]

Father Charles Coughlin was the one conspicuous exception to this trend,
and his seditious antics early in the war were a major embarrassment to the
Church. Although the "Radio Priest" had been taken off the air in 1940,
through his newspaper *Social Justice* he continued to praise Germany's
alleged attempt to erect a "new Christian social order" in Europe. Coughlin
tried to dismiss the mounting criticism leveled at him as a "smoke screen" for
"those who directly or indirectly support communism," but in May 1942
Detroit's Archbishop Edward Mooney used his authority to close down *Social
Justice* and silence Father Coughlin, who then passed into obscurity.[7]

Coughlin's pro-Nazi sympathies were far too obvious for his Communist-
bogey gambit to succeed. However, even patriotic, unsilenced American
Catholic opinion makers refused to draw a clear distinction between the two
ideologies during the war. Msgr. Fulton Sheen of Catholic University claimed
Stalin was not at war with Nazism but with Hitler personally and might
therefore revive the Nonaggression Pact should Germany's generals unexpec-
tedly seize power. Father Edmund Walsh, vice president of Georgetown
University, wrote that the two ideologies had the "identical objective" of
"world revolution"—again, a common enough assumption before the war but
not one widely expressed now. Catholic newspapers did not avoid the
comparison. A Maryknoll missionary, writing in the order's national organ,
The Field Afar, claimed that "Nazism is communism stripped of its messianic
promises"; Indiana's *Our Sunday Visitor* said that "Daily propaganda ... in
behalf of friendship for Stalin" had created an artificial difference between the
two ideologies; and the ever-blunt Brooklyn *Tablet* insisted that "Nazism is
brown Fascism; communism is Red Fascism. Both destroy liberty, peace and
religion."[8]

Though they claimed to hold these ideologies in equal contempt, many
Catholics frequently betrayed a greater loathing for bolshevism. Catholic-

---

*Anticipating the efforts of a later Pope, the Catholic-American press insisted that the
Church in Germany had condemned Nazi atrocities and was still resolutely opposed to
Hitlerism. Nazi officials who criticized the Church were almost gratefully quoted by
Catholic publicists.

American opinion makers tended to assume that dictators like Mussolini and Hitler were the products of legitimate public hatred for communism. As the *Michigan Catholic* put it, communism was a "Fascism of the Left which sometimes brings on Fascism of the Right." More problematic was the Catholic position on fascist Spain, headed by Catholic dictator Francisco Franco. Most Catholic opinion makers agreed with Cleveland's *Catholic Universe Bulletin,* which stated that "decency triumphed" when Franco emerged victorious in the Spanish Civil War. Throughout the war, diocesan editorialists maintained an obvious double standard for Franco, minimizing his faults and excusing or denying the brutality of his rule. One *Tablet* editorial claimed this "Christian statesman" deserved sympathy because Franco was "threatened by the hordes of Hitler"; and even the relatively liberal *America* thought there was "a foundation for maintaining cooperation" with him, based upon such "hopeful signs" as "his insistence upon the supremacy of spiritual values." Such a foundation did not exist with respect to nonmilitary cooperation with the U.S.S.R.[9]

Communism's hostility to organized religion was an especially important issue to Catholic opinion makers. Although not failing to condemn the equally "pagan philosophies" of German nazism, Catholic leaders were determined to counteract claims that religious freedom now existed in the U.S.S.R. *Catholic World* charged that the "recent concessions to religion in Russia have been made, not because the Soviet philosophy has changed, but because of political necessity"—a harsh judgment shared by most Catholic opinion makers. As far as they were concerned, anyone who admired communism had to hate religion, because the Communist millennium could not be achieved so long as organized religion endured. Thoroughly wedded to materialism and atheism, communism sought to destroy the spiritual basis of Western civilization by de-Christianizing Europe. As such, no genuine reconciliation or compromise between communism and Christianity was possible: "God Who is the source of human rights is given no consideration in the Russian ideology," insisted *The Monitor.* "In Russia there is but one criterion—the will of the ruler who creates and destroys rights."[10]

Catholics supported this harsh assessment by repeatedly raising the Soviets' past record of religious intolerance. In one typical editorial, the *Tablet* reminded readers that Lenin and the others had "killed off every public semblance of religion in one swoop"; that clergymen were "liquidated or sent to Siberia"; whereas anyone who still did not get the message "was denied a food card." *The Catholic Transcript,* of Hartford, Connecticut, recalled the Soviets' "history of subversion" of organized religion and concluded "there is as yet no assurances that Stalin does not mean to use it in precisely the same way." Elmer Murphy, whose column appeared in many diocesan papers, wrote that it strained credibility to assume that the Kremlin leaders had "discarded overnight their atheistic convictions."[11]

None of the Kremlin's statements to the effect that religious freedom now existed (or indeed always existed) in the U.S.S.R. placated Catholic suspicions. The *Catholic Universe Bulletin* called one such assertion, made in mid-1943 by the figurehead president of the Soviet Union, "one of the most brutally offensive things that has ever come out of the Red mad-house of irreligion"; and the Brooklyn *Tablet* dismissed the whole "prolonged diet of airy nothings on the subject of religion under the Communist regime." When Polish priests were released from prison to serve as chaplains to soldiers fighting against the Nazis, the *Tablet* asked why Stalin did not immediately release the thousands of other priests still imprisoned in his jails. Unimpressed by this Soviet "strategy of seduction" on the religious issue, Catholics continued to complain about restrictions on the Church within Russian borders and constantly pressed for more information from the Kremlin about the rights, opportunities, and standing of the Catholic population in the U.S.S.R. Believing the Soviets were capable only of cynicism and deceit on the religious issue, Catholics insisted that nothing less than the outright cessation of all religious persecution in the Soviet Union would prove Stalin's supposedly good intentions.[12]

To many observers, this seemed to be just the direction in which Stalin was heading when he resurrected the Russian Orthodox Church, an institution he had once brutally suppressed. This shrewd ploy boosted the morale of a beleaguered people, as attested to by the overflow crowds that flocked to the reopened Russian churches. Again, however, American Catholics remained doubtful, suspecting that Stalin was establishing a dependent, state-dominated institution, not a climate of open religious worship.

Such suspicions were fueled by the early actions of Metropolitan Sergius, restored patriarch of the Russian Orthodox Church. "What were his first words?", Fulton Sheen sarcastically asked. "Thanks to God? No, he asked for a second front." *America* also accused the Soviet regime of using the Metropolitan as a spokesman for their second-front propaganda, and as a mouthpiece for anti-Papal bigotry. At least in part, this last charge reflected the deep-rooted antipathies between the Orthodox and Roman Catholic churches, dating back to the great schism of 1054.[13]

Adding to the present controversy was a preface, supposedly written by the Moscow Patriarchite, to the 1942 book *The Truth About Religion in Russia:*

> This book is primarily a repudiation of the so-called 'crusade' of the fascists ... At the same time an answer is given to the broad question of whether our Church conceives of itself as persecuted by the bolshevists, and hence whether it asks anybody for liberation from such persecution.

In brief, the answer provided was that the Church did not conceive of itself as persecuted, believed that it was an "imperative duty" to support the Soviet government, and wanted help only in liberating the U.S.S.R. from Nazi occupation.[14]

The Catholic press immediately denounced this volume as a fraudulent propaganda effort to improve the Soviet government's image abroad. A National Catholic Welfare Conference press release described the book as a "colossal offense against truth" and "a superlative offense to the very concept of truth." In Boston, *The Pilot* echoed the views of other diocesan papers by upbraiding the book as an "unholy travesty," an "affront to intelligence," a "tissue of audacious lies." It was noted that *The Truth about Religion in Russia* had not been distributed in the U.S.S.R., only to foreign readers. A front-page headline in the *Catholic Universe Bulletin* aptly summarized these attacks: "Red Attempt to 'Prove' Religious Freedom Nailed".[15]

Persuaded that the Communists abroad remained the avowed enemies of God, religion, and Christian morality, Catholic–American leaders were not inclined to think any better of Communists at home. For all its patriotic, high-minded fervor of the moment, the Communist movement still planned to lead America away from its Christian heritage and toward a spiritual Armageddon. As the *Catholic Telegraph-Register* put it, "The American Communist has combed his hair and changed to a clean shirt, but he has not definitely changed his principles. He has not changed his atheism." To the extent that Communist dogma gained credibility among Americans—perhaps including Catholics—traditional Church teachings could become outmoded or discredited. As this opinion was widely shared among Church officials, the *Catholic Universe Bulletin* felt constrained to warn the faithful they "cannot afford to be dormant since the Reds are always wide-awake."[16]

On a more temporal level, Catholic opinion makers still regarded the Communist movement as a serious threat to America's most cherished institutions—indeed more so under present circumstances. This concern was reflected in a *Brooklyn Tablet* cartoon that showed a Communist workman using a power drill (labeled "Our military alliance with Red Russia") to undermine the great pillar of "Our Constitution and our American way of life." Believing the Communists were Quislings at heart, Catholic opinion shapers kept up the rhetorical pressure against them. "The country which smilingly and tolerantly permits a Communist organization within its borders," warned *The Pilot*, "is nursing a viper at the bosom." According to the National Catholic Welfare Conference's youth director, Communists were still directing "their slimy propaganda" at American children. The Reverend Matthew Toohey, pastor of a Newark church and the national chaplain of the Catholic War Veterans, said he put Communists "in the same class with the Bundists who landed here recently from a German submarine to commit acts of violence against our country." Marquette University's president, the Reverend Raphael McCarthy, broadly summarized these disparate charges when he predicted that communism would be "chief among the forces that will assault our American way of life" in the postwar period.[17]

Those American Communists presumed to be leading this "assault" received no quarter from the Catholic press during the war years. "An Unpopular Move" is how an editorial in Davenport, Iowa's *Catholic Messenger* summed up Catholic opinion on Earl Browder's release from federal prison. The delays in Harry Bridges's deportation case also were criticized in the Catholic press. Party members involved in union work were derided as "ideological acrobats" in one Catholic labor paper. "Reds Lay Plot to Capture Colorado" is how the the *Denver Catholic Register* headlined an editorial on Communist labor activity in that state. In addition, few if any Catholic leaders believed that the formal dissolutions of the Comintern and the American Communist party had severed the Communists' ties to Moscow: "every trick in Stalin's bag"; "many Americans may be deceived"; and "cheap, sleasy subterfuge" were some of the reactions to these initiatives. The last phrase might just as well have been directed at the *Daily Worker,* with which the Catholic press always disagreed.[18]

Almost as objectionable to Catholic opinion makers were the various left-wing journals that generally followed the Soviet line; these included *PM, The Protestant,* the *New York Post,* and, especially, *New Republic* and *Nation.* But many journals were writing favorable articles on the U.S.S.R. at this time, so many that not even the most implacable anti-Communist could have rebutted them all, though the Catholic press did its best. For example, a columnist in the *Tablet* chastised the March 1943 issue of *Life* magazine for glorifying the U.S.S.R. Those who criticized the Catholic press for maintaining its tough anti-Soviet/anti-Communist line were in turn accused of harboring pro-Communist sympathies. Some Catholic papers even believed that leftists were behind what *Our Sunday Visitor* called a "planned attack" against the Church. In addition, prominent non-Communist progressives like Albert Einstein, Henry Wallace, Claude Pepper, Archibald MacLeish, and Joseph Davies were taken to task for their effusive support for the U.S.S.R. but not accused of anti-Catholic bigotry. John LaFarge, reviewing in *America* Davies's best-seller *Mission to Moscow,* prophetically wrote that the former ambassador "has written a courteous book and will be believed for a time. When that time is up, he will be forgotten."[19]

At the time, however, a film based on the Davies book provoked an explosion of protest in the Catholic press. An extremely flattering depiction of Stalin's U.S.S.R., *Mission to Moscow* struck most Catholic opinion makers as a deliberate falsification of history served up as fact to a mass audience. As the reviewer in Los Angeles' *The Tidings* put it, the movie was an "example of pictorial propaganda" that left "little or no room for free interpretation." The *Catholic Universe Bulletin,* saying the film could "do great harm to the American way of life," advised readers to "avoid this picture as we would the plague." Chicago's diocesan paper, *The New World,* was less fearful of the movie's likely impact, though the editors did admit that "our historical sensibilities" had been "gently shocked." Elmer Murphy predicted the movie—nicknamed "Submission to Moscow" by its critics—would become an issue in the next presidential campaign. To no one's surprise, the Church's "Legion of Decency," a committee that reviewed all films and rated them according to moral content, condemned *Mission to Moscow* for all Catholic moviegoers.[20]

Catholics could snub Hollywood, but they could not so easily segregate themselves from the political process. Thus, they shared with other anti-Communists the apprehension that party members and sympathizers were infiltrating the U.S. government, with the long-range intention of destroying American democracy. "A Communist is one who has no sense of loyalty to anything but his delusion," stated the *Catholic Standard and Times.* "He will change sides as often as he thinks that the cause will eventually triumph." In an extraordinary May 1942 editorial, *The Pilot* even suggested that Communists—not Nazis—were still America's greatest enemies:[21]

> The Nazis will never destroy us. Even if to suppose the impossible, they win the military decision, they still can not destroy us. A free people may be disarmed and tormented. They can never be conquered by an external foe.

> But these slippery borers-from-within, these plausible pseudo democrats, the Communists, are something else. They are dangerous because they are not recognized as dangerous. Cleverly they seize on the weakness and inconsistencies of 'The democratic way.'

With this perspective on domestic communism, it is not surprising that most Catholic organs of opinion praised the overall objectives, if not always the methods, of the House Committee on Un-American Activities and its controversial chairman, Martin Dies. "We'll take the Dies Committee with its imperfections if any," declared the Reverend Matthew Toohey, of the Catholic War Veterans, "in preference to the American Communistic Party." Portland, Oregon's *Catholic Sentinel,* conceding that the committee "has laid itself open to criticism time and again," nevertheless praised HUAC for having "assumed the role of watch-dog for the liberties and civil heritages of Americans." The comparatively liberal *America* was more critical: It accused the committee of compiling "a disgraceful record" that "scarcely justifies the time and money" expended. Even at that, America admitted that HUAC had "an important function to perform," and that Communists who secured governmental posts would have "an unchecked opportunity to sap and to destroy."[22]

The "Communists-in-government" issue really came to the fore during the 1944 elections, when Republicans used HUAC's charges concerning Communist influence in the Congress of Industrial Organization's pro-Roosevelt

Political Action Committee: As might be expected, many Catholic organs of opinion took this charge seriously and condemned the Communist presence—however great or small it might be—in the PAC. The *Tablet* sharply criticized the "small foreign-minded element" that it said ran PAC with such "militant zeal"; and Father Gillis said those who ignored warnings against PAC were "living in a fool's paradise." However, Catholic opinion makers refused to draw the broader conclusion that the Roosevelt administration was being run by the "Reds"* just because it accepted campaign contributions and other assistance from an organization staffed partly by Communists.[23]

More significantly, three Catholic publications—*Commonweal, America,* and *The Liquorian* expressed sympathy for PAC, for which the *Brooklyn Tablet* branded them as having been "utilized" by the Communists. This was unfair. These journals correctly contended that most of the charges leveled at PAC constituted a red-baiting campaign by the enemies of labor and the New Deal. *Commonweal* accused the "powerful, unscrupulous forces" opposed to PAC of having raised "a howl so loud, so expensive, and for the most part so dishonest" that they did not deserve to be taken seriously. Then, in the midst of the controversy, Father Raymond Ogden, of Catholic University, published a critical history of the Dies committee, wherein he accused HUAC of exaggerating the Communists' power in PAC for political reasons. This merited a lengthy and favorable review in *The Nation* by I. F. Stone,** who thought the book might get "a hearing ... in circles no radical like myself could hope to reach or persuade."[24]

Unfortunately for Stone, Father Ogden's unassuming volume did not substantially reduce Catholic support for vigorous efforts against domestic Communists. But even the most committed anti-Communist realized that the threat to American security was minimal when compared to the situation in Europe. Ever suspicious of the Soviet ally, Catholics wondered whether a defeated Germany would merely be replaced by an equally brutal totalitarian power also bent on expansion. The *Catholic Telegraph-Register* asked the pertinent question: "What territorial wreaths will a triumphant Stalin demand for his victorious brow?"[25]

Of course, Catholic leaders opposed communism's advancement anywhere; this is why the Pope, in late 1943, spoke privately with an American official about Communist penetration into the Mediterranean and Balkan regions. But Catholics focused their concerns on the Baltic States—especially Catholic Lithuania—and Poland. Little Lithuania's demise seemed almost certain, yet

---

*Catholic newspapers did a good job of hiding their preference for specific candidates. With the probable exception of the *Tablet*, no one reading any of the diocesan weeklies could have said for certain whether the editor preferred President Roosevelt or Thomas Dewey in 1944.

**"Izzy" Stone enjoyed Ogden's book so much that he gave it *two* glowing, full-length reviews, in consecutive issues of *Nation*.

Catholic editorialists tried to ensure that the anguish of some 3 million Catholics would not be forgotten. In February 1943 *America* charged the U.S.S.R. was plotting the "wholesale destruction of the Baltic peoples"; later, *The New World* labeled U.S. policy on the Baltic question *appeasement.* A *Catholic World* article discussing this "territory Red Russia covets" sympathized with the "gallant little people whose only fault is that they are small, whose only desire is the not unnatural one of ruling themselves in peace." In late 1944, the Lithuanian Catholic Priests' League of America beseeched Roosevelt not to permit the reincorporation of Lithuania into Stalin's empire, for this would assure the "total annihilation of religion" in this tiny land.[26]

Catholic concerns for the bigger prize, Poland, grew steadily as the Red Army advanced westward against the Nazi invaders. Should Stalin remain in Poland once he got there, 7 million Catholics would be lost to atheistic rule. Early in the war, Monsignor Michael Ready, general secretary of the National Catholic Welfare Conference, hinted at the treatment they would receive when he accused the Soviets of hindering Catholic relief efforts for Poland.[27]

In June 1942, the liberal, lay-edited *Commonweal* provoked a furor in Catholic circles by suggesting that Poland and its East European neighbors unite in a postwar federation, under nominal Russian hegemony. *Commonweal* believed such an arrangement would satisfy Soviet security needs while preserving some home rule in the individual buffer states. Lamentably, "there are times when small nations' hopes for independence simply do not correspond with reality." Somewhat paradoxically, *Commonweal* called for "guarantees and assurances" in keeping with the Atlantic Charter from the "hard-boiled, almost bullet-headed" men in the Kremlin; yet the same editorial said all idealistic war aims speeches should be given a "cold douche" before delivery.[28]

These startling arguments evoked a flurry of outraged retorts, some of which the *Commonweal* editors dutifully published in the letters section. The critics insisted that a Poland (or Lithuania or any other country) that was at all controlled by Stalin would inevitably lose all its freedoms, especially the right to worship freely. In *Catholic World*, a "scandalized" Father Gillis wrote that the *Commonweal* proposal had given him "a sinking at the pit of the stomach as if some tried and true companion in the effort to keep political thinking on a high plane had suddenly surrendered and gone over to the practitioners of moral mediocrity."[29]

Accusing their critics of adhering to an unrealistic and absolutist "give-us-liberty-or-give-us-death" stance on Poland, the *Commonweal* editors refused to disavow their controversial position. They did readily concede "that absorption by Russia undoubtedly constitutes as bitter a pill as any in the international pharmacopoeia" because "again and again the Soviet State has shown its utter disregard for what we conceive to be basic human rights." But these admissions did not mollify the hard-liners, one of whom, editor–publicist Waclaw Bitner, was given a full article in *Commonweal* to rebut the editors' views. Bitner appreciated the gesture but accused *Commonweal* of siding with those wishing to tear up the Atlantic Charter and "break the Shield of Christendom" by destroying Poland.[30]

This was far more typical of how most Catholic opinion makers felt about this issue. They fully concurred with the Polish Roman Catholic Union of America when it accused the U.S.S.R., in April 1943, of advancing "baseless claims" to Polish territory. That same month, Germany implicated the Red Army in the Katyn Forest Massacre; after the Soviets failed to refute the charge persuasively, Elmer Murphy wrote that their behavior indicated "there is something to hide." When Stalin curtailed diplomatic relations with the London Poles for insisting on a Red Cross investigation of the affair, the *Catholic Register* concluded that "we cannot believe that Russia has any more intention of observing the Atlantic Charter than have the Nazis." After Secretary of State Cordell Hull's diplomatic visit to Moscow, the Catholic Bishops of America issued a statement noting how the much-heralded conference had not served to "dispel the fear that compromises on the ideals of the Atlantic Charter are in prospect." Nor was the Big Three communique at Teheran very reassuring. "The rhetorical statement issued . . . meant nothing," concluded *Catholic Review*. *America*, suspecting "it was decided to allow Russia a free hand," demanded "official reassurance that the peace has not already been lost."[31]

As the war entered its last full year, Poland's fate became an issue of paramount importance to Catholic opinion makers. Pope Pius XII told a large gathering of Polish leaders that he hoped "all nations will acknowledge their debt to Poland," and many of his followers foresaw grave consequences were that debt not honored. Archbishop Francis Spellman of New York said, "If there is no resurrection for Poland, there is no hope of resurrection for Christian Civilization after the war"; the *Michigan Catholic* accused the Kremlin of wanting Polish land "as a stepping stone to Europe"; and the Knights of Columbus supreme council passed a resolution branding as "unthinkable" any postwar settlement denying democracy to Poland. All agreed that "The test is Poland," as Buffalo's Bishop John Duffy told a receptive Polish–American congress. It was the test of the Soviet Union's real intentions toward its neighbors and of America's resolve in fulfilling its stated war aims. "As goes Poland, so goes the world," the *Catholic Herald Citizen* apprehensively predicted. "If the Poles are forced to exist in misery and slavery, then only a bitter, cruel world can be expected for all mankind."[32]

Yet, events seemed to be running against Poland. Catholic organs of opinion denounced Winston Churchill's abandonment of the exiled "London Poles," the Red Army's fateful delay in supporting the Polish Underground uprising, Prime Minister Stanislaw Mikolajczyk's fruitless meetings with Stalin, and the U.S.S.R.'s granting of diplomatic recognition to the pro-Communist "Lublin" Poles. But mere expressions of disapproval, however harsh—the *Catholic Transcript* called the situation "Munich All Over Again"—counted for little. Only the President of the United States could rescue Poland. Because he seemed to be avoiding the issue as the crisis grew ever worse, Catholic editorialists regularly reminded him of the high-minded guarantees he had codified in the Atlantic Charter. A betrayal of any innocent country's sovereignty would destroy the moral underpinning to the Allied cause. Given Stalin's likely ambitions for Poland, a policy of continued presidential silence—what one Catholic official dubbed the "Pontius Pilate" approach—could only embolden the Soviet dictator further. Relying on his goodwill, as Roosevelt seemed to be doing in 1944, was a sure prescription for disaster; FDR simply had to make Poland's cause his own, in as public a manner as possible.[33]

Criticizing the president directly was difficult for Catholic opinion makers, especially in this election year. Nevertheless, the frustration and displeasure with what was increasingly regarded as a policy of steady diplomatic disengagement was obvious. The *Brooklyn Tablet* said that "some officials responsible for our foreign policy will barter away principle and justice for expediency, [and] will sacrifice religion and morality for atheism and godless practices." *Catholic Sentinel* observed that American negotiators had allowed Stalin to maneuver "the United States into a position of political dependence upon his personal points of view." The Reverend Edward Dailey of *The New World* called the Polish crisis an "inevitable result of our past appeasement of the Soviet." Some Catholic commentators even contemplated a more terrible third world war, should America's leaders fail to uphold what the National Council of Catholic Women called "our privilege and our sacred duty" to Poland.[34]

Obviously this "sacred duty" could only exacerbate the deep antipathy that the Vatican and Kremlin already had for each other. Regarding the Vatican as a formidable obstacle to the growth of communism in postwar Europe, the Soviet regime sought to undermine the Church's moral and spiritual standing in the world community. The method employed, crude and predictable, was to link the Church to fascism.

The official Soviet newspaper *Izvestia* began the propaganda offensive on 1 February by charging the Vatican with having "earned the hatred and contempt of the Italian masses for supporting fascism." This was a reference to the Holy See's diplomatic relations with the fascist powers, and to its 1929 concordat with Mussolini.* *Izvestia* also acccused the Pope of having endorsed

---

*Like most of their countrymen, Catholic-Americans regarded Mussolini as less brutal and dangerous than Hitler's Nazism. This hardly implied sympathy for the Italian dictator. Even the ultraconservative Father Gillis had called Mussolini "a madman" as early as 1926. (Quoted in the *Tablet*, 21 November, 1942.)

the Italian campaign against Abyssinia, and of betraying its "pro-Fascist" sympathies by keeping silent about other German–Italian aggression. Although there was nothing unusual about Communists calling their enemies Fascists, this attack was notable because it came directly from the Soviet regime, not from its legions of surrogates and sympathizers abroad.[35]

In America, Fulton Sheen provided the most forceful response to these charges, which he said stemmed from a realization that the Church was the only obstacle left in Europe to a Soviet takeover. According to Sheen, "No country in the world has contributed as much to Fascism as Russia" because the 1939 nonaggression pact had allowed the Nazis "to extend their form of fascism all over Europe." Indeed, Sheen believed Stalin might yet conclude a separate peace with his former ally. These attacks on the Church were totally unwarranted, but at least *Izvestia* had revealed "the serpent beneath the flower."[36]

Others in the Catholic community fully agreed: The *Tablet*'s Patrick Scanlan hailed these strong words from a man who "has made the Christian world his debtor"; Bishop Edwin O'Hara, of Kansas City, described the *Izvestia* accusations as "totally false"; and the *Catholic Register* called upon other United Nations to disavow the Soviets' charges. Joining in their outrage were the *Washington Post,* which suspected that the Soviets were trying to breed dissension in home-front America, and the *Philadelphia Inquirer,* which hoped "some good friend whispered . . . to Stalin" that the Grand Alliance was not designed to wage war on religion. Catholics also applauded the New York state legislature for passing a resolution condemning the *Izvestia* attack on the Holy See.[37]

Having tried the stick, Stalin turned next to the carrot. In the early spring of 1944, the Kremlin revealed that Stalin had met privately with Father Stanislaus Orlemanski, an obscure priest from Springfield, Massachusetts. The meetings were described as friendly and informative; Orlemanski reported that Stalin had offered to do "all in his power to cooperate with the Church so that there will be no persecution" in Poland during the difficult period ahead.[38]

It was no accident that Orlemanski had been tapped for this drama. He had written—and, remarkably enough, had avoided detection by his Church superiors—several complimentary articles about the U.S.S.R., at least one of which had been quoted in the *Daily Worker.* In this article, "The Path for Poland," the Springfield priest called upon American Poles to ignore all criticism of the Moscow conference. Clearly this was someone who could be counted on to find Stalin's demeanor "very democratic, very open."[39]

One of Stalin's biographers attributes this bizarre episode to "a streak of naivete in Stalin's character." Although this is not how one generally thinks of Stalin, he surely was naive if he thought this gesture would alter fundamentally the Church's attitude toward his regime. Catholic reaction to Orlemanski's journey, for which no ecclesiastical approval had been granted, was totally negative. A banner headline in the *Catholic Messenger* called the affair a "Communist Trick", which is the way nearly all Catholic opinion makers described the incident. "Fellow Traveler" is how the *Wage Earner* characterized Orlemanski. In addition, the Reverend Wilfrid Parsons of Catholic University noted that this "tricky manipulation" offered no relief to Polish Catholics; and Monsignor Ready said the "burlesque" was an example of Stalin's trying to "divide the orderly march of our forces to victory and a better world." Of course, Orlemanski's visit and comments were immediately disavowed by the Church and condemned by various Polish groups and organizations. Ready was pleased to see the ploy backfire: "So far, the very clever men of Moscow, in this latest inning of the propaganda game have made no hits, no runs and one more error."[40]

Perhaps so, but the well-publicized incident was highly embarrassing to the Church. Orlemanski had to apologize to his bishop, his priestly privileges were suspended, and he was sent to a monastery to do penance, ending his role in the affair. When Representative John Lesinski, of Michigan, asked why a passport had been so readily issued for this unusual expedition, the State Department responded that the request had come from a friendly government, the U.S.S.R., and that the White House had had no involvement in the routine decision.[41]

Watching with considerable amusement was the *New Republic*, which called this "the juiciest story of the year." For his role in the "movie thriller," Orlemanski should be hailed as "the greatest benefactor of the Catholic Church in this generation." *Nation* was a bit tougher on the Church, calling its reaction a "slap in the face for Joseph Stalin at the very moment when . . . he is showing himself particularly kindly disposed toward the Catholic and other religious faiths." This was not Orlemanski's fault, of course; *Nation* called him a "courageous priest," whose approximately 4 hours of conversations with Stalin "entitled him to speak with authority of the Soviet government's intentions toward Poland."[42]

Nation stepped up its attacks on the Church in June 1944, when Pius XII reaffirmed Vatican neutrality and called for a cease-fire and negotiated peace—not an unconditional surrender by Nazi Germany. To be sure, this aroused widespread resentment in America, but *Nation* immediately drew the harshest possible conclusion—that Pius was "serving the cause of Berlin." In addition, the Pope's words "had the familiar ring of that religious total-itarianism that regretted the Reformation because it opened the floodgates of democracy." Presumably this also was why the Holy See opposed commu-nism. In October, a *Nation* article characterized the Vatican's peace hopes as "authoritarian and pro-fascist," as there was no demand for the outright destruction of Nazi Germany.[43]

Nation's main rival had been making much the same charges for at least a year. "To be neutral as between fascism and democracy," *New Republic* intoned in June 1943, "can scarcely be said to qualify anyone for spiritual leadership." *New Republic* did not say if neutrality in the struggle between fascism and communism would also warrant such disqualification, but the journal did call upon American Catholics to pressure the Vatican to adopt "a sensible and moderate political policy," instead of continuing "to slambang away at Russia with their eyes shut."[44]

Realizing that a modus vivendi with the Vatican was impossible, the Kremlin resumed its propaganda offensive against the Vatican in the fall of 1944. The Soviet-controlled magazine *War and the Working Class* was the instrument of attack. In this journal, the Pope was accused of being pro-Hitler and in favor of lenient treatment of Nazi war criminals. Next, the Communist party newspaper *Pravda* said the Pope's Christmas message "was characterized by a policy aimed at the protection of Hitlerite Germany and its delivery from responsibility for crimes." Then, an article in the Soviet journal *Red Star* labeled the Pope a "preacher of a soft peace" and accused the Holy See of trying to "revive Russian–Polish hostility." According to *Red Star,* "Under the slogan, 'Back to Catholic fascism,' terror bands are being organized to fight against democratic Poland." For good measure, a Moscow radio broadcast accused the Vatican of collaborating with Fascist elements in Argentina, and the four Patriarchs of the Orthodox Church issued a statement charging the Vatican with trying to absolve Germany of its international crimes.[45]

The Vatican responded to these criticisms in an editorial, "Intermediaries and Calumnies," in its official newspaper *Osservatore Romano.* These claims "are simply to be ranged among the frequent arbitrary, false and calumnious attacks which," the editorial said, "for some time past a certain propaganda has been employing." Catholic–American editorialists were even more pointed. The *Tablet* argued that the Soviets' propaganda attack "dramatically exposes again not only the dastardly anti-religious menace of organized communism but it makes ridiculous all the pious hopes of the star-gazers who think Russia has changed." The *Catholic Register* contended that the Soviets were trying to "discredit" the papacy because they recognized it "as the strongest opposition in Europe to its apparent attempt to control that continent." *The New World* believed that "this flood of invective was geared to the Crimean conference, [and] especially to Catholic attitudes towards the sacrifice of Poland on the altar of expediency." As we shall see, if the Soviets assumed their criticisms would intimidate Catholics into remaining silent on the Yalta settlement, or postwar developments in general, they were very badly mistaken.[46]

After this historic Big Three meeting, Catholic opinion makers immediately concluded that Poland had been cruelly abandoned by the Anglo–American negotiators. A sampling of headlines from Catholic press news accounts and editorials graphically conveys their anger: "Big Three Cast Lots For Poland;

Russia is Given Her Share"; "Poland's Desertion Means Jungle Law Still Lives"; "Crimean Tragedy"; "Smaller Nations Lose Out"; "Poland 'Sold Down the River' at Yalta Conference, Leaders Charge"; "President and Churchill Throw 9,000,000 Catholic Poles to Reds." Indeed, it was hard for Catholic opinion makers to mask their bitterness over the turn of events. *America,* although conceding there was no "practicable means" of dislodging the Red Army from Polish soil, noted that "no adroitness of phrasing can conceal the fact that the Polish settlement is distinctly a Stalin victory" and a disavowal of the Atlantic Charter. Predictably, the *Brooklyn Tablet* was even more disconsolate: asserting that "might rather than right" had triumphed at the bargaining table. Poland, "the first and most valiant champion of liberty," had been sacrificed to "Russian imperialism." Indeed, "the rights of small nations, the voice of the people, the cries of the stricken defenders of liberty went unheard." As such, "liberty, justice, democracy, representative government, national sovereignty—all went by the boards" at the Crimea conference, with grim, disquieting ramifications for the forces of liberty in their already-escalating competition with communism.[47]

Strongly in agreement with Catholics on the Soviet/communism issue were their doctrinal rivals and frequent antagonists, the Protestant fundamentalists. Their unstinting militancy against communism was maintained not only by the extremists in their midst, but among such comparatively moderate organizations as the National Association of Evangelicals and the American Council of Christian Churches.* For example, in March 1943 *Christian Beacon,* the ACCC's news organ, insisted that nothing in the U.S.S.R.'s past history justified America's trust and that "Germany and Russia are [still] closer together in their philosophy . . . than Russia is to democracy." In the same year NAE President Harold Ockenga also condemned the two systems as one, saying that "such systems as Nazism, Fascism, communism, and other ideologies challenging democracy for world rulership" had arisen "on the decaying ruins of western civilization." Now, "the kings of the rising of the sun" in the U.S.S.R. had emerged, as prophesied in the Bible. Ockenga lamented these developments, saying "this could never come to pass had we clung to the belief in God, for each of these theories is fundamentally built upon the denial of the Christian tradition."[48]

At least implicitly, this dismissed the Soviets' moves toward religious freedom as a hoax. *Christian Beacon* further charged the Soviet regime with

---

*The two organizations did not disagree on doctrinal grounds; their dispute centered around the confrontational personality and methods of ACCC founder Carl McIntire. See Jerry Falwell, ed., *The Fundamentalist Phenomenon* (Garden City, NY: Doubleday and Company, 1981, pp. 121–24; Carl McIntire, *Servants of Apostacy* (Collingswood, NJ: Christian Beacon Press, 1955); and J. D. Murch, *Cooperation without Compromise, A History of the National Association of Evangelicals*(Grand Rapids, MI: Eerdmans, 1956).

striving "to protect herself from the influence of the democratic ways; while in the United States the barriers are down as never before for the reception of Russian propaganda ... now flooding our country." Though the *Christian Beacon* was confident that "true Americans will never say, 'Give me a job or I'll take Communism.'" Such propaganda was always to be feared because "under Marxianism and Prussianism you may have the blessed tranquility and the superb security of slaves!" It was with much regret, then, that *Christian Beacon* concluded after the "appeasement" and "surrender" at Yalta that "it looks more and more as if this Second World War has been fought to make the world safe for communism!"[49]

United Evangelical Action, principal organ of the National Association of Evangelicals, expressed similar concerns about the Communists, left-wing educators, and even some liberal clergymen still active in this war-distracted American society. Though others considered this issue "too hot to handle" just now, *United Evangelical Action* insisted that "this is the hour when we must speak out on these matters." This apprehension was reflected in a report by Dr. William Ward Ayer to a 1942 NAE convention:[50]

> Not only is there surreptitious entrenching of radicals in high places in our governmental life, but a tendency is manifest even on the part of high officials to smear any who call attention to these cancerrous adhesions to our body politic.

> It is not boasting to declare that evangelical Christianity has the America of our fathers to save. While our army and navy fight the enemy without, we have the enemy at home to battle, and he is in some ways more dangerous than the enemy abroad.

In full agreement was *Moody Monthly,* which ran several articles and editorials during the war asserting that "in essence, communism and Nazism are the same" and that the Soviet regime had not changed its essential nature. The improved religious climate came about because "Russia is so intent on the intense prosecution of the war that she has no time to give to the persecution of religious people." The Soviet alliance was an immediate necessity, but inevitably it created doubt about the purpose and goals of the war. An article by *Moody Monthly's* editor Will Houghton in April 1944 bluntly posed a central question: Were U.S. servicemen fighting and dying to extend American democracy, or were their sacrifices primarily going to benefit Soviet communism? Houghton decried all the "muddled thinking" passing for policy on this issue and openly wondered if the philosophy of Stalin and Marx would be allowed to prevail, worldwide, over that of Washington, Lincoln, and Jefferson.[51]

Moody Monthly also feared that the Communist menace remained alive and well on American soil. Indeed, "they are digging in for a grand campaign when the war is over." Their goal was to use "the situation in Russia to sponsor their destructive plans for this country." This concern almost prompted *Moody Monthly* to abandon its policy of political neutrality during the 1944 presidential campaign. A pointed editorial question in the November issue betrayed the journal's unhappiness with the incumbent, President Roosevelt: "How can any Christian give encouragement or consent to a candidate when he has the all-out backing of Sidney Hillman and Earl Browder, Communists of the deepest dye and of the most destructive type."[52]

Other fundamentalists in this era carried the war against communism to more zealous extremes, adding the poison of anti-Semitism to their sweeping charges. One of these was the Reverend William Herrstrom, Minneapolis editor of *Bible News Flashes*. Using what he called "prophetic analysis," Herrstrom mangled scriptural quotations to demonstrate that God opposed international cooperation, Great Britain, the Soviet Union, and the Jews. Herrstrom accused anyone who criticized his prophecies of helping the international Communist conspiracy. No less extreme was the Reverend Harvey Springer, of Englewood, Colorado. His weekly hate sheet, *The Western Voice*, constantly eviscerated the Jews, the Federal Council of Churches, the New Deal "fascist dictatorship," the proponents of a world state, and especially the "spread of communism." According to him, the attacks on native fascists like the Reverend Gerald Winrod constituted a struggle between "the white forces of Christianity" and "the black forces of communism and Modernism."[53]

Winrod, of Wichita, Kansas, was much better known than Herrstrom or Springer. As the director of the right-wing Defenders of the Christian Faith and editor of the monthly magazine *The Defender*, Winrod had maintained a small national following among anti-Semitic fundamentalists since the mid-1920s. His views grew steadily more extreme, until he became an open sympathizer of Nazi Germany in the 1930s. Well before the Pearl Harbor attack, the FBI had listed Winrod among those "to be considered for custodial detention." In late July 1942, he was indicted, along with 27 others, for conspiracy to cause insubordination in the military.* Somewhat surprisingly, a highly toned-down version of *The Defender*—it ran flattering articles on General Douglas MacArthur and other military heroes—continued to be published. Of course, Springer and other extremists publicly expressed sympathy for him; however, the distraction and unfavorable publicity generated by his conspiracy trial and pro-Nazi views could only narrow Winrod's already very limited effectiveness and appeal during these years.[54]

Gerald L. K. Smith, who like Winrod had deservedly acquired a reputation as a leading far-right figure, was a much shrewder—and potentially more

---

*Winrod would be indicted three times during the war. Eventually he and a motley group of 29 other pro-Nazis and seditionists were put on trial in Washington, DC for conspiracy. The prosecution had trouble proving its case, the trial quickly degenerated into a circus, and a mistrial had to be called after the harried presiding judge died of a heart attack. The charges were dismissed in 1947.

dangerous—extremist. Well-known since the mid-1930s as a gifted rabble-rouser with a small but devoted following of right-wing fundamentalists, isolationists, Roosevelt haters, and anti-Semites, Smith had enough sense to publicly express unqualified support for the war effort against Germany. This posture shielded him from formal sedition charges, much to the annoyance of his most "dangerous enemy," President Roosevelt. FDR's displeasure was well founded: With Winrod and Father Charles Coughlin effectively neutralized, Smith quickly became the country's most prominent clerical extremist.[55]

Though his patriotic bombast and anti-Nazi protestations gave him legal cover, Smith's credentials as a far-right agitator are hardly in doubt. Demagogic speeches against the U.S.S.R. and Moscow-directed conspiracies poured effortlessly from his lips. Anticommunism was a lifelong fixation of his, though at times he also asserted that a "diabolical conspiracy" was afoot "to destroy private enterprise as a prelude to Fascism." The New Deal was a product of this pro-Fascist enterprise. Although he readily likened Franklin Roosevelt to Adolf Hitler, it was Smith who imitated the Fuehrer by imagining that much of America's troubles were the fault of "international Jewry." His "solution" to the nation's ills had a familiar ring: "If we'd herd all Reds and Communists into concentration camps, outlaw about two-thirds of the movies and turn to Christian statesmanship, the problem would be solved—well, ninety-five per cent solved." Of course, Smith tried to dismiss the fascist charge so frequently leveled at him as a Communist smear. "America is full of propagandists," Smith exclaimed, "who insist that if one does not throw his arms around the Christ-killing Stalin and embrace him with a holy kiss and crawl right into his political bed, he must of necessity be a Fascist." Left alone by the U.S. government (one can only imagine what his fate would have been in some of the other warring nations), Smith was determined to oppose these "propagandists" and thereby prevent "the American way of life from disappearing from the earth."[56]

To that end, he maintained his leadership in the so-called "Committee of One Million," a right-wing organization with a misleading name he had established to promote "Christian nationalism" and defeat communism. The Inner Circle, another group Smith sponsored during the war, lobbied for the near-defunct isolationist cause. For part of the war, Smith had a weekly radio program on Detroit's station WJR, which he used to vilify the British, the Soviets, the Roosevelt administration, international bankers, and Communists, all of whom were supposedly involved in various schemes against the American people.

To combat these conspirators directly, Smith entered the 1942 Republican primary for U.S. senator from Michigan. Claiming to be "the voice of the speechless," Smith sought the support of "old-fashioned Christian, American people" and patriots. He welcomed the opposition of "the Reds, the Pinks, the New Dealers, the subversionists, the Nazi Communists, the racketeers, the profiteers and countless other groups of sadists, revolutionists and scandalmongers." Though he never was considered the favorite to win this election, the possibility of Smith's capturing at least the nomination was taken seriously by some political observers. An article in *Nation* discussing his chances called him "perhaps our most dangerous professional defeatist"; and a writer in *American Mercury* predicted that Smith, if elected, "would at once become the magnetic center for all the desperations and discontents engendered by the war and the New Deal." By all accounts, he ran a vigorous campaign, crisscrossing the state and speaking to as many groups, often hostile, as possible. On primary day, he received 120,000 votes but lost to the ultimate winner, Judge Homer Ferguson. Annoyed when Ferguson refused to receive him after the primary, Smith entered the general election as an "Independent Republican," receiving a token 32,000 votes.[57]

This tail off in support did little to diminish his appetite for public affairs, but now Smith had to rely on his magazine, *The Cross and the Flag,* as the chief forum for his views. A monthly with perhaps 7,000 subscribers, *The Cross and the Flag* was filled with scurrilous attacks on Roosevelt, accolades to right-wing congressmen in both major parties, warnings about American Jews and their "Gestapo" organizations, and, especially, Smith's incendiary commentary on the evils of communism and the U.S.S.R.[58]

At this time, the "Red" menace seemed to be his greatest fear, especially as the Soviet–American alliance had made it so fashionable to "bootlick" the Communist movement. Smith made it clear that he, at least, still hated the "wire-whiskered Communists who embrace atheistic Marxism, whether we be at war or at peace." He accused American Communists of promoting subversion, free love, and the 1943 race riot in Detroit. His solution to their disruptive influence had an air of finality: "If they like Russia so well, let's send them over to Russia and tell them to stay there."[59]

As for the U.S.S.R., he refused to acknowledge it as an ally of the United States. Like other anti-Soviets, he attached much significance to the recent Nazi–Soviet pact and the U.S.S.R.'s present friendship with Japan. The future looked ominous, too, and Smith demanded that the problem posed by Soviet ambitions "be settled right now," not after the war. After the Teheran conference, he remarked that "the only people who seem to be real sure of what happened are the Communists." A free Poland, he said, would be a real "symbol of victory"; this important issue revealingly divided the American people "into two factions—the Communists and the anti-Communists." Unfortunately, Smith soon concluded that the former group had won: The Atlantic Charter had been relegated to "the bottom of the Atlantic" by the administration and other friends of the Stalin regime.[60]

Thoroughly frustrated by the direction in which he saw the country drifting, Smith elected to run for president as the candidate of the "America First" party, of which he was the founder.* His leadership was needed to ease the "almost hysterical apprehension" among the people about "the growth of Communism in America," the expanding "bureaucratic dictatorship," and "internationalism." During the campaign, Smith repeatedly raised these themes, flavoring his remarks with increasingly virulent attacks on Jews.[61]

Anti-Semitism was nothing new for Smith, but in 1944 (and from then on) it would dominate Smith's political rhetoric, distinguishing him from most, if not all, anti-Communist office seekers and commentators. "We must admit that there is a Jewish problem," read America First's party platform. This problem needed to "be solved honestly, realistically, and courageously," and to this end questions needed to be answered. For example, "Is it true that ninety-five per cent of the founders of communism were apostate Jews?" And was the New Deal staffed mainly by Jewish bureaucrats? Smith inserted both questions into his party's platform. He also emphasized the ethnoreligious heritage of Sidney Hillman, an important figure in the Roosevelt campaign. Smith falsely accused this "obnoxious, atheistic, Communist Jew" of having been involved in "the first Communist revolution in Russia" and of trying to inspire another in the United States. However, "real Democrats," Smith sneered, "do not want a Jew immigrant from Russia to run their party."[62]

Smith may well have expected that many disaffected Democrats would join his cause, but what he got was a total repudiation by the GOP's candidate, Thomas Dewey, who said "rodents" like Smith should not be "permitted to pollute streams of American life." Smith retorted that Dewey's attack was an attempt to curry favor with wealthy Jewish voters, but this gambit fooled almost no one. Indeed, Smith was rapidly losing all semblance of credibility. Protesters hounded him at every stop. Local authorities in several cities denied him municipal facilities for his rallies and meetings. He no longer had his radio program. *The Cross and the Flag,* cited by the Justice Department as a purveyor of material harmful to American morale, was refused by many news vendors. Conservative figures in both parties—including many who were every bit as anti-Communist as the Reverend Smith—rushed to distance themselves from this "Dean of American Anti-Semitism." On election day 1944, he received 1,530 votes in Michigan and 251 in Texas, the only states in which the America First party had secured places on the ballot. Never again would Smith be regarded as a significant force in American politics. He continued to speak out on the major issues—"Stalin had his way with everything" at the Yalta conference, Smith concluded—but almost no one (not even, apparently, a majority of the fanatics) was listening any longer.[63]

The Catholic and fundamentalist activities we have examined are difficult to evaluate as a whole; the record is mixed and uneven. Of course, Smith and the

---

*Smith's party should not be confused with the earlier "America First" organization that tried to keep the United States out of the war. Some of the original America Firsters protested Smith's usurpation of their name, to no avail.

other radical fundamentalists deserve nothing but condemnation, for their false and outrageous charges against the administration and their brutish anti-Semitism. Catholic opinion makers, for the most part, were not guilty of these excesses, though like most anti-Communists they sometimes exaggerated the size and potential danger of the domestic Communist movement. In addition, the Church's amicable relations with the fascist powers, its silence on the atrocities committed by those regimes, and its admiration for General Franco undercut the moral force behind Catholic condemnations of communism.* Probably it would be accurate to conclude that Pius XII disliked nazism less than he feared communism. And for all their insistence that Communists and Fascists were equally evil, American Catholic leaders also believed the Communists were just a bit worse.

Obviously, any assessment of this perspective will be heavily influenced by one's own attitudes about communism, the Soviet Union, and the East–West struggle as a whole. Surely, though, Catholics and some of the moderate fundamentalists correctly perceived that the ideals for which millions were dying would not automatically materialize from an Allied victory. The Atlantic Charter was fine-sounding propaganda, but would it be honored when the shooting stopped? This extremely important question was ignored, in some cases deliberately, by many Americans, causing enormous shock and disillusionment later. Catholics, however, were outraged but probably not very surprised by what happened to their beloved Poland. On that vital issue, events fully vindicated their suspicions of Russian and Anglo–American intentions: The Atlantic Charter was torn up and ignored at Yalta, and Poles still live under a Soviet-controlled dictatorship. Catholics' worst foreboding—that World War III would break out over Poland—did not come to pass. However, the Soviet takeover of Eastern Europe helped launch the Cold War, now more than 40 years old and still dominating international relations.

During the height of the Cold War, Catholic leaders such as Francis Cardinal Spellman of New York City fully backed the government's hard-line policies against the U.S.S.R. and American Communist party. Many in the Catholic community were proud to call Senator Joe McCarthy one of their own; The *Brooklyn Tablet* remained loyal until the end.[64] America's only Catholic President was a cold warrior of a different stamp, but no less determined to root out communism wherever he thought it possible. Today, Catholic opinion about the Communist threat is divided; Pope John Paul II has openly sympathized with the Solidarity movement in his native Poland, but more liberal American Catholics, particularly the Jesuit and Maryknoll Orders, have been among the most vocal supporters of Marxist Nicaragua.

---

*Of course, such matters are rarely this simple: Franco was a dictator, but if the Communists had triumphed in the civil war, they, too, would have established a dictatorship, and probably one with little chance of undergoing the reforms now slowly taking place in Spain.

However, their activities have been counterbalanced by the emergence of a highly politicized Christian fundamentalist movement, led by such conservative evangelists as Jerry Falwell and Pat Robertson, both devout anti-Soviets. The full impact of Robertson's personal political ambitions has yet to be determined, but he and others like him may exert a greater influence on the Republican party than many now believe. What *is* certain is that, one way or another, communism and the U.S.S.R. will remain the focal point of U.S. foreign policy debates—debates that will be enlivened and enriched by the ever-growing involvement of America's religious community.

NOTES

1. *Catholic Universe Bulletin*, 2 January 1942; "With Regard to Russia," *Catholic World*, May 1942, p. 130; "The Truth is Out—At Long Last," *Roman Catholic Register*, 2 March 1944.
2. *Catholic Messenger*, 7 May 1942.
3. "The Election," *Moody Monthly*, November 1944, p. 121; "Americans Fear Russia. Why?" *The Cross and the Flag*, May 1944, p. 398.
4. "Second Front—Too Little and Too Soon," Denver *Catholic Register*, 30 July 1942; *Catholic Herald Citizen*, 18 July 1942; "Wilkie's Front," *America*, 10 October 1942, p. 15; "Erratic Playing," *America*, 17 October 1942, p. 42; "Japan," *The Monitor*, 9 October 1943; "Russia No Ally," *Catholic Standard and Times*, 27 March 1942; J. C. Maier-Hultschin, "The Collapse of Marxism," *Catholic World*, p. 307; "Mr. Wilkie and His Second Front," Denver *Catholic Register*, 8 October 1942; *Catholic Herald Citizen*, 7 November 1942.
5. "Consistency," Brooklyn *Tablet*, 7 March 1942; Papers of the American Civil Liberties Union (Princeton University), Vol. 2384, p. 101; *Catholic Herald Citizen*, 18 March 1944; *Catholic Herald Citizen*, 15 April 1944; Brooklyn *Tablet*, 11 November 1944; "The Russian Enigma," *Catholic Telegraph-Register*, 6 February 1942; "China's Program," *The Monitor*, 6 January 1945.
6. Carlo Falconi, *The Silence of Pius XII* (Boston: Little, Brown and Company, 1970); Saul Friedlander, *Pius XII and the Third Reich* (New York: Alfred A. Knopf, 1966); "The Nazi God," *Catholic Telegraph-Register*, 14 August 1942; "Hitler 'Protects' the Vatican," *Catholic Review*, 17 September 1943; "Feeding World after the War," Denver *Catholic Register*, 2 July 1942.
7. Papers of Charles Coughlin (Northwestern University), Box 6, "World War II" File; Alden Brown, *The Tablet, The First Seventy-Five Years* (New York: The Tablet Publishing Company, 1983), p. 37; Sheldon Marcus, *Father Coughlin* (Boston: Little, Brown and Company, 1973), pp. 208–24.
8. *Catholic Universe Bulletin*, 8 October 1943; *The Pilot*, 28 October 1944; *The Field Afar,* quoted in *Michigan Catholic*, 30 June 1942; "What's the Difference between Nazism and Communism?" *Our Sunday Visitor*, 5 March 1944; "Red Fascism," Brooklyn *Tablet*, 21 October 1944.
9. "World Peace Requires Just Social Order," *Michigan Catholic*, 14 September 1944; "The Reds Again Turn Their Eyes on Spain," *Catholic Universe Bulletin*, 17 November 1944; "A Concise Definition," Brooklyn *Tablet*, 28 November 1942; "General Franco's Address," Brooklyn *Tablet*, 12 December 1942; *America*, 19 December 1942, p. 282.

10. "Tale of Three Cities," *Catholic Telegraph-Register*, 29 January 1943; "Religious Freedom!" *Catholic World*, June 1942, p. 264; "Russian Apologists," *The Monitor*, 14 August 1943.

11. "Bigotry's Technique," Brooklyn *Tablet*, 19 December 1942; "Not Religious Freedom," *Catholic Transcript*, 17 August 1944; *Catholic Universe Bulletin*, 1 October 1943.

12. "Religion in Russia," *Catholic Universe Bulletin*, 25 June 1943; "Religion in Russia," Brooklyn *Tablet*, 3 October 1942; "Thoughts on Liberalism," Brooklyn *Tablet*, 5 September 1942; *Catholic Review*, 21 July 1944.

13. *Michigan Catholic*, 14 October 1943; *America*, 22 April 1944, p. 57.

14. *The Truth about Religion in Russia* (London: Hutchinson and Company, 1942), pp. 5, 7.

15. *Catholic Messenger*, 4 March 1943; "The Truth about Religion in Russia," *The Pilot*, 13 March 1943; *Catholic Universe Bulletin*, 5 March 1943.

16. *Catholic Telegraph-Register* quote found in *Michigan Catholic*, 9 July 1942; "Communist Still Remains America's Enemy," *Catholic Universe Bulletin*, 10 November 1944.

17. Brooklyn *Tablet*, 11 April 1942; "Congratulations to Our Next President," *The Pilot*, 8 November 1944; *Catholic Universe Bulletin*, 15 October 1943; Brooklyn *Tablet*, 11 July 1942.

18. "An Unpopular Move," *Catholic Messenger*, 16 July 1942; "Liberals Echo Nazi Propaganda," *The Wage Earner*, 28 May 1943; "Reds Lay Plot to Capture Colorado," Denver *Catholic Register*, 21 January 1943; "Above Ground," Brooklyn *Tablet*, 7 October 1944; "Dissolution of the Comintern," *The Wage Earner*, 28 May 1943; "The Comintern No Longer Exists?" *The Pilot*, 29 May 1943.

19. "*Life* Canonizes Stalin," Brooklyn *Tablet*, 3 April 1943; "Is There a Planned Attack on the Catholic Church?" *Our Sunday Visitor*, 18 June 1944; "All's Rosy in Russia," *America*, 7 February 1942, p. 497.

20. "'Mission to Moscow' Falsifies History," Denver *Catholic Register*, 27 May 1943; "Mission to Moscow," *The Tidings*, 21 May 1943; "Mission to Moscow," *Catholic Universe Bulletin*, 11 June 1943; "From the Desk," *New World*, 11 June 1943; *Catholic Universe Bulletin*, 11 June 1943.

21. "Totalitarianism Is the Menace," *Catholic Standard and Times*, 5 June 1942; "Promoting National Unity," *The Pilot*, 23 May 1942.

22. Brooklyn *Tablet*, 20 February 1943; "No Free Hand," *Catholic Sentinel*, 21 January 1943; "Comment," *America*, 12 September 1942, p. 619; "Aid for Communism," *America*, 14 March 1942, p. 631.

23. "N.C.P.A.C.," Brooklyn *Tablet*, 29 July 1944; Gillis quote in Brooklyn *Tablet*, 9 December 1944.

24. "Upholding PAC," Brooklyn *Tablet*, 25 November 1944; "Hillman, CPA and PAC," *Commonweal*, 20 October 1944, p. 9; August Ogden, *The Dies Committee* (Washington, DC: Catholic University of America Press, 1945), pp. 295–98; I. F. Stone, "A Catholic Looks at the Dies Committee," *Nation*, 27 May 1944, pp. 642–43; *Nation*, 3 June 1944, pp. 642–43.

25. "Let Stalin Speak," *Catholic Telegraph-Register*, 24 February 1943.

26. "Lithuania Hopes and Fears," *America*, 20 February 1943, p. 537; "From the Desk," *New World*, 5 November 1943; Joseph Brusher, "The Bear at the Conference Table," *Catholic World*, February 1944, p. 469; "Lithuanians Fear Future," *Catholic Messenger*, 14 September 1944.

27. "Soviet-Russians," *Catholic Telegraph-Register*, 7 August 1942.

28. "The Rub," *Commonweal*, 12 June 1942, p. 172; "War Aims in the Raw," *Commonweal*, 19 June 1942, pp. 195–96.
29. "Without So Much as a Blush," *Catholic World*, August 1942, pp. 519–20.
30. "The Moral," *Commonweal*, 3 July 1942, p. 243; "The Frontier Issue," *Commonweal*, 15 October 1943, p. 627; "The Shield of Christendom," *Commonweal*, 12 November 1943, p. 93.
31. "Appeal for Poland," *Catholic Messenger*, 6 May 1943; *Catholic Universe Bulletin*, 7 May 1943; "Russian Attitude on Poland Outrageous," Denver *Catholic Register*, 29 April 1943; "Teheran," *America*, 18 March 1944, p. 659.
32. *Michigan Catholic* guest editorial in "Poland Remains a Test," *Catholic Universe Bulletin*, 18 August 1944; Brooklyn *Tablet*, 4 March 1944; "What Does Russia Really Want?" *Michigan Catholic*, 5 October 1944; "Unthinkable," *Catholic Herald-Citizen*, 26 August 1944; Brooklyn *Tablet*, 3 June 1944; "Men and Affairs," *Catholic Herald-Citizen*, 22 January 1944.
33. "Munich All Over Again," *Catholic Transcript*, 11 January 1945; *Catholic Universe Bulletin*, 8 December 1944.
34. "Latest Polish News," Brooklyn *Tablet*, 6 May 1944; "Stalin Holds the Big Stick," *Catholic Sentinel*, 2 November 1944; *San Francisco Examiner*, 7 October 1944; *Catholic Universe Bulletin*, 27 October 1944.
35. Brooklyn *Tablet*, 5 February 1944; *Catholic Universe Bulletin*, 25 February 1944.
36. *New York Times*, 2 February 1944; Brooklyn *Tablet*, 5 February 1944; *Michigan Catholic*, 17 February 1944.
37. "Commendation," Brooklyn *Tablet*, 12 February 1944; Brooklyn *Tablet*, 5 February 1944; "We Protest," Denver *Catholic Register*, 3 February 1944; "Russian Lies Rejected," *The Messenger*, 17 February 1944; *Catholic Universe Bulletin*, 3 March 1944.
38. *New York Times*, 13 May 1944.
39. *Catholic Universe Bulletin*, 5 May 1944; *New York Times*, 13 May 1944.
40. *The Messenger*, 11 May 1944; *The Wage Earner*, 12 May 1944; *Catholic Universe Bulletin*, May 1944; Brooklyn *Tablet*, 6 May 1944.
41. Brooklyn *Tablet*, 6 May 1944; *New York Times*, 6, 7 May 1944.
42. "A Priest Goes to Moscow," *New Republic*, 22 May 1944, pp. 696–97; *Nation*, 20 May 1944, p. 582; Eric Estorick, "Polish American Politics," *Nation*, 20 May 1944, p. 591.
43. *Nation*, 10 June 1944, p. 666; G. A. Borgese, "The Pope and the Peace," *Nation*, 14 October 1944, p. 429.
44. "The Vatican's Neutrality," *New Republic*, 21 June 1943, p. 812; "Catholics and Liberals," *New Republic*, 7 June 1943, p. 752.
45. "For What Do Men Die?" Brooklyn *Tablet*, 14 October 1944; *New York Times*, 1 January 1945; *New York Times*, 8 February 1945; *New World*, 16 February 1945; *Catholic Standard and Times*, 16 February 1945; *Catholic Herald-Citizen*, 17 February 1945.
46. *New World*, 16 February 1945; Brooklyn *Tablet*, 14 October 1945; Denver *Catholic Register*, 4 January 1945; "From the Desk," *New World*, 23 February 1945.
47. Brooklyn *Tablet*, 17 February 1945; *Catholic Universe Bulletin*, 2 March 1945; *Catholic Herald-Citizen*, 24 February 1945; *Michigan Catholic*, 15 February 1945; *Catholic Messenger*, 1 March 1945; *The Tidings*, 23 February 1945; "Poland," *America*, 24 February 1945; "Might versus Right," Brooklyn *Tablet*, 17 February 1945.

48. "Practical Religion in the World of Tomorrow," *Christian Beacon*, 18 March 1943; *United Evangelical Action*, 4 May 1943.
49. "Practical Religion in the World of Tomorrow," *Christian Beacon*, 18 March 1943; "The Yalta Conference," *Christian Beacon*, 22 February 1945; "San Francisco," *Christian Beacon*, 3 May 1945.
50. *United Evangelical Action*, August 1943; *Evangelical Action, A Report on the Organization of the National Association of Evangelicals for United Action* (Boston: United Action Press, 1942), p. 46.
51. "The Spirit of Hitler," *Moody Monthly*, January 1944, p. 255; F. J. Miles, "Is There Religious Liberty in Russia?" *Moody Monthly*, February 1944, p. 323; Will Houghton, "Is America Facing Sunrise or Sunset?" *Moody Monthly*, April 1944, p. 432.
52. "They Are Still Active," *Moody Monthly*, September 1942, p. 4; I. V. Neprach, "The Soul of Russia," *Moody Monthly*, November 1942, p. 136; "The Election," *Moody Monthly*, November 1944, p. 121.
53. Heinz Eulau, "False Prophets in the Bible Belt," *New Republic*, 7 February 1944, pp. 169–71; Morris Schonback, *Native American Fascism during the 1930s and 1940s* (New York: Garland Publishing, Inc., 1985), p. 226; Charles Higham, *American Swastika* (Garden City, NY: Doubleday and Company, Inc., 1985), pp. 51–52; Ralph Roy, *Apostles of Discord* (Boston: Beacon Press, 1953), pp. 53–55, 166–67, 199–200; John Carlson, *The Plotters* (New York: E. P. Dutton and Company, 1946), pp. 94–96; Carlson, *Under Cover* (New York: E. P. Dutton and Company, 1943), p. 496.
54. Clifford Hope, Jr., "Strident Voices in Kansas between the Wars," *Kansas History*, Spring 1979, pp. 54–64; G. H. Montgomery, *Gerald Burton Winrod* (Wichita, KS: Mertmont Publishers, 1965); Leo Ribuffo, *The Old Christian Right*, pp. 80–127.
55. *The Cross and the Flag*, August 1942, p. 16; Ribuffo, p. 162; see also Ribuffo, pp. 154–77.
56. "American Foreign Policy," *The Cross and the Flag*, June–July 1944, p. 404; *Hearings*, U.S. House of Representatives Committee on Un-American Activities (79th Congress, 2nd Session), 30 January 1946, p. 20; David Bennett, *Demagogues in the Depression* (New Brunswick, NJ: Rutgers University Press, 1969), p. 285; "Blame Stalin," *The Cross and the Flag*, April 1942, p. 5; William Huie, "Gerald Smith's Bid for Power," *American Mercury*, August 1942, p. 156.
57. "A Statement by the Editor," *The Cross and the Flag*, June 1942, p. 16; "Enemies at Home," *New Republic*, 13 July 1942, p. 55; Maxine Block, ed., *Current Biography, 1943* (New York: H. W. Wilson Company, 1944), p. 709; "My Hat's in the Ring," *The Cross and the Flag*, May 1942, p. 9; Will Chasan and Victor Riesel, "Keep Them Out! The Reverend Gerald L. K. Smith," *Nation*, 16 May 1942, pp. 566–68; *American Mercury*, August 1942, p. 156.
58. Walter Davenport, "The Mysterious Gerald Smith," *Collier's*, 4 March 1944, p. 15; "Gestapo Methods," *The Cross and the Flag*, March 1944, pp. 367–68.
59. "Moscow Honors Me," *The Cross and the Flag*, July 1943, p. 231; "Sex Appeal, Free Love and the Communist Party," *The Cross and the Flag*, November 1943, p. 294; "Race Riots! An Interpretation," *The Cross and the Flag*, July 1943, p. 233; "Comintern Dissolved," *The Cross and the Flag*, June 1943, p. 211.
60. "Stalin and Tito," *The Cross and the Flag*, March 1944, p. 362; "What Is Teheran?" *The Cross and the Flag*, February 1944, p. 340; "What about

Poland?'' *The Cross and the Flag*, December 1943, p. 312; "News Distorted," *The Cross and the Flag*, June–July 1944, p. 415.

61. "America First Leaders Challenge Republican Leaders," *The Cross and the Flag,* September 1943, p. 258.

62. "Platform," *The Cross and the Flag*, September 1944, p. 440; *The Cross and the Flag*, October 1944, p. 455; Gerald L. K. Smith, *Besieged Patriot* (Eureka Springs, AR: Elma M. Smith Foundation, 1978), p. 48; "Low Down on Democratic Convention," *The Cross and the Flag*, August 1944, p. 432.

63. *New York Times*, 1 April 1944; "An Open Letter," *The Cross and the Flag*, August 1944, p. 418; Maxine Block, ed., *Current Biography, 1943* (New York: H. W. Wilson Company, 1944), p. 710; Seymour Martin Lipset and Earl Raab, *The Politics of Unreason: Right-Wing Extremism in America, 1790–1970* (New York: Harper & Row, 1970), p. 244; "'Big Three'," *The Cross and the Flag*, March 1945, p. 532.

64. Vincent DeSantis, "American Catholics and McCarthyism," *Catholic Historical Review*, April 1965, pp. 2, 13, 15, 29–30.

8

The Socialist Perspective

The Socialists are the rogue elephants of our study. Unlike the other groups we have examined, Socialists believed that America's capitalist system was inherently unjust to the great majority of citizens. They preferred a collectivist society in which the government, not private enterprise, managed the production and distribution of goods and services for the people's welfare. In the broadest ideological sense, this aligned them with the Communists, many of whom had impatiently broken away from the Socialist movement in the heady aftermath of the Russian Revolution. From then on the two groups were at odds, each competing for the allegiance of "leftist" intellectuals, activists, and trade unionists.

Even as misinformed anti-Communists condemned Socialists and Communists together, they bitterly accused each other of having betrayed the class struggle. Communists argued that the Socialists' program of cautious, limited reform was a sellout to the capitalists. Socialists responded that their goal was democratic socialism, an alien concept to those who had "sold out" to Stalin's U.S.S.R. During the U.S.–Soviet alliance, this war on the left reached its greatest intensity when Soviet authorities announced the execution of Victor Alter and Henryk Erlich, prominent Polish Socialists who were well known in American Socialist circles. Killed because Stalin wanted no Socialist opposition to a Soviet takeover of Poland, Alter and Erlich were lionized as martyrs by a Socialist community united in outrage over this latest reminder that the Soviet ally and its defenders had not forsaken their totalitarian past.

To be sure, among democratic Socialists[1] there was perpetual bickering and division of opinion, but hostility to the Communist party and the Soviet Union was a shared value, cutting across many sectarian lines. Within the democratic Socialist ranks, the Norman Thomas-led Socialist party and the "right-wing" Social Democratic Federation (SDF) had the largest popular followings. The *Call* and *New Leader,* the official organs, respectively, of these two groups, continued to criticize both the home-grown and Allied varieties of communism. David Dubinsky of the International Ladies' Garment Workers' Union maintained close ties with the SDF; his union's organ, *Justice,* qualified almost as a sister paper to the *New Leader.* In addition, a clutch of independent thinkers and writers—many former Communists, all at various stages of faith, hope, or disillusionment in Socialism—also remained vigorously anti-Stalinist during the war. Their material appeared in *Common Sense, Politics, Partisan Review* (then principally edited by anti-Stalinist Philip Rahv), and other top intellectual journals of the day. Of course, the Communists lambasted their rivals as pro-Hitler agents, deserving the same fate that Soviet justice accorded to Erlich and Alter. Hardly more numerous than the Communists themselves, anti-Communist Socialists were truly a minority within a minority during the Soviet-American alliance. Yet they persevered and contributed in a small but distinctive way to the undercurrent of anti-Communist/anti-Soviet opinion in wartime America.

Unlike most conservative anti-Communists, democratic Socialists did not reflexively exaggerate the power and size of the American Communist party. Indeed, most Socialists regarded Martin Dies, William Randolph Hearst, and other anti-Communist conservatives as dangerous reactionaries in their own right. *Fundamentally,* however, Socialists agreed with the likes of Dies on at least one point: the Communist party *was* a destructive force in American society. Slavishly devoted to the Soviet Union, party members and fellow travelers had no mission or agenda of their own. Yet they postured as the champions of the workers. Now, even more hypocritically they were posing as ardent American patriots. "The ease with which they could turn round and round," Dubinsky wrote after the war, "simply confirmed the feeling I had always had about their untrustworthiness as allies." Norman Thomas acidly called them "totalitarian liberals"—unwilling to acknowledge Stalin's crimes, yet perfectly willing to employ "basically fascist" types of "propaganda and social controls" to achieve their ends. About the Communist party proper, Thomas in 1944 was even blunter: "Now it merely seeks power, by any means. It has one principle left and that is to advance the immediate interests of Russia, no matter what that seems to require." Even collaborating with "Boss" Frank Hague's Democratic machine—a maneuver the New Jersey Socialist party called an "all-time low" in political cynicism—was apparently not beneath the Communists. When the U.S.S.R. announced the dissolution of the Comintern in 1943, Socialists saw the move to cynicism played out on an international stage. Louis Fischer belived that "Stalin hopes that the Comintern's death will make us more receptive to his territorial claims." The *Call's* columnist Lillian Symes correctly predicted the Communist party would remain a "highly disciplined agency of Soviet power."[2]

Because Soviet "power" now depended so heavily on American industry, the Communists had abandoned the class struggle and embraced the corporate interests. For pure shamelessness, this surpassed everything except the Communists' support of the Nazi–Soviet Pact. As the *Call* put it, the

Communists had "offered their services without charge to American reaction-aries" just to satisfy the current "Kremlin directives." Maurice Goldbloom, writing in *Common Sense,* noted that this latest transmogrification had put American communism "to the right of center . . . [and] in favor of things [like monopoly capitalism] progressives are and always have been against." This point, duly made in the Socialist party's 1944 platform, was not destined to attract many converts amid the unique conditions of World War II. Thomas garnered only 80,518 votes in the 1944 election. The Social Democratic Federation also suffered a humiliating setback that year, losing control of the American Labor party in New York to a coalition dominated by Sidney Hillman and his temporary allies, the Communists. *Justice* predicted this would "sound the death knell of independent labor political action in America," even though the Labor party fully intended to support President Roosevelt. The prediction was quite premature, as the defeated SDF and its supporters promptly abandoned the Labor party and organized yet another minority organization, the Liberal party. Led by David Dubinsky of the Ladies' Garment Workers' Union, the Liberal party also worked for FDR in 1944.[3]

Significantly, Socialists did not share the Right's delusions about President Franklin Roosevelt. They knew he was no Communist, and they knew the New Deal was no blueprint for Communism. Dubinsky was not the only democratic Socialist who admired the President. But when FDR commuted Earl Browder's prison sentence to promote "national unity," the SDF angrily declared that such reasoning "offends and wrongs all who are on principle opposed to dictatorship and who are working and fighting for democracy." Similar gestures of good fellowship provoked additional protests from democratic Socialists. The former Communist intellectual Max Eastman, turning increasingly more conservative, wrote that Vice President Henry Wallace had become an "apologist for Communism" during the war. Sidney Hook also derided the Vice President's "foolish and dangerous words" about the comparative states of democracy in the U.S.S.R. and the United States. Nor was FDR's foreign policy immune from Socialist attack. "At the Teheran conference," wrote Louis Fischer, "Roosevelt and Churchill apparently acquiesced in Russia's power politics; that is why 'Teheran' has become the nub of the world for foreign Communists." In March 1944, Harry Paxton Howard, a regular contributor to the *Call,* suggested that FDR was providing "ever-increasing tribute to the new Colossus of Europe"; perhaps an "uncon-ditional surrender to Stalin" already had been tendered. The subsequent Yalta accords were savaged by the *Call* as a "sellout," a "pattern for slavery," and a "program for World War III."[4]

Even at this late date, these were distinctly minority views; the idealized image of the Soviet Union would survive a few months longer. Socialists had been resisting the pro-Soviet trend from the start. For example, they took a leading role in protesting the 1943 film *Mission to Moscow.* The *New Leader* considered "Submission to Moscow" a "national scandal" that had been "manufactured for the deception and bamboozling of the American public." Edmund Wilson jeeringly observed how this "fraud on the American public" was not even true to the book by Joseph Davies, on which it was based. Sidney Hook warned that "unless a storm of opposition arises ... it will serve as precedent for more and worse films of this type." In an effort to counteract the film's propaganda effect, some 52 prominent Socialists, writers, and educators— including Hook, Thomas, and Eastman—publicly denounced *Mission to Moscow.* Their statement noted that the film "glorifies dictatorship" and "falsifies history"— particularly in its portrayal of Leon Trotsky and its account of the 1930s' show trials. Were it to be popularly accepted as fact, *Mission to Moscow* could help create "an impression in the minds of tens of millions of Americans that the methods of Stalin's dictatorship are nowise incompatible with genuine democracy." Roosevelt, too, was deified in the movie as an all-knowing "Leader." Targeted to a mass audience, such a film had "the most serious implications for American democracy."[5]

It was "not only unnecessary but dangerous," the philosopher John Dewey wrote in 1942, "to present the totalitarian despotism of Stalin in any but its true light." Dwight MacDonald, editing the first issue of *Politics* in February 1944, prodded readers to remember that the U.S.S.R.'s "bureaucratic collectivism" had created "a form of society profoundly repugnant to the ideals ... shared by most radicals, bourgeois or socialist." No amount of heroism by the Red Army could change the fact that the regime they were defending permitted no political rights or freedoms whatsoever. Such an environment could not possibly foster socialism. As Louis Fischer put it, "socialism without liberty, which is today the Russian way of life, cannot be a free man's free choice."[6]

Of course, other anti-Soviet critics we have examined did not support *any* kind of Socialist agenda. Yet, on other points the Socialists were in complete agreement with conservative anti-Communists. Nazi Germany and Stalin's U.S.S.R. were still more alike than different. Sidney Hook, an atheist himself, mocked the Godless Stalin regime for having discovered—immediately after the German invasion—"that Nazism is a movement which seeks to destroy Christianity." Stalin was an ally of pure expedience; assuming that he would eventually assist in the Pacific war might be a dangerous mistake. As James Burnham put it, once the Soviet ruler had saved himself in Europe, American Communists might well discard their prowar fervor for a new line: "Don't Let Our Daddies Die in the Jungles!" Socialists frequently recalled the infamous Nazi–Soviet Pact of 1939–1941, and did not discount the possibility of a surprise separate peace between Hitler and Stalin.[7]

In the event of a total Soviet victory, Socialists feared that Stalin would crush the democratic aspirations of liberal elements in Eastern Europe and elsewhere. The Baltic states and Poland would be the first victims of his expansionist ambitions. Bertram Wolfe said that if the Allies acquiesced in such a takeover it would be "a violation of all the most decent pledges and promises under which our people are being summoned to fight and die." John Chamberlain, reviewing Jan Karski's *Story of a Secret State* for *Harper's,* wrote that "it is impossible to escape the conviction that the fate of his nation [Poland] is the test of a righteous peace, no matter what the 'realists' may say." However, the prospects—realistically speaking—were not encouraging. In the summer of 1944, Lillian Symes referred to the developing Polish situation as "the most incredibly brutal betrayal in a war that has been one long series of betrayals." When the Red Army failed to aid General Bor during the Warsaw uprising, Dwight MacDonald disgustedly wrote that all "honest doubts one might have had as to the nature of the Soviet regime and the direction in which it is heading must be resolved." William Henry Chamberlin, too, was "reasonably sure" that "pro-Soviet regimes" would be established on the Russian border. Even more pessimistic was Harry Paxton Howard, who considered it entirely possible that "Stalin and his satellites will dominate all Europe with its crushed peoples under their heels forever."[8]

If there was a single incident that confirmed all these apprehensions among democratic Socialists, it was the dismal Erlich–Alter affair, which came to a head in March 1943. Unimportant to most Americans, the execution of these two Polish labor leaders by the Soviet Union provoked an enormous protest among fellow democratic Socialists around the world, and especially in New York City. From an historical standpoint, the incident encapsulates the Socialists' distrust and hatred for Stalin's Communist regime, despite the wartime alliance against Nazi Germany.

Henryk Erlich and Victor Alter were prominent in the Socialist and labor internationals and respected leaders in the Socialist Jewish Bund of their native Poland. Though never pro-Soviet, in the 1930s they had called upon the international Socialist community to join in an anti-Fascist "popular front" with the Stalin regime. When Germany invaded Poland in September 1939, Erlich and Alter helped organize a workers' resistance movement. The Gestapo had orders to liquidate both of them. Fleeing to eastern Poland, the two were promptly arrested by Soviet troops occupying this region, under the terms of the Nazi–Soviet nonaggression pact. They were charged with "working for the forces of international Fascist reaction." Erlich and Alter remained in a Russian prison until the Soviet-Polish treaty of July 1941, a product of course of Hitler's surprise attack on the U.S.S.R. Soviet officials even admitted that a "terrible mistake had been made and that the charges against them were false." Liberated, Erlich and Alter appealed to Polish Jews in the U.S.S.R. to assist in repelling the Nazi invaders from Russian soil.

They had a role in the organization of the Moscow-based Jewish Anti-Fascist Committee. In recognition of their anti-Nazi activities, Erlich and Alter were named to the Polish National Council by the London government in exile. However, before leaving the U.S.S.R. the two were again arrested, on 4 December 1941.[9]

Dismayed labor officials in the United States, England, and elsewhere demanded an explanation from the Soviet government—which initially denied that Alter and Erlich had been rearrested. Other prominent figures—including Eleanor Roosevelt, Reinhold Niebuhr, Albert Einstein, Wendell Wilkie, and General Sikorski of the Polish provisional government—appealed unsuccessfully for information about the fate of the two leaders. Their case, Norman Thomas wrote to presidential advisor Harry Hopkins, was "symbolic"; Stalin could do much "to abate suspicion and increase good will" by ensuring that Erlich and Alter were treated with justice. Yet for more than a year, silence was the only Soviet response to inquiries about this matter. Then, AFL President William Green received a letter, dated 15 February 1943, from Soviet Ambassador Maxim Litvinov, stating that Erlich and Alter had been executed in December 1942.[10]

Widely quoted in the New York press, the letter claimed that the two men had been arrested the first time for "active subversive work against the Soviet Union." Sentenced to death, they were released only because the U.S.S.R. honored the request of the Polish provisional government to set them free. However, Erlich and Alter allegedly repaid this merciful gesture by resuming "their hostile activities, including appeals to the Soviet troops to stop bloodshed and immediately to conclude peace with Germany." This treachery occurred "at the time of the most desperate battles of the Soviet troops against the advancing Hitler Army." Accordingly, Erlich and Alter were again arrested and sentenced to death. "This sentence," Litvinov's letter informed Green, "has been carried out in regard to both of them."[11]

Almost no one who knew of these men believed the Soviets' incredible charges. It was assumed that Stalin, no longer fearing for his country's survival, was already proceeding against potential opposition in a postwar Poland. He must have known that Erlich and Alter despised the U.S.S.R. almost as much as Nazi Germany and were cooperating with his regime only to defeat Hitler. Once this occurred, obviously things would be different. However, by late 1942, Hitler's eventual defeat seemed far more likely, freeing Stalin to make some preemptive decisions with respect to his western neighbor. By executing Erlich and Alter, Stalin had eliminated two certain barriers to establishing a postwar Polish government that would be friendly to the U.S.S.R. This was why the *New Leader* attributed the executions to "Soviet vindictiveness" and why a *Justice* editorial called the killings "an act of vengeance" and "a political assassination."[12]

This was the unanimous view of the democratic left. The twin killings absolutely convinced Norman Thomas that the Soviet leader was a barbarian without equal.* James Weschler, writing in *Common Sense,* noted how "each time that we launch this pretense" of inherent Soviet–American compatibility "an Alter–Erlich case arises to remind us of the past and of the unsolved problems." Chamberlin wrote that if these executions finally awakened everyone to the real nature of the Soviet government, then "Erlich and Alter[13] will not have died in vain."

Even some of the leading fellow-traveling journals of opinion expressed dismay over the murder of these undoubtedly innocent men. Alexander Uhl, analyzing the affair in *PM,* wrote that "no one who knew the men personally will accept the thought that these two Jewish leaders ... could possibly have been working with the Nazis." But Max Lerner, also writing in *PM,* insisted that this minor episode should not impede continued good relations between the two allies. The *Nation* said, "The execution of Erlich and Alter was not only bad justice; it was also bad propaganda." Perhaps it was the latter point that most disturbed the *Nation* editors—who apparently viewed the event as at least as much a public-relations snafu as a state-sponsored murder. *New Republic* bravely admitted that "Both Henryk Erlich and Victor Alter were consistently and vigorously anti-fascist and ... anti-Nazi," which meant the Soviets were guilty of a frame-up and cold-blooded murder. Still, the incident needed to be put into proper fellow-traveling perspective: Cooperation with the U.S.S.R. remained paramount, and anyway "All the chief United Nations have sins on their consciences like the Erlich–Alter case."[14]

This was heavily qualified criticism, but at least it was more than the total silence that the Roosevelt administration maintained about the slayings. Asked to comment upon the incident, a spokesman for the Office of War Information stated: "Our agency does not concern itself with matters that are divisive and serve to harm the unity of the United Nations. Disruption is not considered grist to our mill." Hillman and Philip Murray, labor leaders with close ties to the administration, also had nothing to say about the murdered Erlich and Alter.[15]

Many democratic Socialists believed that this tragedy could not be so casually dismissed and forgotten. Dubinsky, a member of the Polish Bund himself as a youth, took the lead in organizing a public rally—"war or no war," as he put it—to honor the martyred heroes and to protest their state-sponsored murder. Three thousand people filled Mecca Temple in New York

---

*Because he was the best-known Socialist, Thomas was especially detested by the Communist party, which called him a "spearhead of fascism." The *Daily Worker* called for the cancellation of his radio program (*The Communist,* June 1942, pp. 450–57; *Worker,* 28 April 1942). This disdain for his civil liberties contrasts sharply with Thomas's condemnation of the treatment of the Nisei—to say nothing of his opposition to the abridgments of the Communist party's civil liberties after the war.

City on 31 March 1943, for the rally. Similar meetings were held in London, Chicago, Boston, and Newark. At the main rally in Mecca Temple, the prominent figures in attendance included New York City's legendary Mayor Fiorella LaGuardia, the theologian Reinhold Niebuhr, William Green and Matthew Woll of the AFL, James Carey and Emil Rieve of the CIO, and Luigu Antonini, a Dubinsky associate and president of the Italian American Labor Council. They listened as Dubinsky, who presided over the gathering, flatly declared that Alter and Erlich[16]

> were executed because they were democratic Socialists, champions of trade union-ism, and opponents of all dictatorships, including Communist dictatorship . . . . The Comintern could not afford to permit them to remain alive and return to Poland after the war.

Other speakers also alluded to the ongoing alliance that made this gathering all the more awkward and difficult. James Mead, speaking by telephone from Washington, DC, declared that "an acknowledgment of the part Russia is playing as our ally, does not mean, however, that we must close our eyes to these terroristic methods." The executions of Erlich and Alter, Dr. Niebuhr said, "is a proof of the fact that Russia has not established anything like democratic justice." Green, noting the "disposition in some quarters to accept all the acts of the Soviet Government as sacred and beyond the sphere of debate," emphatically demurred: "Murder has been committed by the Soviet Government. We cannot stop our ears, blind our eyes, or silence our protests." Carey, the highest-ranking CIO official at the rally, said that although much of "man's hope rests upon the incomparable heroism of the Russian people," this war was "not merely a negative crusade against the evils of fascism."[17]

No representative of the Socialist party spoke at the memorial. However, everyone who attended the meeting received a party leaflet, which read in part: "By the murder of Erlich and Alter, Stalin has once more sealed in blood his complete betrayal of democratic socialism, his acceptance of aggressive imperialism." Added the *Call*:[18]

> Russia's plans for Eastern Europe—unifying it under a Stalinist dictatorship—make it a matter of absolute necessity to win the workers and peasants of that area to an acceptance of Stalinism as their political expression . . . .

> The Jewish Socialist Bund is the living proof that the workers do not have to choose between reformist Socialism and Stalinism . . . The growing strength of the revolutionary socialism represented by The Bund transcended the national bound-aries of Poland and was an influence in Socialist thought throughout the world. All this must have figured in the carefully thought-out plans of Stalin and his lieutenants.

Needless to say, Stalin's defenders in the United States hastily accepted the Soviet explanation for the Erlich–Alter slayings. The Communists also attempted to squelch the memorial rally at Mecca Temple. LaGuardia, who was then politically aligned with pro-Communist Representative Vito Marcantonio, almost did not attend. (In his speech, he referred to the affair as "Russia's Sacco-and-Vanzetti case" and otherwise trimmed as much as possible.) The New York CIO Council, over which the Communists had considerable influence, rejected a motion to support the Mecca Temple rally. Once the meeting was held, there was little for Earl Browder to do except denounce it as "a conspiratorial effort of American citizens, organized on American soil, to overthrow the government of the Soviet Union."[19]

To support their claims of a Socialist conspiracy against the U.S.S.R., Browder and other Communists frequently cited a comment by one "N. Chanin," in the obscure Socialist magazine *Friend*. In January 1942, Chanin had written that the "last shot" of the war "will be fired from free America— and from that shot the Stalin regime, too, will be shot to pieces." The Communists assumed that this was the message that Erlich and Alter had received from "their paymasters in New York." Chanin's remark was certainly inflammatory, as was the Communists' own rhetorical counteroffensive, which was typically overwrought and weighted with inaccuracies. For example, the two men were depicted as "counter-revolutionary conspirators"—and all the "hulla-baloo" was "a conspiracy against the United Nations, against victory itself." Party officials also claimed "that no Jew in the Soviet Union has fallen a victim of anti-Semitism," meaning that Erlich and Alter had not been singled out on religious grounds. Indeed, Jews had been given "special protection" against Nazi persecution by the Soviet government. But none of this mattered to Erlich, Alter, and their co-conspirators in the United States, who firmly opposed "the aspirations of the peoples of America and Europe for a people's peace." Exposing and defeating this conspiracy was essential: no less than "The future of our country, and the world, is at stake."[20]

That anyone could seriously believe that Joseph Stalin, in the darkest hours of his nation's history, gave special thought to the plight of Russian Jews is almost beyond belief. Nevertheless, the Communists were probably correct in claiming that anti-Semitism, as such, was not a factor in the murder of these men. Erlich and Alter were executed because of their hostility to Soviet totalitarianism and because of their influence among Polish Jews and Socialists. The reaction of many American Jews informed on this issue is instructive. At the Erlich–Alter Mecca Temple rally, Adolph Held, chairman of the Jewish Labor Committee, asserted that "no one in this wide world in whom there is still a spark of human decency will believe the monstrous charge which has been leveled against them by their brutal executioners." *The Ghetto Speaks*, a publication issued by the American Representation of the General Jewish Workers' Union of Poland, simply exclaimed: "We Shall Never Forget This Bloody Crime."[21]

The Socialist–Communist dispute over the deaths of Henryk Erlich and Victor Alter did not interest most Americans. Representative John Rankin was an exception. Momentarily setting aside his anticommunism, he used the episode to mock the American Jewish community.[22] But a majority of Americans probably did not even know of the slayings. Nevertheless, this parochial quarrel belongs in our review of anti-Communist/anti-Soviet opinion in wartime America. Democratic Socialists were as militantly opposed to communism as were the more conservative American critics of the Communist party and the U.S.S.R. Indeed, the Socialists probably had a better overall understanding of their enemy than did Martin Dies or John Frey or Colonel Robert McCormick. On the specific matter of the Erlich–Alter executions, no evidence exists to support the Soviets' claim that these men were Nazi agents. The Socialists were entirely justified in denouncing the U.S.S.R.'s cold-blooded murder of these martyred activists. One does not need to accept the Socialists' critique of capitalism to acknowledge and respect the consistency and sense of moral purpose with which they opposed the totalitarian ideologies encamped on both ends of the political spectrum.

NOTES

1. Among the secondary works consulted for this chapter were the following: W. A. Swanberg, *Norman Thomas, The Last Idealist* (New York: Charles Scribner's Sons, 1976); Sidney Hook, *Out of Step* (New York: Harper & Row, 1987); Louis Fischer, *The Great Challenge* (New York: Duell, Sloan and Pearce, 1946); Dwight MacDonald, *Memoirs of a Revolutionary* (New York: Farrar, Straus and Cudahy, 1957); Max Eastman, *Reflections on the Failure of Socialism* (New York: Devin- Adair, 1955); John Chamberlain, *A Life with the Printed Word* (Chicago: Regnery Gateway, 1982); William Henry Chamberlin, *The Evolution of a Conservative* (Chicago: Henry Regnery Company, 1959); Chamberlin, *America's Second Crusade* (Chicago: Henry Regnery Company, 1950); Bertram Wolfe, *A Life in Two Centuries* (New York: Stein and Day, 1981); Edmund Wilson, *Letters on Literature and Politics, 1912–1972* (New York: Farrar, Straus and Giroux, 1977); James Burnham, *Suicide of the West* (New York: John Day Company, 1964); Philip Rahv (Arabel Porter and Andrew Duosin, eds.), *Essays on Literature and Politics, 1932–1972* (Boston: Houghton Mifflin, 1978); Alan Wald, *New York Intellectuals: The Rise and Decline of the Anti–Stalinist Left* (Chapel Hill: University of North Carolina Press, 1987).

2. David Dubinsky and A. H. Raskin, *David Dubinsky: A Life with Labor* (New York: Simon & Schuster, 1977), p. 272; Norman Thomas, "Totalitarian Liberals," *Commonweal*, 22 January 1943, p. 342; *Call*, 21 January 1944; *Call*, 23 July 1943; "Will Russia's Abolition of the Comintern Help Win the Peace?" Transcript of the radio program "Town Meeting of the Air," 27 May 1943, p. 9; *Call*, June 4, 1943.

3. *Call*, 1 January 1945; Maurice J. Goldbloom, "American Communism: Party of the Right," *Common Sense*, September, 1944, p. 305; Donald Johnson and Kirk Porter, eds., *National Party Platforms, 1840–1972* (Urbana: University of Illinois Press, 1973), p. 450; Harry Fleischman, *Norman Thomas* (New York: W. W. Norton and Company, 1969), p. 207; "A Challenge to Working America," *Justice*, July 1, 1943.

4. New York *Journal–American*, 18 May 1942; San Francisco *Examiner*, 13 July 1943; Sidney Hook, "The Failure of the Left," *Partisan Review*, March–April

1943, p. 174; Louis Fischer, "Laski Should Know Better," *Common Sense*, August 1944, p. 290; *Call*, 17 March 1944; *Call*, 19 February 1945.

5. *New Leader*, 1, 8 May 1943; Edmund Wilson, "Mr. Joseph E. Davies as a Master of Prose," *Partisan Review*, Winter 1944, p. 116; *New Leader*, 8 May 1943; *Call*, 28 May 1943.

6. John Dewey, "Can We Work with Russia?" *Frontiers of Democracy*, 15 March 1942, pp. 179–80; "Why Politics?" *Politics*, February 1944, p. 7; *Common Sense*, August, 1944, p. 291.

7. Sidney Hook, "The New Failure of Nerve," *Partisan Review*, January–February, 1943, p. 23; James Burnham, "The Sixth Turn of the Screw," *Partisan Review*, Summer 1944, p. 366.

8. "Should We Support Russia's Plans for Poland?" Transcript of the radio program "Town Meeting of the Air," 4 January 1944, p. 10; *Harper's*, Vol. 190 (December 1944– June 1945), p. 696; *Call*, 25 August 1944; "Warsaw," *Politics*, October 1944, p. 259; *Call*, 10 November 1944; *Call*, 3 September 943.

9. Max Danish, *The World of David Dubinsky* (Cleveland: World Publishing Company, 1957), p. 144.

10. Danish, pp. 144–5; Norman Thomas to Harry Hopkins, 4 September 1942, Norman Thomas Papers (New York City Public Library), Box 23A.

11. *The Living Record of Two Leaders of Labor* (New York: Erlich–Alter Memorial Conference, 1943), *passim*.

12. *New Leader*, 6 March 1943; *Justice*, 15 March 1943.

13. Swanberg, p. 282; James Wechsler, "Failure of Two Missions," *Common Sense*, April 1943, p. 131; *New Leader*, 13 March 1943.

14. *PM*, 18 March 1943; William O'Neill, *A Better World* (New York: Simon and Schuster, 1982), p. 98; *Nation*, 13 March 1943, p. 362; "The Erlich–Alter Executions," *New Republic*, 15 March 1943, pp. 336–37; "Helping Soviet Russia," *New Republic*, 12 April 1943, p. 460.

15. Maurice Isserman, *Which Side Were You On?* (Middletown, CT: Wesleyan University Press, 1982), p. 160; *Daily Worker*, 27 March 1942.

16. Dubinsky and Raskin, p. 249; Danish, p. 145.

17. *New Leader*, 3 April 1943; Biography File, "Erlich Alter Case," Tamiment Institute (New York University); *New Leader*, 3 April 1943.

18. *Call*, 9 April 1943; *Call*, 12 March 1943.

19. Dubinsky and Raskin, p. 250; *New Leader*, 3 April 1943; Isserman, p. 160; Earl Browder Papers (Syracuse University), Series VI, Reel 12, Item 51, "A Conspiracy against Our Soviet Ally," 1943.

20. Browder, "A Conspiracy against Our Soviet Ally"; Chanin's quote first appeared in *Friend*, January 1942, and was cited frequently thereafter in Communist literature; Earl Browder Papers, Series II, Reel 4, Item 71, "Facts of the Alter Erlich Case," 1943; Max Steinberg, "Under a 'Socialist' Mantle," *Communist*, May 1943, p. 471.

21. Biography File, "Erlich Alter Case," Tamiment Institute; *The Ghetto Speaks*, April 1, 1943.

22. *Congressional Record*, 78th Congress, 1st Session, p. 2878.

9

Conclusion

We have examined an interesting group of people—those Americans who resisted majority opinion during World War II by remaining publicly hostile to the U.S.S.R. and communism. These were controversial, often cross-grained individuals, hardliners whose actions do not lead readily to an unqualified label or verdict. They possessed both courage and conviction, traits admired in a general way but that do not necessarily lead to ennobling actions. Our subjects surely were not always noble or infallible on the issues. Yet they endured much unfair criticism and were in fact more often right than not. An appraisal of their mixed record to posterity is in order.

A convenient starting point for such an assessment is provided by a review of the relevant poll data, which indicate that a respectable portion of the general public agreed with the more widely known figures we have studied. For example, in February 1942, a *Fortune* poll surveyed Americans on the question, "Regardless of how you feel toward Russia, which of these policies do you think we should pursue toward her now?" Respondents were given a choice of four answers: end all assistance; "don't know"; "work along with Russia and give her some aid if we think it will help beat the Axis"; and "treat Russia as a full partner along with Britain in the fight against the Axis nations." A mere 4.4 percent of the respondents favored a total cutoff of aid. But the last two choices provide an interesting distinction. Only 41.1 percent favored treating the U.S.S.R. "as a full partner along with Britain," as opposed to 43.2 percent who preferred the more pragmatic approach of assisting the Russians only if this served America's own objectives. The plurality who gave the latter response do not seem to have harbored any special goodwill for the U.S.S.R., a country they did not even regard as a "full partner" in the ongoing struggle.[1]

This same suspicion is reflected in a pair of polls taken by the National Opinion Research Center (NORC) in September and November 1943, asking Americans whether the Soviet Union "will continue fighting and help us beat Japan" if Germany were defeated first. Forty percent answered "No" in

September, a figure that dropped to 31 percent by November. The affirmative totals were 39 and 49 percent, respectively, with the rest expressing no opinion; the intervening Moscow conference probably explains the rapid shift in favorable opinion of Soviet intentions. Significantly, about a third of those polled just after this much-heralded conference still believed the Russians would not help in the Pacific theater—meaning they were not America's "full partners" against the Axis, after all. It also is interesting that only half of the respondents expressed confidence that such assistance would be forthcoming.[2]

Of course, the Soviets' *post*war behavior was an even more vital matter. According to monthly polls by the American Institute of Public Opinion and the Office of Public Opinion Research, between 30 and 40 percent of the American people did not believe that Stalin's regime could be trusted to cooperate with the United States once the shooting stopped. As might be expected, Republicans and Catholics registered greater suspicion than did Democrats or Protestants; however, Polish–American opinion apparently was more divided than one might expect, especially while German troops still occupied Poland. In August 1943, the AIPO asked those (34 percent of the respondents) who said they mistrusted the U.S.S.R. why they felt this way. A quarter of this group answered that the Soviets were not interested in cooperating with the United States; about a fifth said that unbridgeable differences between the U.S.S.R. and the West precluded any prolonged harmony between them; and some 45 percent claimed, in so many words, that the U.S.S.R. was inherently immoral and not worth the risk of seeking permanent good relations.[3]

Of course, none of this should obscure the fact that millions of Americans were friendlier to the U.S.S.R. during World War II than at any other time. Yet, the fragility of this pro-Soviet opinion should have been obvious to any discerning wartime observer. A mid-1943 *Fortune* poll suggested that anxieties about Soviet intentions were real, indeed. When asked if the U.S.S.R. wanted basically the same kind of peace as the United States, only 30 percent believed this to be the case, whereas 48 percent predicted that "she will make demands that we can't agree to." *Fortune* also found that 41 percent of the people thought the Soviets would "try to bring about Communist governments in other European countries," whereas only 31 percent disagreed. The NORC's November 1943 poll provides another indication that anti-Soviet suspicions lay just below the surface in homefront America. Asked if "Russia will want more territory after the war than she had before the war started," 59 percent answered affirmatively, whereas 24 percent said No. At the same time, only 27 percent agreed that "Russia should have more territory than she had before the war," while a 56 percent majority did not think the Soviets deserved to expand their borders. Indeed, when asked "If Russia wants some land that belonged to Poland before the war, do you think that the United States and other Allied countries should try to stop her from getting it?", 38 percent answered No, 39 percent said Yes.[4]

Yet another *Fortune* poll, taken just as the war ended, clearly points to the difficult times ahead. Asked to select the statement most representative of their views about U.S.–Soviet relations, respondents provided the following results:

> It is going to be very important to keep on friendly terms with Russia after the war, and we should make every possible effort to do so 22.7%
> It is important for the U.S. to be on friendly terms with Russia after the war, but not so important that we should make too many concessions to her 49.2%
> If Russia wants to keep on friendly terms with us after the war, we shouldn't discourage her, but there is no reason why we should make any special effort to be friendly 11.3%
> We shall be better off if we have just as little as possible to do with Russia after the war 9.3%
> Don't know 7.5%

Already, the undercurrent of suspicion was building momentum, soon to become a tidal wave of anti-Soviet resentment, hostility, and fear.[5]

For our purposes, what these poll data reveal is that the views expressed by the high-profile anti-Soviet figures we have studied were *not* thoroughly rejected by the American people. This alone would seem to refute the most serious charge leveled against these individuals—that they were pro-Axis sympathizers trying to weaken the United States with their divisionist propaganda. Yet, no less a figure than President Franklin Roosevelt believed that his vociferous anti-Communist critics cared more about their vendetta against him and the Communist party than the need for national unity. Their "divided counsels," he said, "are serving as obliging messengers of Axis propaganda." As we have seen, many of the president's mainstream and more liberal supporters echoed this complaint, as did the Communist party, whose spokesmen used every opportunity to portray their foes as fifth columnists seeking "defeat for America and world domination for the slave-state of Hitler."[6]

These charges cannot be sustained. For one thing, the anti-Communist holdouts were not a monolithic, tightly disciplined pressure group. Indeed, there was surprisingly little ideological cohesion among them: Anti-Communist labor leaders did *not* generally support anti-Communist conservatives; partisan loyalties often separated Southern Democrats from the Republican right; centuries of mistrust divided Catholics and conservative Protestants; and the Socialists broke ranks with nearly everyone else we have studied. Not even in the broadest sense can the activities of such diverse groups be construed as a conspiracy. William Green, Walter Reuther, Robert McCormick, Robert Taft, to name only a few of our chief subjects—not one can responsibly be accused of failing to support an American victory. Although many internationalist-minded Socialists mustered only a "critical" support for the war, their aversion for nazism and its ultranationalistic fervor was unqualified. Even the Reverend Gerald L. K. Smith, widely regarded as a "native Fascist" and perhaps the most scurrilous individual we have examined, did not desire a Nazi victory over the United States. It would be fair to conclude that many anti-Soviet hardliners regarded Stalin's regime as a greater long-term danger to mankind than the immediate Nazi threat, a line of thinking that many regard as impolitic or wrong. But the conviction itself did not imply a latent sympathy for Nazi Germany, or a proclivity for fifth-column activity against the American people.

Indeed, with the possible exception of the Socialists, our subjects regarded themselves as the true American patriots, the guardians of their country's interests above even those of its most helpful ally.* As Senator Burton Wheeler put it, Stalin's "first concern was for Russia, so I have no regrets or apologies to make for placing the welfare of America ahead of that of any other country." Perceived self-interest was the basis for the second-front controversy and the "Pacific first" argument, although it is likely that some Japan firsters also hoped to see the U.S.S.R. bled even more deeply by a delay in the western front. But Father James Gillis of *Catholic World* expressed the main concern when he asked: "When Josef was howling for a second front in Europe did Uncle Sam say sure, Joe, but how about a second front in Asia? . . . Do we get it? Do we even ask it?"[7]

Self-interest may not be an especially ennobling basis on which to formulate foreign policy, but few nations ever do otherwise. Certainly Stalin did not send his Red Army on an altruistic crusade to save the world from Hitler, as some of his American sycophants pretended. The U.S.S.R.'s participation in World War II began with its annexation of eastern Poland, as its share of the spoils from the Nazi–Soviet pact. Next, the Soviet Union invaded Finland and took possession of the Baltic states. Suddenly, the Soviets were forced to defend themselves against a surprise German attack—a struggle in which they received more than 10 billion dollars worth of lend lease assistance from the United States. Given these facts, the basic posture of the anti-Soviets does not seem unreasonable or unwarranted. As such, the American people did not owe the Russians any special gratitude or convenient memory lapse during the alliance. Pure circumstance, and not anything remotely resembling noblesse oblige, had made the Red Army the benefactors of the free world.

Critics of the U.S.S.R. correctly reasoned that Stalin's government was no less a dictatorship merely because Nazi Germany was attempting to impose its brand of tyranny on the Russian people. In the most fundamental sense, this is why the AFL refused to pretend that Soviet trade unions were not state-

---

*This statement is not meant to impugn the loyalty of democratic Socialists. However, to the extent that a "patriot" is someone who tends to think in nationalistic, as opposed to internationalistic, terms, many Socialists would reject the label.

controlled entities; it is why the Hearst and McCormick–Patterson papers would not alter their anti-Soviet editorial policies; and it is why politicians as different as Norman Thomas and Senator Robert Reynolds continued to speak out as they did during the war. In so doing, they emphatically rejected the popular new assumptions that the Nazi–Soviet pact should be forgotten, that the U.S.S.R. was no longer a dictatorship, that Stalin was not such a bad fellow, and that all argument or evidence to the contrary was a Nazi-inspired plot to wreck the Allied cause. It is likely that many Americans did not believe these baseless claims so much as they dared not come to terms with them— lest their patriotism be challenged—and make the logical deduction that the U.S.S.R. was not a friend but an embarrassing, if necessary, battlefield ally against the Germans. It is unfortunate that the likes of Martin Dies saw through and admitted to this reality although so many better people of his time did not. Still, the conclusion seems inescapable: for rejecting what Senator Styles Bridges called the "pernicious theory" that "a padlocked mouth is the symbol of a new patriotism," wartime critics of the U.S.S.R. deserve a measure of praise from those respectful of the truth.[8]

A supposed commonality of ideals between the Allies was another groundless assumption given temporary currency by the Soviet–American alliance. For this dangerous falsehood, the president of the United States must bear much of the blame. Early on, Roosevelt had claimed that America was fighting to preserve the values proclaimed in the Atlantic Charter, a document also endorsed by the U.S.S.R. Although his precise thoughts can never be known, FDR probably knew the charter would never be honored in full; yet apparently he naively hoped he could charm his Soviet counterpart into cooperating with him after the war. But until such time, the president was determined to downplay the difficult issues, the ones that cut against his charter's lofty principles. At this the wily Roosevelt generally succeeded, except with the anti-Soviets. They insisted on asking all the troubling questions, particularly with respect to Poland. Because no one seriously believed that the Baltic states would regain their sovereignty, ravaged Poland would be the key test of the charter's credibility. FDR's harshest critics claimed that he had given Stalin secret assurances about Poland's fate at the Teheran conference, in cynical violation of his own stated principles. History has vindicated these suspicions. Poland, whose invasion by a totalitarian power had touched off World War II, remained at war's end under the control of a dictatorial regime. Not Nazi Germany, of course, but the Soviet Union, which dominates Poland and her East European neighbors to this day, confirming all the wartime predictions and fears.

On the other hand, the anti-Soviets offered no solutions of their own to the problem of Eastern Europe. Indeed, logistically the matter was a foregone conclusion, given the lengthy delay in the Anglo-American front in Europe. The Russians, burdened with most of the ground fighting against the Nazis, would not be denied the satisfaction of arriving in Poland well before their allies. Once there, the Red Army would be impossible to displace, short of a military conflict that was unthinkable to most war-weary Americans, including those who most despised the U.S.S.R. Here the anti-Soviets can be faulted for refusing to face unpleasant facts and for wanting it both ways. We have seen how many of them preferred a "Japan-first" strategy, which could only have reduced American influence in Europe all the more. In addition, many confirmed anti-Soviets had not even fully abandoned their isolationist longings and therefore did not *want* the United States to play an assertive role in Europe after her involvement in this latest foreign entanglement. Yet, such people still expected Roosevelt to rescue Poland and the rest of Eastern Europe from the Soviets.

In more practical moments, FDR's opponents simply accused him of being dishonest about the prospects for a non-Communist Poland. Congressman Fred Bradley, of Michigan, once referred to "the idealistic—but hardly realistic—Atlantic Charter." Even this was a little unfair, as it failed to take into consideration the president's need to preserve both the coalition abroad and good morale at home. At other times, the temptation to blame Roosevelt outright for the impending but near-inevitable disaster in postwar Eastern Europe proved irresistible. Thus, to the *Chicago Tribune,* he was "the boob of the century," for not having played his lend lease card to extract various commitments from Stalin. Yet, more than anyone else, the anti-Soviets should have appreciated the absurdity of assuming that Stalin would feel bound to honor such promises once Germany was defeated.[9]

In short, FDR's critics blamed him for not possessing a magic wand that would have transformed all Europe into an American sphere of influence, cost free. To some extent this thinking was the product of frustration, a sense of helplessness to prevent the flow of unwanted events. Had the critics left it there, they might be more deserving of our sympathy. Unfortunately, the president's enemies often went much further and irrationally accused him of desiring a communized Europe, on the grounds that this was the fate he also had in mind for the United States.

The agitation against domestic Communism* is somewhat less easily

---

*Pollsters were much intrigued by public attitudes about the U.S.S.R., but less data are available on what homefront America thought about domestic Communism. In late 1943, *Fortune* found that 58.5% of the people agreed there were dangerous groups in America that "might be harmful to the future of the country unless they are curbed." (*Fortune*, November 1943, p.14) One in six who answered this way named the Communists as people they had in mind. Only labor unions—regarded by many as Communist-influenced—were cited more often. Perspective is important: this was at a time when fascists were killing American soldiers in a war the Communists were militantly supporting. Of course, there is also much impressionistic evidence suggesting that mass opinion about domestic Communism did not entirely change for the better. Examples include the CP's decision to change its name, FDR's public disavowal of Communist defended than the anti-Soviet commentary of the war years. Unlike the U.S.S.R., the American Communist party—or association, as it temporarily called itself—possessed little power or influence. Yet, many conservatives regarded this small political sect as a major threat to the survival of the United States. In our period, the specter of "New Dealism" most excited the anti-Communist fears of those on the political right. Some, like Westbrook Pegler, held that the "empire of the irresponsible which President Roosevelt has set up in this country" was a greater menace than the Axis.[10] FDR's landslide victories, the fact that the New Deal had become an accepted part of American life, and of course the Soviet–American alliance made no difference to those who just knew that a Communist lived in the White House. This was a preposterous assumption based on outworn ideas, provincialism, and prejudice. More moderate critics like Governor Tom Dewey probably knew better, but red baiting was just too useful a political tactic against the commander-in-chief for them to disavow. This too was highly irresponsible behavior, particularly while Nazi Germany still threatened the world.

For these failings, it is possible to indict the anti-Communists with having indirectly served the Axis cause with their shrill and largely unfounded claims of Communists in the White House. Yet, the subject as a whole cannot be so easily dismissed. First, the anti-Communist ranks included some—principally the democratic Socialists and many of the trade-union leaders—who did *not* oppose the reformist thrust of the New Deal. Most anti-Communists did, of course, but there was nothing new about their antiradical extremism; we have seen how its roots reached back to the earliest days of the Republic. Again, this undercuts the claim that anti-Communists hectored Roosevelt because they sided with Germany, the favorite false accusation of their enemies.

In addition, the charge that Communists and fellow travelers had penetrated the federal government was *not* entirely without basis.[11] Few serious historians now deny the existence of Communist cells and spy rings within the Roosevelt administration. By no means does this excuse or legitimize the demagogic excesses of the Dies Committee and its most rabid followers; for example, their vicious and politically motivated crusade against the CIO–PAC was grossly overblown. Yet, even these charges were not pure fiction, as some wished to believe. CIO–PAC was staffed with many Communists, and Roosevelt knew it. But he was willing to accept their assistance as long as it did not cost him or the Democratic party votes overall. Thus, from FDR's standpoint the less the general public knew about his temporary collaboration with the Communist party, the better. The smear campaign launched by the GOP and the Hearst/McCormick–Patterson newspapers should not be permit-

support (which he nevertheless continued to receive) in 1944, and the logical assumption that those who were suspicious of the U.S.S.R. maintained similar doubts about American Communists.

ted to obscure this connection between the Communist party and FDR's bid for yet another term in the White House.

Most importantly, although the majority of anti-Communists were wrong about the *size* of the Communist party, they were right about the *motives* of this group. As anti-Communists realized from the start, the Communist party supported the war exclusively because the U.S.S.R. also was Hitler's enemy, at this time. Had the United States joined the war in, say, 1940—while the Nazi–Soviet pact was in force—the Communist party would have rivaled the conservative–isolationist America-First movement in opposing the venture. But whereas the America Firsters resisted intervention out of misplaced fealty to a now dangerously antiquated policy, the Communists supported isolationism out of loyalty to their favorite country's agreement with Germany. This explains the Communist party's immediate abandonment of isolationism when Hitler launched his invasion of the U.S.S.R. in June 1941. The Communists tried to explain their sudden calls for U.S. intervention by arguing that the *nature* of the war had been changed by the invasion of the U.S.S.R., and in an ironic way they were right. Initially, the war was a reasonably clear-cut struggle between the democracies France and England against the dictatorships Germany and Italy; but Hitler's betrayal of Stalin blurred this distinction considerably, at least to most anti-Communists.

When the United States finally entered the war after the Japanese attack on Pearl Harbor, the Communists expected their countrymen to forget the Pacific theater and launch an all-out assault on Fortress Europe—a strategy guaranteed to produce frightfully high casualty lists. This meant nothing to the Communists; what mattered to them was the survival of the Stalin dictatorship, at any cost. The piecework controversy involving the United Automobile Workers union is an excellent example of the party's willingness to cast aside principle for the sake of the beleaguered U.S.S.R. Of course, the Communists justified their demands for sacrifice with anti-Hitler rhetoric coupled with accusations of disloyalty against those who disagreed with the Communist party's program of the moment. Had Stalin concluded a separate peace with Hitler in 1943 or 1944, the Communists would have terminated their support for the war unless ordered to do otherwise by the Kremlin. When the United States found itself at war—a Cold War, fortunately—with the U.S.S.R. after the Axis' demise, choosing sides in this latest struggle was not a decision likely to give the Communists any pause, except that the new circumstances again made their allegiance to the U.S.S.R. impossible to disguise. This was why World War II had been so wonderful to them. It had allowed them to pretend to be American patriots without compromising their ideological submissiveness to the Soviet Union. As we have seen, many Americans were fooled by the ruse. The subjects of our study were not.

A minority point of view during World War II, anticommunism swiftly emerged as a dominant political and social credo of the postwar period. All the goodwill and optimism born of the alliance disintegrated in caustic Cold War America. Never entirely discredited or abandoned, the old image of the U.S.S.R. as Godless Menace resurfaced with a vengeance. Aided of course by their traitorous American henchmen, the Red Terror now seemed closer, more threatening than ever.

None of this surprised or confused the groups of Americans we have studied. Their warnings had been ignored; now their predictions were coming true. "Begging nobody's pardon," the *New York Daily News* boasted, "this newspaper never did get suckered into believing that Bloody Joe was fighting for anything but eventual Communist domination of the world."[12] At least now the American people realized it, as well—thanks initially to the Soviet takeover of Eastern Europe and the House Un-American Activities Committee's sensational investigations of Communist subversion. Unfortunately, this Cold War climate of suspicion and fear permitted Republican Senator Joseph McCarthy, of Wisconsin, and others to wreak havoc on the civil liberties of countless American citizens, in the name of anticommunism. Supporters of this notorious crusade included other political conservatives—including Robert Taft and others who had kept the cause alive during the war, the right-wing press, and key elements in the Catholic church, some of whom lionized McCarthy long after his censure in 1954.

More sensibly, democratic leftists denounced McCarthyism even as they continued to oppose communism and the U.S.S.R. Many joined the Americans for Democratic Action, a liberal anti-Communist group founded in 1947. Sidney Hook and other prominent left-liberal figures organized the Congress of Cultural Freedom, an international body dedicated to the anti-Communist struggle—and secretly subsidized by the American Central Intelligence Agency. Like the Congress of Cultural Freedom, organized labor also refused to support McCarthy, who had an antilabor voting record. But the American Federation of Labor remained vigorously anti-Soviet, also to the point of collaborating with the CIA in resisting Communist factions in the European trade unions.[13] In the CIO, Walter Reuther and his supporters joined such ventures, as well. At home, they took advantage of the Cold War to drive their enemies the Communists out of organized labor for good; frequent reminders of the party's wartime program of sacrifice and "sellout" made the job that much easier.[14]

These "Cold War liberals" in the labor and Socialist-intellectual communities had little in common with American conservatives except opposition to communism and its home country. But together, often in an unacknowledged semialliance, they struggled throughout the 1950s and beyond against their common foe. For them the enemy had been there all along, even during the aberrant Soviet–American alliance. Clearly, the Cold War as such had not inspired these individuals to enlist as Cold Warriors. They had joined the fight long ago.

NOTES

1. Ralph Levering, *American Opinion and the Russian Alliance, 1939–1945* (Chapel Hill: University of North Carolina Press, 1976), pp. 60–1.
2. Jerome Bruner, *Mandate from the People* (New York: Duell, Sloan and Pearce, 1944), pp. 116, 249–50.
3. Bruner, pp. 109–11, 113, 118–20, 250; Levering, pp. 131, 153.
4. Hadley Cantril, ed., *Public Opinion, 1935–1946* (Princeton, NJ: Princeton University Press, 1951), p. 131; Bruner, pp. 117, 121–22, 250.
5. Peter Filene, ed., *American Views of Soviet Russia, 1917–1965* (Homewood, IL: The Dorsey Press, 1968), p. 162.
6. Robert Dallek, *Franklin D. Roosevelt and American Foreign Policy, 1932–1945* (New York: Oxford University Press, 1979), p. 334; "The U.S.–USSR Alliance—Is It an Accident?" (11 June 1942), Papers of Earl Browder (Syracuse University), Series III, Reel 7, No. 126.
7. Burton Wheeler and Paul Healy, *Yankee from the West* (Garden City, NY: Doubleday and Company, 1962), p. 398; James Gillis, "The Gullible Yank," *Catholic World*, August 1944, p. 389.
8. *Congressional Record*, 78th Congress, 2nd Session, p. 185.
9. *Ibid.*, p. A1004; "Their Faces are Red," *Chicago Tribune*, 20 March 1946.
10. Oliver Pilat, *Pegler, Angry Man of the Press* (Boston: Beacon Press, 1963), p. 185.
11. Earl Latham, *The Communist Controversy in Washington* (New York: Atheneum, 1969), pp. 101–216.
12. Paul Willen, "Who 'Collaborated' With Russia?" *The Antioch Review*, September 1954, p. 278.
13. Thomas Braden, "I'm Glad the CIA is 'Immoral,'" *Saturday Evening Post*, 20 May 1967, pp. 10–12.
14. David Oshinsky, *Senator Joseph McCarthy and the American Labor Movement* (Columbia: University of Missouri Press, 1976), p. 94.

Bibliography

Manuscript Collections

America First Papers, Northwestern University
American Civil Liberties Union MSS, Princeton University
American Federation of Labor MSS, University of Wisconsin-Madison
Joseph Barnes MSS, Library of Congress
Earl Browder MSS, Syracuse University
Tom Connally MSS, Library of Congress
Charles Coughlin MSS, Northwestern University
Thomas Dewey Papers, Williams Press
Erlich-Alter Biography File, Tamiment Institute, New York Unversity
James Farley MSS, Library of Congress
Fight for Freedom Archives, Princeton University
Finnish Relief Fund Papers, Rutgers University
John Frey MSS, Library of Congress
John D. Hamilton MSS, Library of Congress
Arthur Krock MSS, Princeton University
David Lawrence MSS, Princeton University
John L. Lewis MSS, Library of Congress
Walter Reuther MSS, Wayne State University
Franklin Roosevelt Papers (S. I. Rosenman, ed.)
H. Alexander Smith MSS, Princeton University
Robert Taft MSS, Library of Congress
Norman Thomas MSS, New York Public Library
Arthur Vandenberg Papers (A. Vandenberg, Jr., ed.)
Henry Wallace MSS, Library of Congress
Wallace White MSS, Library of Congress

Oral Histories

George F. Addes, Wayne State University
Earl Browder, Columbia University Oral History Project
James Carey, Columbia Oral History Project
Thomas Dewey, John Foster Dulles Oral History Project in Princeton University
Julius Emspak, Columbia Oral History Project

Richard Frankensteen, Wayne State University
John Frey, Columbia Oral History Project
Nat Ganley, Wayne State University
Carl Haessler, Wayne State University
Frances Perkins, Columbia Oral History Project

Government Publications

Congressional Record, 1941–1945
Hearings and Reports, U.S. House of Representatives Committee on Un-
American Activities, 1941–1945

Convention Proceedings

Proceedings of the Amalgamated Clothing Workers, 1941–1945
Proceedings of the American Federation of Labor, 1941–1945
Proceedings of the Congress of Industrial Organizations, 1941–1945
Proceedings of the International Ladies' Garment Workers' Union, 1941–1945
Proceedings of the United Automobile Workers CIO, 1941–1945
Proceedings of the United Mine Workers, 1941–1945
Proceedings of the Democratic Party National Convention, 1944
Proceedings of the Republican Party National Convention, 1944

Unpublished Dissertations

Prickett, James. "Communists and the Communist Issue in the American
Labor Movement, 1920–1950." UCLA, 1975.
Ward, Richard. "The Role of the Association of Catholic Trade Unionists in
the American Labor Movement." University of Michigan, 1958.
Wenger, Robert. "Social Thought in American Fundamentalism, 1918–33."
University of Nebraska, 1973.

Newspapers

A. *General Newspapers* (1941–1945)

Chicago *Tribune*
Detroit *News*
Milwaukee *Sentinel*
New York *Daily Mirror*
New York *Daily News*
New York *Journal-American*
New York *Times*
San Francisco *Examiner*
Washington *Times-Herald*

B. *Catholic Newspapers* (1941–1945)

Brooklyn *Tablet*
Catholic Messenger
Catholic Sentinel
Catholic Telegraph–Register
Catholic Transcript
Denver Catholic Register
Michigan Catholic
The Monitor
New World
Our Sunday Visitor
The Pilot
The Tidings

C. *Labor Newspapers* (1941–1945)

The Advance
Aero-Notes
AFL Weekly News Service
American Federationist
American Photo-Engraver
The Carpenter
CIO News
The Elevator Constructor
International Teamster
Justice
Railway Carmen's Journal
Timber Worker
UE News
Union Leader
United Auto Worker
United Construction Worker News
United Mine Workers Journal
Wage Earner

D. *Other Newspapers* (1941–1945)

The Call
Christian Beacon
Daily Worker
Deseret News
PM
United Evangelical Action

Periodicals (1941–1945)

Amerasia
America
American Mercury
Catholic World
Commonweal
The Communist
The Cross and the Flag (1942–1945)
Fortune
Life
Moody Monthly
Nation
Nation's Business
New Republic
Newsweek
Partisan Review
Politics (1944–1945)
Reader's Digest
Time

Selected Books and Articles

A *Century of Tribune Editorials, 1847–1947*. Chicago: *Chicago Tribune*, 1947.

"The A. F. of L. is Still Obstructing." *The New Statesman and Nation*, 20 March 1943, pp. 182–83.

Beitzell, Robert. *The Uneasy Alliance: America, Britain, and Russia, 1941–1943*. New York: Knopf, 1972.

Bell, Daniel. "The Background and Development of Marxian Socialism in the United States." Available in Egbert, Donald, and Persons, Stow, eds., *Socialism and American Life*, I (Princeton, NJ: Princeton University Press, 1952), pp. 215–405.

Beyer, Barry. *Thomas E. Dewey, 1937–1947*. New York: Garland Publishing, Inc., 1979.

Browder, Earl. "Hitler's Secret Weapon—The Bogey of Communism." *The Communist*, March 1943, pp. 198–204.

Browder, Earl. "Production for Victory." *The Communist*, January 1943, pp. 10–29.

Browder, Earl. "The Strike Wave Conspiracy." *The Communist*, June 1943, pp. 483–94.

Browder, Earl. *Victory—And After*. New York: International Publishers, 1942.

Brown, Alden. *The Tablet, The First Seventy-Five Years*. New York: The Tablet Publishing Company, 1983.

Bruner, Jerome. *Mandate from the People*. New York: Duell, Sloan and Pearce, 1944.

Burns, James MacGregor. *Roosevelt: The Soldier of Freedom.* New York: Harcourt Brace Jovanovich, 1970.

Carlson, John. *Under Cover.* New York: E. P. Dutton and Company, 1943.

Chamberlin, William Henry. *America's Second Crusade.* Chicago: Henry Regnery Company, 1950.

Cochran, Bert. *Labor and Communism.* Princeton, NJ: Princeton University Press, 1977.

Cole, Wayne. *America First, The Battle Against Intervention, 1940–1941.* New York: Octagon Books, 1971.

Dallek, Robert. *Franklin D. Roosevelt and American Foreign Policy, 1932–1945.* New York: Oxford University Press, 1979.

Danish, Max. *The World of David Dubinsky.* Cleveland: World Publishing Company, 1957.

Davies, Joseph. *Mission to Moscow.* New York: Simon and Schuster, 1941.

Dewey, Thomas. *Public Papers of Thomas E. Dewey, Fifty-first Governor of the State of New York, 1944.* New York: Williams Press, 1946.

Dies, Martin. *Martin Dies' Story.* New York: Bookmailer, 1963.

Dies, Martin. *The Trojan Horse in America.* New York: Dodd, Mead and Company, 1940.

Divine, Robert. *Foreign Policy and U.S. Presidential Elections, 1940–1948.* New York: New Viewpoints, 1974.

Draper, Theodore. *American Communism and Soviet Russia.* New York: Viking Press, 1968.

Dubinsky, David, and Raskin, A. H. *David Dubinsky: A Life with Labor.* New York: Simon & Schuster, 1977.

Eulau, Heinz. "False Prophets in the Bible Belt." *New Republic*, February 1944, pp. 169–71.

Filene, Peter, ed. *American Views of Soviet Russia, 1917–1965.* Homewood, IL: The Dorsey Press, 1968.

Fish, Hamilton. *FDR, The Other Side of the Coin.* New York: Vantage Press, 1976.

Fleischman, Harry. *Norman Thomas.* New York: W. W. Norton and Company, 1969.

Flynn, George. *Roosevelt and Romanism.* Westport, CT: Greenwood Press, 1976.

Foster, James Caldwell. *The Union Politic, The CIO Political Action Committee.* Columbia: University of Missouri Press, 1975.

Foster, William Z. *History of the Communist Party of the United States.* New York: Greenwood Press, 1968.

Gies, Joseph. *The Colonel of Chicago.* New York: E. P. Dutton, 1979.

Goldbloom, Maurice. "American Communism: Party of the Right." *Common Sense*, September 1944, pp. 305–09.

Goodman, Walter. *The Committee.* New York: Farrar, Straus and Giroux, 1968.

Griffith, Robert, and Theoharis, Athan, eds. *The Specter.* New York: Franklin Watts, 1974.

Guerin, Daniel. *100 Years of Labor in the USA*. London: Ink Links, 1979.

Herring, George. "Lend-Lease to Russia and the Origins of the Cold War, 1944–1945." *Journal of American History*, June 1969, pp. 93–114.

Hoge, Alice Albright. *Cissy Patterson*. New York: Random House, 1966.

Hook, Sidney. "The New Failure of Nerve." *Partisan Review*, January–February 1943, pp. 22–23.

Hook, Sidney. *Out of Step*. New York: Harper & Row, 1987.

Hoover, Herbert. *The Memoirs of Herbert Hoover*, Vols. 2 and 3. New York: Macmillan, 1952.

Howe, Irving, and Coser, Lewis. *The American Communist Party, A Critical History*. New York: DaCapo Press, 1974.

"Incentive Wage Schemes." *American Federationist*, October 1943, p. 4.

Isserman, Maurice. *Which Side Were You On?* Middletown, CT: Wesleyan University Press, 1982.

Jaffe, Philip. *The Rise and Fall of American Communism*. New York: Horizon, 1975.

Josephson, Matthew. *Sidney Hillman, Statesman of American Labor*. Garden City, NY: Doubleday and Company, 1952.

Kampelman, Max. *The Communist Party vs. the CIO*. New York: Frederick Praeger, 1957.

Keeran, Roger. *The Communist Party and the Auto Workers Union*. Bloomington: Indiana University Press, 1980.

Klehr, Harvey. *The Heyday of American Communism*. New York: Basic Books, 1984.

Latham, Earl. *The Communist Controversy in Washington, From the New Deal to McCarthy*. New York: Atheneum, 1969.

Lens, Sidney. *Left, Right and Center, Conflicting Forces in American Labor*. Hinsdale, IL: Henry Regnery Company, 1949.

Levenstein, Harvey. *Communism, Anticommunism, and the CIO*. Westport, CT: Greenwood Press, 1981.

Levering, Ralph. *American Opinion and the Russian Alliance, 1939–1945*. Chapel Hill: University of North Carolina Press, 1976.

Lichtenstein, Nelson. *Labor's War at Home, The CIO in World War II*. New York: Cambridge University Press, 1982.

Lipset, Seymour, and Raab, Earl. *The Politics of Unreason*. Chicago: University of Chicago Press, 1978.

The Living Record of Two Leaders of Labor. New York: Erlich-Alter Memorial Conference, 1943.

Markowitz, Norman. *The Rise and Fall of the People's Century: Henry A. Wallace and American Liberalism, 1941–1948*. New York: Free Press, 1973.

Morgan, Ted. *FDR, A Biography*. New York: Simon & Schuster, 1985.

Murray, Robert. *Red Scare, A Study of National Hysteria, 1919–1920*. New York: McGraw-Hill, 1955.

Neal, Steve. *Dark Horse, A Biography of Wendell Wilkie*. Garden City, NY: Doubleday and Company, 1984.

Ogden, August. *The Dies Committee.* Washington, DC: Catholic University of America Press, 1945.

O'Neill, William. *A Better World.* New York: Simon & Schuster, 1982.

Oshinsky, David. *A Conspiracy So Immense.* New York: Free Press, 1983.

"Party of the Right." *Common Sense,* February 1944, p. 43.

Pegler, Westbrook. "What Strange Bedfellows!" *American Legion Magazine,* November 1939, p. 10.

Perrett, Geoffrey. *Days of Sadness, Years of Triumph.* New York: Coward, McCann, and Geoghegan, 1973.

Polenberg, Richard. *War and Society, The United States 1941–1945.* Philadelphia: J. B. Lippincott Company, 1972.

Preis, Art. *Labor's Giant Step, Twenty Years of the CIO.* New York: Pioneer Publishers, 1964.

Prickett, James. "Communism and Factionalism in the United Automobile Workers, 1939–1947." *Science and Society,* Summer 1968, pp. 257–77.

Prickett, James. "Some Aspects of the Communist Controversy in the CIO." *Science and Society,* Summer–Fall 1969, pp. 299–321.

Puddington, Arch. "Business, Labor, and the Anti-Communist Struggle." *National Review,* 27 January 1984, pp. 29–37.

Reuther, Victor. *The Brothers Reuther.* Boston: Houghton Mifflin, 1976.

Ribuffo, Leo. *The Old Christian Right.* Philadelphia: Temple University Press, 1983.

Riesel, Victor. "The Communist Grip on Our Defense." *American Mercury,* February 1941, pp. 202–10.

Robinson, Archie. *George Meany and His Times.* New York: Simon & Schuster, 1981.

The Roosevelt Record in Red! Washington, DC: Republican National Committee, 1940.

Rosenman, Samuel, ed. *The Public Papers and Addresses of Franklin D. Roosevelt.* (Vols. I–XIII) New York: Harper and Brothers, 1938–1950.

Roy, Ralph. *Apostles of Discord.* Boston: Beacon Press, 1953.

Roy, Ralph. *Communism and the Churches.* New York: Harcourt, Brace and Company, 1960.

Seidman, Joel. "Labor Policy of the Communist Party." *Industrial and Labor Relations Review,* October 1950, pp. 55–69.

Small, Melvin. "How We Learned to Love the Russians." *The Historian,* May 1974, pp. 455–78.

Smith, Gerald L. K. *Besieged Patriot.* Eureka Springs, AR: Elma M. Smith Foundation, 1978.

Smith, Richard Norton. *Thomas E. Dewey and His Times.* New York: Simon & Schuster, 1982.

Swanberg, W. A. *Citizen Hearst.* New York: Charles Scribner's Sons, 1961.

Swanberg, W. A. *Norman Thomas, The Last Idealist.* New York: Charles Scribner's Sons, 1976.

Tebbel, John. *The Life and Good Times of William Randolph Hearst.* New York: E. P. Dutton and Company, Inc., 1952.

Tolstoy, Nikolai. *Stalin's Secret War*. New York: Holt, Rinehart & Winston, 1981.

The Truth about Religion in Russia. London: Hutchinson and Company, 1942.

"The U.S.S.R." *Life*, 29 March 1943, p. 20.

Vandenberg, Arthur, Jr. *The Private Papers of Senator Vandenberg*. Boston: Houghton Mifflin, 1952.

Waldrop, Frank. *McCormick of Chicago*. Englewood Cliffs, NJ: Prentice-Hall, Inc., 1966.

Wallace, Henry. "Our Friendship to Russia." *Vital Speeches of the Day*, 8 November 1942, pp. 71–3.

"Warsaw." *Politics*, October 1944, pp. 257–59.

Wendt, Lloyd. *Chicago Tribune, The Rise of a Great American Newspaper*. Chicago: Rand McNally and Company, 1979.

Westerfield, Bradford. *Foreign Policy and Party Politics*. New Haven, CT: Yale University Press, 1955.

Wheeler, Burton, and Healy, Paul. *Yankee from the West*. Garden City, NY: Doubleday and Company, 1962.

Wilkie, Wendell. *One World*. New York: Simon & Schuster, 1943.

Willen, Paul. "Who 'Collaborated' with Russia?" *The Antioch Review*, September 1954, pp. 259–83.

Winkler, John. *William Randolph Hearst*. New York: Hastings House, 1955.

Young, Roland. *Congressional Politics in the Second World War*. New York: Columbia University Press, 1956.

Ziegler, Abraham. "Russia." *Modern Socialism*, Fall 1941, p. 6.

Index